ONLY THE VALIANT

ONLY THE VALIANT

True Stories of Decorated Heroes

EDITED BY LAMAR UNDERWOOD

LYONS
PRESS

Guilford, Connecticut

An imprint of The Rowman & Littlefield Publishing Group, Inc.
4501 Forbes Blvd., Ste. 200
Lanham, MD 20706
www.rowman.com

Distributed by NATIONAL BOOK NETWORK

Bronze Star and Purple Heart medals © iStock.com/RCarner

British Library Cataloguing in Publication Information available

Library of Congress Cataloging-in-Publication Data available

ISBN 978-1-4930-3732-2 (hardcover)
ISBN 978-1-4930-3733-9 (e-book)

♾™ The paper used in this publication meets the minimum requirements of American National Standard for Information Sciences—Permanence of Paper for Printed Library Materials, ANSI/NISO Z39.48-1992.

Printed in the United States of America

Contents

Foreword

Alan Axelrod

THE NATURE OF WAR HAS BEEN DISCUSSED, DEBATED, AND DISSECTED, often brilliantly, by military theorists from Sun Tzu in sixth-century China through Clausewitz, Jomini, and Mahon in the nineteenth century, to Liddell-Hart and John Kegan among many others in our own time. Yet one element has stubbornly evaded meaningful analysis.

It is valor, individual courage.

Courage is to warfare what the Higgs bosun is to physics: the most elementary element, the ultimate topic, the indispensable piece of the universal puzzle. And yet, as elusive as the "God particle" of physics proved to be, we know far more about it than we do about courage as an element in war. Well, we do know this much, and it is key. Defeat generally follows when courage fails, even though courage is no guarantee of victory.

In any context, courage is a mystery, wonderful and terrible, but nowhere more than in war. When the U.S. Supreme Court handed down its decision in *Jacobellis v. Ohio* (1964), a case of obscenity and the First Amendment right to free speech, Justice Potter Stewart memorably wrote concerning pornography that he could never "intelligibly" define it, "but I know it when I see it . . ."

So is the case with courage in war. Neither Sun Tzu nor Clausewitz nor all their colleagues and progeny could define it, and so we need not be ashamed to say that neither can we. But we know it when we see it.

Lamar Underwood has diligently searched for *it*, has collected *it*, and presents *it* to us in *Only the Valiant*. This is a magnificent collection because courage is magnificent. It is magnificent when it is at its most awesomely noble. And in this book, examples abound of John 15:13: "Greater love hath no man than this, that a man lay down his life for his friends." But it is equally magnificent in the stories told here of warriors who fight despite the naked squalor of their frank and frankly confessed terror. Perhaps these instances of courage are, in fact, the most magnificent of all.

Lamar Underwood included so much great writing here, great because it is true writing, unvarnished and uncooked. The raw clarity is crystal, and yet the mystery remains essential. You will not come away from this book capable of defining courage in warfare. You will not be able to reduce *that* God particle to an equation. But you will see courage, through history, in many conflicts, through the experience of many warriors, and you will know that what you have seen is *it*.

Introduction

Lamar Underwood

WHEN THE REALIZATION THAT SOMEBODY IS TRYING TO KILL THEM strikes most men, they react variously—from following the time-honored advice "Keep your head down!" to fleeing the danger as fast as possible. Sometimes another mode kicks in. It comes to men under fire like lightning striking, illuminating sensory channels and nerve-ends, bringing muscles and awareness to unknown brinks. These are men who will fight back. The hunted becomes the hunter, armed and ready to destroy the enemy. Hiding without fighting is not the answer. Fleeing is not the answer. The answer, if there is one, is apparent for combat-trained troops: Kill the enemy before they can kill you.

"Where did we get such men?" an aircraft carrier admiral asks himself when news of one of his jet pilots being shot down in the Korean War reaches the flight deck. Reflecting on the loss, the admiral muses, "Why is America lucky enough to have such men? They leave the tiny ship and fly against the enemy. Then they must seek the ship, lost somewhere on the sea. And when they find it, they have to land upon its pitching deck. Where did we get such men?"

This graphic scene from James Mitchener's *The Bridges at Toko-Ri*, and the movie that captured the story, asks an important question.

Where, indeed, did we get Alvin York, who single-handily captured over 100 German soldiers in WWI? Where did we get the Ninth Air Force B24 pilots whose planes were hit and burning in the raid on the oil fields of Ploesti, Romania, but continued on to bomb the targets before their planes blew up and crashed? Where did we get the Marines at Khe Sanh, called the most savage fight of the Vietnam War?

Only the Valiant is meant to be a book that takes readers beyond the citations, past the words that outlined the acts of bravery, and into a "felt life" of the acts themselves. Here are battle scenes ranging from the Civil War to Iraq and Afghanistan.

The emotional surge that can turn people who find themselves doing their duty under fire into heroes of inspirational levels, decorated for bravery with our country's highest medals, is almost beyond description. It cannot be issued to our troops; it cannot be ordered by commanding officers.

When we read descriptions of acts of valor, like those related in this book, we can picture vivid examples of individual heroism. But they are all so different that defining the words "courage" or "hero" leaves us spinning under the plethora of definitions. Writers, generals, politicians, and citizens have tried to sum up the essence of the words since men first clashed in battle. Their quotations are stirring, and they show that heroes have answered strange and mysterious clarion calls not heard by those who are listening to words like "Keep your head down."

A book could be filled with quotes on heroes and courage, and perhaps these few will help make my point that acts of valor have many faces, each described by the time and the events, each above and beyond the call of duty:

Uncommon valor was a common virtue.
—ADMIRAL CHESTER NIMITZ, ON IWO JIMA, 1945

It doesn't take a hero to order men into battle. It takes a hero to be one of those men who goes into battle.
—GEN. H. NORMAN SCHWARZKOPF, ON DESERT STORM

No sane man is unafraid in battle, but discipline produces in him a form of vicarious courage.
—GEN. GEORGE S. PATTON JR., 1941

It was easy. They sank my boat.
—PRESIDENT JOHN F. KENNEDY,
WHEN ASKED HOW HE BECAME A HERO

The history of our nation makes it obvious that we have never lacked heroes. The causes that propelled them into acts of "uncommon valor" are as diverse as the individuals themselves. Is it a sheer adrenaline rush that propels the hero to risk sacrificing his own life to deliver a blow to the enemy?

Yes, of course. Sometimes it seems to happen that way.

Can it be anger that has reached the detonation point, the irresistible urge to hurt those who have hurt us?

Yes, absolutely.

Can it be the bond between men, unit pride, the commitment to giving everything in your strength and ability to achieving the mission?

Of course it can.

The citations of valor, even those of the most-celebrated Medals of Honor, usually tell us what the heroes did, not what they were thinking. Most such medals were awarded posthumously. In the rare cases where the heroes survived the action, interviews and manuscripts sometimes offer a glimpse at the moments that inspired the acts of uncommon valor, but more often we are offered an accounting of the action details. We can only wonder and guess what emotional fireworks sent these individuals storming the very face of death itself.

In many battles, the fast action and twists of fate have obscured acts of valor that have gone into history without medals to celebrate them. Lt. Gen. Harold Moore describes the situation in the Ia Drang valley in Vietnam, where the 500 men of his 1st Battalion, 7th Cav, were surrounded by 2,000 North Vietnamese soldiers:

"We had problems with awards. We had few who could type, so many of the forms were scrawled by hand by lanternlight. Many witnesses had been evacuated with wounds or had already rotated for discharge. Too many men have died bravely and heroically, while the men who had witnessed their deeds had also been killed. . . . Acts of valor and sacrifice that on other fields, on other days, would have been rewarded with the Medal of Honor or Distinguished Service Cross or Silver Star were recognized only with a telegram saying, 'The Secretary of the Army regrets . . .' The same was true for our sister battalion, the 2nd of the 7th."

The annals of American military history, the accounts of the battles that have kept our country alive, are no doubt filled with similar situations, where heroes whose bravery will never be recognized. We cannot salute them with medals; even so, their sacrifices must never be forgotten.

This book is dedicated to heroes whose acts of courage have been recognized with appropriate medals. Their stories make irresistible reading. As we relive their experiences, we can only speculate on the forces of willpower that inspired them. They did not hide, they did not flee, they did not quit. They deserve our praise—and our memory.

ABOUT THE MEDALS

Lamar Underwood

WHAT WOULD YOU DO WITH MEDALS FOR MILITARY SERVICE, IF YOU had them?

If you were still on active duty, you would no doubt be wearing them on your uniform. The colorful bars that symbolize the larger real medals and certificates stand out on every soldier, sailor, or airman. Their meanings, the achievements they represent, are instantly identifiable to military professionals. For most civilians, pictures and explanations bridge the gap between a glimpse that tells a story, or an array of silent ribbons, albeit splashes of great color and sources of pride to those who wear them.

Veterans who have put aside their uniforms for good, but retain great affection for medals earned, usually display them in their homes, framed and prominently placed, or sometimes wear them when participating in parades and military events.

Some veterans tuck their medals away in drawers and cubby-holes where they hope they will be forgotten. The experiences that earned them were so horrific, the memories so like the rage of the battles themselves, they demand to be forgotten . . . if possible. These vets don't want to remember the experiences; and they damned sure don't want to talk about them. I once knew an airman, gunner on an Eighth Air Force B-17 Flying Fortress in World War II, who flew bombing raids over Germany. His Purple Heart was tucked away in a drawer somewhere. He did not want to remember his last mission, when his plane limped home to England, with bleeding and dying crew on board. I only know about it because his wife told me, privately.

Another airman acquaintance who flew in the Eighth eagerly described every mission of the 25 he flew—the color of the flak, the sound of it hitting the Fortress, the exact types of Luftwaffe fighters attacking the B-17s. He did not have a Purple Heart, but I don't think it would have mattered. He just didn't mind talking about the war.

Medals for distinguished service, worn with honor, are one thing. Medals for bravery in combat reflect maximum efforts and great sacrifices. Behind every medal and its certificate, there are great stories about individuals who gave far more of themselves than required by their oaths when they entered the service.

The Medal of Honor is the greatest military recognition awarded by the military.

The Congressional Medal of Honor, as it is commonly called, was created back in Civil War days, when we had no Medal of Honor. Congress created the Medal to honor the Union soldiers who stole the Confederate locomotive and ended up being hanged as spies. [See Chapter 6 for that story.]

Ceremonies of presidents draping the Medal of Honor over a courageous and fortunate recipient are usually given the full blast of coverage in all media. Often, the awards are posthumous, given to the survivors of heroes who didn't make it home. The medals themselves are quite striking in appearance, symbolizing sacrifices far beyond "the call of duty."

Next to the Medal of Honor come the Distinguished Service Cross awards of Army, Navy, Air Force and Coast Guard, followed by the Silver Star, the Distinguished Flying Cross, and the Bronze Star. The differences between the action described in each award category are often so slight that it seems the award could have been moved to a higher rank. As Lt. Gen. Harold Moore explains in his book *We Were Soldiers Once*, a lot of paperwork went into award citations, and sometimes there just weren't enough clerks or survivors around to complete the forms. The acts of many combat heroes in every U.S. battle went unrecognized—except in the minds of those who survived the experiences.

And always, as a medal for bravery, in my opinion, the Purple Heart ranks very high. When your blood is spilled for your country, the nation should be grateful. The Purple Heart shows that gratitude.

There is one more, and again this is a personal opinion: The Honorable Discharge is a medal in itself—for every man and woman who served in the Armed Forces of the United States of America.

CHAPTER ONE

The Brave Men

William Manchester

Before the sands of Iwo Jima, there was Tarawa. In 1943, already fully blood-ied in places like Guadalcanal, and long before they would ultimately plant the flag on the summit of Mt. Suribachi in Iwo in February 1945, the U.S. Marines floundered through tidal flats into hell on Tarawa.

This account of one of the most devastating battles ever fought is from William Manchester's brilliant and gripping book on his service as a Marine in World War II, Goodbye Darkness. *The book is a mixture of memories of actual fighting in which Manchester was involved, histories of other battles, and impressions of battlefields as he visits them long after the war. The title is an expression of Manchester's ultimate relief from the frequent nightmares of the war he endured for many years.*

Reading Manchester's account of the Marine landings at Tarawa fills one with awe and wonder—awe over the horrific casualties suffered by the first waves, wonder that they ever got ashore at all. Manchester's prose pulls no punches. This is a portrait of the battlefield in graphic detail, as written by an experienced journalist who wasn't just covering the war—he was part of it, a Marine sergeant in the landing forces. As is well known now, the battle at Iwo Jima that took place in 1945 had more Medal of Honor awards than any single attack of the war. But the landing at Tarawa in November 1943 saw as much heroism as it did bloodshed and suffering. Four Medals of Honor were awarded, three posthumously; 46 Navy Cross awards, 22 posthumously; and 248 Silver Stars. The Marines suffered 1,000 dead, 2,300 wounded. They killed an estimated 97 percent of the 4,800 Japanese defenders.

AMERICANS AT HOME THOUGHT ALL THE ISLAND BATTLEFIELDS IN THE Pacific were pretty much alike: jungly, rainy, with deep white beaches ringed by awnings of palm trees. That was true of New Guinea and the Solomons, but most of Admiral Nimitz's central Pacific offensive, which opened in the autumn of 1943, was fought over very different ground. Only the palms and the pandanus there evoke memories of the South Pacific, and the pandanus do not flourish because rain seldom falls. A typical central Pacific island, straddling the equator, is a small platform of coral, sparsely covered with sand and scrub bush, whose highest point rises no more than a few feet above the surf line. Tarawa (pronounced *TAR-uh-wuh),* like most of the land formations in this part of the world, is actually an atoll, a triangular group of thirty-eight islands circled by a forbidding coral reef and sheltering, within the triangle, a dreamy lagoon. The fighting was on one of Tarawa's isles, Betio *(BAY-she-oh),* because that was where the priceless Japanese airstrip was. Betio is less than half the size of Manhattan's Central Park. No part of it is more than three hundred yards from the water. A good golfer can drive a ball across it at almost any point.

Tarawa is in the Gilbert Islands. Nimitz's real objective was Kwajalein, in the Marshall Islands, over five hundred miles to the northwest. The largest atoll in the world, sixty-five miles long, Kwajalein would provide the Americans with an immense anchorage and a superb airdrome.

But Tarawa and its sister atoll Makin (pronounced *MUG-rin)* had to fall first. Unlike the Marshalls, which had been mandated to Japan in the Treaty of Versailles, and which Hirohito's troops had spent twenty years arming to the teeth, the Gilberts, where Tarawa was, had been a British crown colony. The Nips had arrived there two days after Pearl Harbor. Colonel Vivien Fox-Strangeways, the resident British administrator, had fled Tarawa in a small launch, dashing from island to island by day and holing up in coves by night until a British ship picked him up in the Ellice Islands, to the south. Since then the only Allied contact with the Gilberts had been the ineffectual foray by Carlson's Raiders on Makin. Carlson reported that he hadn't encountered much resistance. By the autumn of 1943 that was no longer true. Carlson, ironically, had been the agent of change. Warned by his strike, the enemy had strengthened the defenses of the Gilberts, particularly those on Tarawa's Betio. The Japanese needed that airstrip there. It is a sign of their determination that they had chosen Betio's beach to site the British coastal defense guns they had captured at Singapore.

Everyone knew that Tarawa—which is to say Betio—would be tough. The reef was formidable. The enemy had mined it. The beach bristled with huge guns, concrete obstacles, and barbed-wire concertinas designed to force invaders into the fire zone of cannon and machine guns. That was only part of the problem, but it was the part known to Spruance and his staff before the first wave of Marines went in. The greater problem was the reef. The only craft which could cross a jutting reef, even after the mines had been defused, were what we called "amphtracs"—amphibious tractors. Driven by propellers, they could move through water at four knots; their caterpillar tracks would carry them over land, including the reef ledge, at twenty miles per hour. Twenty Marines could ride in each amphtrac. The landing force needed all it could get. But there were few available, and Spruance's staff, notably Rear Admiral Turner, took a sanguine view of the tidal problem anyway. Using 1841 charters, they assured the Marines that at H-hour the reef would be covered by five feet of water, which meant that a loaded Higgins boat, drawing between three and four feet, could cross it. Therefore there would be enough amphtracs for the first wave, though, they conceded, there would be none for those following.

This defies understanding. A landing in spring would have been another matter, but Fox-Strangeways had described Betio's low, dodging autumn tides to the Americans. Major F. L. G. Holland, a New Zealander who had lived on Tarawa for fifteen years, said the tide might be as little as three feet. And the night before the Betio attack Rota Onorio, now Speaker of the Gilberts' House of Assembly and then a fourteen-year-old boy, paddled his dugout out to the Allied fleet and told naval officers that tomorrow the reef would be impassable, even at high tide. He, Fox-Strangeways, and Holland were ignored. Then, in the morning, the situation worsened when the fleet's timetable began to come apart. The transports carrying the Marines were trapped between Spruance's battleship bombardment and the replying fire from the enemy's shore guns. They moved, delaying the landing and missing the tide. Next it was discovered that the battleship captains and the carrier commanders had failed to consult one another; the ships' thirty-five-minute salvos ended to permit the carrier planes to come in, but the planes, whose pilots had been given another schedule, were a half hour late. That permitted the Jap batteries to open up on the transports, further delaying the landing waves. The air strike was supposed to last thirty minutes. It lasted seven. Finally, everyone awaited what was supposed to be the last touch in softening up the beach defenses, a massive B-24 raid from a base in the Ellice Islands. They waited. And waited. The B-24s never arrived. H-hour was delayed by forty-three more precious minutes.

Both the American and the Japanese troops were commanded by admirals—the defenders of the atoll were members of the Japanese Special Landing Forces: Japanese Marines, wearing the distinctive chrysanthemum-and-anchor emblem on their helmets—and confidence was high, both on the flagship offshore and in the beach's headquarters bunker. The admiral commanding the American bombardment told Marine officers: "Gentlemen, we will not neutralize Betio. We will not destroy it. We will obliterate it!" A Marine general, Julian C. Smith, replied: "Even though you navy officers do come in to about a thousand yards, I remind you that you have a little armor. I want you to know that Marines are crossing that beach with bayonets, and the only armor they will have is a khaki shirt." But despite scheduling blunders the warships and warplanes seemed to be doing their best to prepare the way for the landing force. Three U.S. battleships, five cruisers, and nine destroyers had plastered the shore with three thousand tons of high explosives—roughly ten tons per acre. Yet the Japanese admiral remained confident. He had said that "a million men cannot take Tarawa in a hundred years." Each of his underground pillboxes was built with steel and reinforced concrete, covered with coconut logs and coral, invisible to the American bombers and warships. Underground tunnels, invulnerable even to direct hits, connected the pillboxes and blockhouses. Fourteen huge coastal guns, including the eight-inchers from Singapore, led an orchestra of fifty fieldpieces. Over a hundred machine-gun nests were zeroed in on the lip of a four-foot coconut-log and coral-block seawall. The Japs doubted that any of the U.S. assault troops would ever reach the beach, however. The reef standing between them and the Allied fleet was wider than Betio itself. And the Japanese, unlike the Americans, possessed accurate tide tables.

The struggle for the island began in the early hours of Saturday, November 20, 1943. By 4:30 a.m. the Marines assigned to the first wave had descended their cargo nets, jumped into Higgins boats, and transferred to amphtracs, which began fanning for the assault. Japanese ashore were aware of dark hulks in the night but were waiting until the Americans committed themselves to the isle's sea beach or its lagoon side. At 4:41 a.m. a Nip coastal defense gun fired a red-star cluster over the six U.S. transports. Now they knew: it was to be the lagoon side. Our naval gunfire had been stunning—one Marine said, "It's a wonder the whole goddam island doesn't fall apart and sink"—but it had ended an hour earlier. Two U.S. destroyers laying down a smoke screen for the Marines were shelling the beach, but against such defenses tin-can fire was ineffectual. Japs who had been braced for an approach from the sea leapt into prepared positions facing the lagoon. Now the American Marines would confront 4,836 Japanese, most of them Jap Marines.

Amphtrac coxswains found the seventeen-mile-long, nine-mile-wide lagoon choppy, its current strong, and their screws baffled by a riptide, a tug created by large volumes of water being sucked through underwater gaps in the reef. Instants later, they discovered that the Japs had somehow survived the bombardment. At three thousand yards from shore enemy artillery opened up on them; at two thousand yards they came under fire from long-range machine guns; and at eight hundred yards, as their awkward vehicles, half tanks, half boats, waddled over the reef, they were greeted by everything the enemy had, including sniper fire and heavy mortars. The amphtracs, performing as expected, came on. The Higgins boats behind them were stranded on the reef. They lowered their ramps, and the Marines stepped into chest-deep water. Robert Sherrod, then a *Time* war correspondent, has recalled: "It was painfully slow, wading in such deep water. And we had seven hundred yards to walk slowly into this machine-gun fire, looming into larger targets as we rose onto high ground." Aboard one of the American warships a naval officer wrote in his log, "The water seemed never clear of tiny men . . . slowly wading beach-ward. . . . They kept falling, falling, falling . . . singly, in groups, and in rows." Yet they trudged on, keeping their formations, "calm," in Sherrod's words, "even disdainful of death . . . black dots of men, holding their weapons high above their heads, moving at a snail's pace, never faltering." As Balaklava Pierre Bosquet had said of the Light Brigade: "*C'est magnifique, mais ce n'est pas la guerre.*" And at Sedan in the Franco-Prussian War, where the French cavalry charged the Krupp guns again and again, until the last of them lay writhing in their own blood beside the carcasses of their slaughtered mounts, the King of Prussia had lowered his spyglass and murmured: "*Ah, les braves gens!*" Tarawa was more ghastly than magnificent, and it was certainly war, yet after all these years the bravery of its men is still wondrous.

There was a ramshackle, cribwork pier, long and narrow, jutting out from the beach. As shelters, the pier's coconut stanchions were pitifully inadequate, but they were better than nothing, and those who reached them unwounded thought themselves lucky. There they crouched, with shellfire pealing in their ears, amid geysers of water from new shells and the smaller splashes from machine guns in the bunkers and Jap snipers tied in the trees overhead, while the precise American invasion plan fell apart. The troops in the amphtracs were luckier than those jumping from the Higgins boats stranded on the coral-reef apron, but in this fire storm danger was merely relative; there was no real safety for anyone. Unprotected by counterbattery fire from the U.S. fleet, which could not risk hitting Americans, five out of every six amphtracs were destroyed or disabled. Some reached the wrong beaches. Some, their coxswains dead, ran amok, spinning crazily and hurling seasick men into the surf. Some toppled into shell holes. And some blew up when enemy bullets pierced their fuel tanks. A survivor of the first wave remembers: "Amphtracs were hit, stopped, and burst into flames, with men jumping out like torches." Craft which survived were shuttling back and forth from the reef, carrying the wounded out and reinforcements in. The commander of the assault, Colonel David M. Shoup, a bullnecked, red-faced fighter who was also a scholar and poet, was wading toward shore when he hailed an amphtrac, ordered its crew to help him toss the Marine corpses in it overboard, rode in, and then set his command post in the shadow of the pier pilings, issuing orders while standing waist-deep in water with two other officers and a sergeant. Shrapnel riddled Shoup's legs; he winced and then braced himself, waving away a corpsman. Other drenched Marines who had made it ashore huddled, terrified, beneath the four-foot seawall. Two brave amphtrac coxswains punched a gap in the long wall. Marines following them actually established a precarious toehold at the edge of the airstrip, about fifty yards inland, but their waterlogged radios didn't work and so Shoup was unaware of their position. Closer to him, another coxswain trying to climb the wall succeeded only in jamming his amphtrac treads against it. The men who had reached the beach alive seemed doomed. One later said that it felt "like being in the middle of a pool table without any pockets."

It was now noon. Because the tide had been misjudged, the Higgins boats couldn't even mount the reef now. Most of the amphtracs had been destroyed. One of them completely disappeared in a shell burst. "It had been there," recalls a Marine who was nearby, "and then suddenly it was not. In its place, for a split second, there was a blur in the air, and then there was nothing." One horrified coxswain lost his mind. On his way in, with bullets rattling on his hull, he screamed, "This is as far as I go!" He dropped his ramp and twenty Marines bowed by weapons and ammunition drowned in fifteen feet of water. A battalion commander elsewhere raised his pistol as he waded in and cried to the men behind him: "Come on, these bastards can't stop us!" A Nambu ripped open his rib cage, killing him instantly. Another battalion commander, gravely wounded in shallow water, crawled on top of a pile of dead Americans to avoid drowning in the incoming tide. He was found there the following afternoon, still alive but raving.

Enemy fire, writes Morison, "was horribly accurate; several times it dropped a shell right on a landing craft just as the ramp came down, spreading a pool of blood around the boat." The Marine dead became part of the terrain; they altered tactics; they provided defilade, and when they had died on barbed wire obstacles, live men could avoid the wire by crawling over them. Even so, the living were always in some Jap's sights. There were many agents of death on Tarawa: snipers, machine gunners, artillery shells, mortar bursts, the wire, or drowning as a result of step-ping into holes in the coral. As the day wore on, the water offshore was a grotesque mass of severed heads, limbs, and torsos. If a body was intact, you could tell which wave it had been in; the freshly killed were limp, with only their scalps and arms visible in the swells, but those who had died in the first hour floated stiffly, like kayaks, showing faces, or pieces of faces. If they had lost all their blood they were marble white, and the stench of their putrefaction soon hung over them. Most of those still alive cowered where they were. One who didn't, a corporal and a pro-fessional baseball pitcher in civilian life, crouched beside an amphtrac that Japs were trying to stop with hand grenades. As the grenades sailed in, he fielded them and flung them back as fastballs. Then one took a home-team bounce. Before he could grab it, it exploded. Later his hand was amputated. His example awed his men but did not inspire them. Real leadership was impossible. In a typical company, five of six officers were dead and all the sergeants dead or wounded. The survivors were bunched in little groups of three or four, trembling, sweating, and staring the thousand-yard stare of combat.

By early afternoon, with the tide falling, virtually all in the fourth wave, including 37-millimeter guns and their crews, were blocked by the reef. Some coxswains found holes in the coral; the others would be unable to move until night fell and the tide rose. The fifth wave landed its Sherman tanks on the reef; they plunged into four feet of water on the lee side and churned gamely on. Ashore, the survivors of four assault battalions held a lumpy arc about 300 yards wide which at places, owing to individual acts of heroism, reached a maximum depth of about 150 yards. Shoup had moved his command post fifteen yards in from the surf. His legs streaked with blood, he was standing exactly three feet from a Japanese blockhouse, but owing to the angle of its gun ports, he couldn't reach the enemy and they couldn't reach him. Here and there officers and NCOs were shoving and kicking—literally kicking dazed Marines inland. All the news was bad. The most dismaying reports came from the west, or right, of the island. The seawall was useless in the cove there; a sweeping cross-fire enfiladed our riflemen. The battalion commander in the cove, seeing that his men ashore were being scythed by machine gunners, held the rest of them on the reef. He radioed Shoup: "Unable to land. Issue in doubt." After a silence he radioed: "Boats held up on reef of right flank Red One. Troops receiving heavy fire in water." Shoup replied: "Land Red Beach Two"—to the left—"and work west." Another silence from the battalion commander, then: "We have nothing left to land." The officers around Shoup stared at one another. There had been seven hundred men in that battalion. How could there be *nothing* left?

In fact about a hundred of the men were still alive, but in the chaos on the beach, with most radios still sodden or jammed, no one, including Shoup, knew of local successes. There was that tenuous hold on the end of the runway. It lay on the left flank of the assault, east of the pier. There was also the battalion of Major Henry P. "Jim" Crowe, a redheaded mustang, and it had landed intact, thanks to the covering fire of two destroyers. Except for the force on the runway tip, Crowe's men were pinned down on the beach by fire from Jap pill boxes, but he could have silenced them with flamethrowers and TNT satchel charges if he had had enough of them. Chagrin yielded to alarm when an enemy tank appeared, clanking toward the battalion. Two U.S. 37-millimeter antitank guns were off shore in a sunken landing craft. The men hauled them through the languid surf and then, with all hands lifting, the two nine-hundred-pound guns were thrown over the seawall just in time to drive the tank back. On the other end of the Marine position, Major Michael P. Ryan, leading a ragtag force of men who had made it ashore and supported by the 75-millimeter guns of two tanks, overran several enemy positions.

But Ryan, too, lacked flamethrowers and TNT. Finding that he couldn't reach Shoup to call for reinforcements, he pulled back to a defense perimeter about five hundred yards deep. On Tarawa that was a victory.

Messages between the troops ashore and the hovering fleet also went astray. In desperation, Shoup sent out an officer (Evans Carlson) in an undamaged amphtrac to beg for men, water, and ammunition. Carlson didn't reach the battleship *Maryland* until late in the evening. By then, however, the plight of the force ashore had become obvious to General Smith, who had been anxiously following the sketchy reports from his CP on the battleship. Smith radioed his senior, Marine General Holland M. Smith, who, aboard the *Pennsylvania,* was commanding both the Makin and Tarawa assaults. His message to Holland Smith was: "Issue in doubt." He wanted the Sixth Marines, which were being held in reserve. Meanwhile he was organizing cooks, field medics, typists, motor transport men, specialists, and staff officers into an improvised battalion which he intended to lead ashore if reinforcements were denied him. But he got the Sixth Marines. At the time it was thought they might just swing the balance, but Shoup's position was at best precarious, and the Japanese were by now notorious for their night counterattacks.

As darkness fell, five thousand Marines on the beach awaited death or terror. Ryan's and Crowe's men were wired in and Shoup held a shallow, box–like perimeter at the base of the pier. Everything, including ammunition, was in short supply. The beach was covered with shattered vehicles, the dead, the dying, and the wounded awaiting evacuation. Five 75-millimeter pack howitzers were ashore and a few medium tanks; that and the 37-millimeter guns was about it. The tropical moon was only a quarter full, but fuel dumps burning all over Betio provided a lurid, flickering light. Corpsmen worked through the night, ferrying casualties to the reef in large rubber rafts; other rafts brought water, blood plasma, ammunition, and reinforcements to the pier. The men on the perimeter, who thought they were ready for anything, were shocked to find their foxholes raked by machine-gun fire from the sea. Japs had swum out to disabled amphtracs abandoned there and were firing at the Marines' backs. To the Americans that seemed the ultimate blow. Demoralized, they expected a banzai charge at any moment. To their astonishment it didn't come. The night passed quietly. The Japanese had problems, too. Naval gunfire hadn't obliterated the island, but it had inflicted very heavy casualties on the Nips outside their bunkers. And it had destroyed their communications. Great as Shoup's radio problems were, the Japanese commander's were worse. He couldn't get *any* messages through.

Seawalls are to beachheads what sunken roads-as at Waterloo and Antietam-are to great land battles. They provide inexpressible relief to assault troops who can crouch in their shadows, shielded for the moment from flat trajectory fire, and they are exasperating to the troops' commanders because they bring the momentum of an attack to a shattering halt. On Tarawa the survival of the American force depended upon individual decisions to risk death. Wellington said, "The whole art of war consists of getting at what is on the other side of the hill." If no one vaulted over the wall, no Marine would leave Betio alive. Naturally everyone wanted others to take the chance. In the end, some did—not many, but a few—and they were responsible for the breakthrough. In defense of those who chose to remain until the odds were shorter it should be said that Tarawa was exceptional. In most instances frontal attacks are unnecessary. Cunning is more effective than daring. Even on Betio, even after the reef blunder and the failure to bombard the enemy until the last possible moment, permitting the shift of defenders to prepared positions on the lagoon side, there was a way out. Ryan provided it. He had turned the Jap flank. If Shoup's radio had worked he would have known that and could have strengthened Ryan, rolling up the Nip defenses from the rear. So the instincts of the rifleman who hides behind the wall are usually sound. At least that is what I tell myself whenever I think of Tubby Morris.

My seawall was on Oroku. There was no reef to speak of, and though enemy fire was heavy as the Higgins boats brought us in—we were soaked with splashes from near misses, and we could hear the small-arms lead pinging on our hulls—we lost very few men in the landing. Then we saw the seawall and thanked God for it. It was built of sturdy logs and stood over five feet high. Incongruously, an enormous scarlet vine rioted over the lower half of it. Between there and the surf line the beach was about ten feet deep. It looked wonderful. I was prepared to spend the rest of my life on those ten feet. A braver man, I knew, would try to skirt the wall and find Jap targets. But enemy machine gunners knew where we were. Nambus were chipping at the top of the wall; you could see the splinters. Even if I hadn't been determined to save my own skin, which I certainly was, there were other reasons for staying put. I was surrounded by the Raggedy Ass Marines, the least subordinate of fighters. I knew that if I went up I would be alone. Furthermore, it seemed possible, even probable, that the First Battalion, on our extreme right, could envelop the Nips. The seawall tapered off in that direction, and the map showed an inlet where our men had room to move around. Anyhow, I was going to give them their chance and all the time they wanted.

That was when Tubby arrived in the third wave. He had been in my officer candidate class at Quantico, and unlike me he had been commissioned. Now he was a second lieutenant, a replacement officer making his debut as a leader, or presumed leader, of seasoned troops. If there is a more pitiful role in war, I don't know it. Troops are wary of untested officers, and the Raggedy Ass Marines were contemptuous of them. Some of them, like me, remembered him from Quantico. He hadn't changed since we had last seen him; he was a stubby, brisk youth, in his early twenties but already running to fat around the jowls and belly. He had the sleek peach complexion of a baby and a perpetual frown, not of petulance but of concentration. I hadn't known him well. He had the megalomania of undersized men. He was like one of those boys who always do their homework at school and never let you copy. He had been an overachiever, determined to please his superiors, but there had been many like him at Quantico. Here, however, he was unique. Among men who prided themselves on the saltiness—shabbiness—of their uniforms, his was right off the quartermaster's shelf. I wondered whether he had been disappointed when they told him not to wear his bars in combat, for whatever his other failings he was, and was soon to prove, courageous.

He caught his breath, looked around, and said, "I'm your new officer." I grinned, held out my hand, and said, "Hi, Tubby." That was stupid of me. He glared and kept his own hand on his trouser seam. Standing cockily like a bantam rooster—the wall was just high enough to let him stand— he crisply asked, "Sergeant, are these your men?" The Raggedy Asses grinned at one another. The very thought of belonging to *anyone* amused them. I felt cold. This wasn't the good-natured Tubby I had known. This was trouble. I said, "Tubby—" and he cut me off: "Slim, I am an officer and expect to be treated with proper military courtesy." That broke the men up. He heard their stifled chuckles and looked around furiously. It was an insane situation. Here we were, in the middle of a battle, and Tubby seemed to expect a salute, if not homage, from me. There wasn't much room, but I said in a low voice, "Let's talk this over," moved away a few feet, and knelt. He bridled, but came over and squatted beside me. I told him that I didn't want to undermine him, that I hadn't meant to sound familiar, and that I was sorry. His jaw muscles were working. He said, "You should be." Anger stirred in me. Looking back, I see that my motives were less selfless than I thought then. My sympathy for his position, though genuine, was tainted by resentment at taking orders from this little man whose background was no different from mine, by irrational scorn of junior officers who hadn't yet proved themselves, and by the arrogance which combat veterans feel toward all green replacements, especially platoon leaders. At that moment, however, all I saw was that there was bound to be a certain stiffness between us which we would probably work around in time. Then I learned that for Tubby there wasn't much time. He said, "Don't tell me. Show me. I'm going to lead these people over the top, and I want you with me."

He actually said "over the top." We didn't talk like that. He must have heard it from his father. World War I soldiers left their trenches to go over the top, over the parapet, into no-man's-land. Then the implication of what he had said hit me. I whispered, "You mean over this wall?" He nodded once, a quick little jerk of his head. He said, "That's where the Japs are. You can't kill them if you can't see them." I felt numb. I said, "Look, Tubby—Lieutenant—I think—" He snapped, "You're not paid to think. You're paid to take orders." I considered saying the hell with it. But this was literally a matter of life or imminent death. I tried again, earnestly: "Going up there would be suicide. The First Bat's down there," I said, pointing. "Give them a chance to turn the Nips' flank and roll up those machine-gun nests." He growled, "What's the matter with this battalion?" I said, "We're pinned down, so the action is on the flanks." I could see I wasn't convincing him, and I said hoarsely, "Tubby, I know they didn't teach you that at Quantico, but that's how we do it here. You're not on some fucking parade ground. You can't just pump your fist up and down and expect the men to spring up. They won't do it. *They won't do it.* I've been out here a long time, Tubby. I *know.*"

He stared at me for a long time, as though waiting for me to blink first. I blinked and blinked again. Letting his voice rise, he said, "You're scared shitless, aren't you?" I nodded emphatically. His voice rose higher. All the guys could hear him now. He said, "That's why I put up bars and you're just an NCO. They could tell the difference between us in O.C. I've got balls and you haven't." There was just a tremor in his voice, and it dawned on me that he himself was petrified—he was masking his fear with his rudeness to me. But what he said next smothered my compassion. He sneered, and keeping his voice in the same register, he said: "I know your kind, Bub. You think we couldn't hear you back there in the squad bay, masturbating every night? Did you think they'd give a Marine Corps commission to a masturbator? Only thing I couldn't make out was how you dried the come. I figured you had a handkerchief." I heard a titter from Bubba. I'm sure Bubba had never masturbated. His father, the Alabama preacher in whose steps he hoped to follow, had shown him the way to what he called "Nigra poontang" when he reached adolescence. But I wasn't interested in Bubba's good opinion. What Tubby had done, and it was unforgivable, was make me look ridiculous in the eyes of all my men. He knew that was wrong. They had taught that at Quantico. By mocking me he had contaminated both of us. I thought: *Since I am a dog, beware my fangs.* He and I were through. He was past saving now. His longevity would be less than a Jap's. No one could lengthen it for him. I've kept telling myself that all these years, but there will always be a tug of guilt.

Rising in one swift motion, he wiped his hands on his sturdy thighs, stood with, arms akimbo, and barked: "Men, I know you'd like to stay here. I would myself. But those yellow bastards down the beach are killing your buddies." He didn't even realize that a combat man's loyalty is confined to those around him, that as far as the Raggedy Ass Marines were concerned the First Battalion might as well have belonged to a separate race. He said, "Our duty lies up there." He pointed. He went on: "That's what we call a target of opportunity, lads." He paused, and his pouter-pigeon breast swelled. I wondered if he was trying to imitate Chesty Puller, that legendary Marine hero who is said to have boasted that he would win a Medal of Honor if he had to bring home a seabag full of dog tags. Tubby said, "I'm not going to ask any of you people to do what I don't do. I'm going up first. Your sergeant will—" He checked himself. "It's your sergeant's job to see that every man follows me." I was still down on one knee, eyes averted, running sand through my fingers. I wanted no part of this. He asked, "Any questions?"

They looked up at him glassily. He hesitated, probably wondering whether he should threaten them with courts-martial. Then he turned and sprang at the seawall. He was too short. He couldn't get a footing. He tried to stick one boondocker in a vine crotch, but the V was too tight. He could only wedge his toe in sideways, and that didn't give him the right leverage. Panting, he tried again and again. He turned to me, his face flushed. He said, "Help me." He must have hated to ask. I certainly hated his asking. I felt an insane urge to laugh, which I knew would turn into weeping. I looked into his wide eyes and said, "My legs are too shaky." It was true. He said between his teeth, "I'll take care of you later." He turned, pointed to Bubba, and said, "You, over here." Bubba came over and linked his hands. Tubby put in a foot, as if into a stirrup, swung up, rolled atop the wall, and rose till he stood sideways. Both his hands were pointing. His left forefinger was pointed down at us, his right forefinger at the Japs. It was a Frederic Remington painting. He breathed deeply and yelled, "*Follow me!*"

The men's faces were turned up, expressionless. Nobody moved. I stood beneath the wall, my arms outstretched, waiting to catch what would be left. At that moment the slugs hit him. It was a Nambu; it stitched him vertically, from forehead to crotch. One moment he was looming over us in that heroic pose; in the next moment red pits blossomed down him, four on his face alone, and a dozen others down his uniform. One was off center; it slammed in the Marine Corps emblem over his heart; the gunner knew his job. Blood had just begun to stream from there, from his face, from his belly, and from his groin, when he collapsed, tottering on the edge and falling and whumping in my arms face up. His features were disappearing beneath a spreading stain, and he was trying to blink the blood out of his eyes. But he could see. He saw me. He choked faintly: "You . . . you . . . you. . . ." Then he gagged and he was gone.

I looked away, feeling queasy. My blouse was wet with gore. Mo Crocker and Dusty Rhodes took Tubby from me and gently laid him out. There was no malice in the section. They mourned him as they would have mourned any casualty. They—and I above all—had merely been unwilling to share his folly. It was followed by savage irony. We had scarcely finished trussing him up in a poncho when we heard the sound of cheering to our right. The First Bat had turned the Jap flank. You could just see the bobbing of the camouflaged helmet covers and the moving line of smoke, and you could hear the snuffling of the tanks as their drivers shifted gears. I raged as I had raged over the death of Zepp. It was the sheer futility of it which was unbearable. Then I was diverted, as death in its grisly mercy diverts you, by the necessity of disposing of the corpse. I said to Knocko, "Pass the word to Buck Rogers—" Suddenly I realized that Buck might not still be alive, and that because Tubby had arrived so recently, his name might be unknown at the CP anyhow. Instead, I said, "The new lieutenant is dead. Pass the word to the nearest officer."

One of the problems at Tarawa was the uniforms. When General Smith said the Marines' armor would be limited to khaki, he was speaking figuratively. The men actually wore new jungle suits, camouflaged green on one side and brown on the other, presumably for use if the Marine Corps found itself fighting in the Sahara Desert. But the designers of the suits had neglected to make them porous. Wearing them was like being wrapped in plastic. The men would have sweated that first night on Betio whatever they wore—they were just ninety miles from the equator—but in those suits they lost pounds, and greeted the dawn gaunt and shrunken. In the early light, they saw that their lines were intact. That heartened them, and led many to conclude that the crisis was past. They were wrong. As the struggle resumed its ferocity, Sherrod heard on all sides the *pi-ing* of enemy rifles rippling the air and the *ratatatata* and the *brrrp* of their machine guns. In five minutes he saw six Marines die. He wrote: "This is worse, far worse than it was yesterday." The battleship *Maryland*, with communications restored, radioed Shoup, asking him if he had enough men. He said he didn't and added: "Imperative you land ammunition, water, rations and medical supplies. . . . Imperative you get all types of ammunition to all landing parties immediately." The corpsmen ran out of bandages. Shoup ordered them to wade out to the reef and strip dead Marines of first-aid kits that all men carried on their belts. At midmorning he told Sherrod: "We're in a mighty tough spot." At 11:00 a.m. he radioed General Julian Smith: "Situation doesn't look good ashore."

The immediate problem was bringing in reinforcements from the Sixth Marines. They had been waiting in Higgins boats for nearly twenty hours, trying to find a way past or over the reef. The Japs on the stranded amphtracs were still in position, firing seaward now, their .303-caliber copper bullets hitting with remarkable accuracy whenever men on the landing craft peered over their bulkheads. Nambus seemed to be firing on all sides. One was set up on a Jap privy built over the water. The greatest danger, however, came from the hulk of an old freighter to the right of the pier, about seven hundred yards out. From here the enemy could smash the fuel tanks of landing craft, exploding them, and zero in on the Sixth Marines as they jumped out into the water and started trudging in. There were 800 Marines when they started; 450 made it to the beach.

Marines already ashore rocked the freighter with 75-millimeter pack howitzers and 81-millimeter mortars, and dive-bombers from U.S. carriers tried to take it out, but it seemed indestructible. A naval officer on one Higgins boat suggested to debarking men that they keep the boat between them and the hulk, as a shield, but, as the officer recalls, "They told us to follow the plan and retire so other waves could get to help them." It was at this point that the erratic Betio tide began to rise, threatening the wounded men lying on the reef with drowning. A salvage crew from the transport Sheridan, rescuing them, encountered about thirty-five Marines, unharmed but lacking weapons. The skipper offered to evacuate them. They shook their heads, asking only that the crew "bring back something to fight with." During the five hours needed to land the First Battalion of the Eighth Marines—the last of the reinforcements—its casualties were greater than those of any battalion reaching shore the day before.

The survivors strengthened Ryan's end of the beachhead. At daybreak, his communication with the fleet reestablished, he had called in a barrage of five-inch shells from a destroyer offshore. With those salvos and fire from two tanks, he recovered the ground that he had yielded the previous afternoon; pushing on, he crossed the airfield and established an anchor on Betio's south shore. This time Shoup learned of Ryan's progress and altered his tactics to exploit it. As Tarawa's tide turned, the tide of the battle was at last turning with it. The freighter hulk was annihilated by concentrated fire. Jim Crowe's mortars and a seemingly invincible tank christened "Colorado" were cracking pillboxes open. Flamethrowers, suddenly plentiful, licked at spider holes and bunkers. One two-story concrete blockhouse, intact despite point-blank fire from a destroyer, was knocked out when a Marine tank crawled up to the entrance and blasted away. Over three hundred charred corpses were later found inside. The western half of Betio was now in American hands. Shoup radioed the fleet: "Casualties many; percentage dead not known: we are winning."

The Japanese didn't think so. They laid down such heavy howitzer fire on Shoup's left flank, resting on a Burns-Philip Company wharf, that any U.S. advance there was out of the question. The enemy didn't know about the cargoes of equipment, supplies, and plasma coming in over the now-submerged reef, or that another battalion had reached Ryan—the first to stream ashore with few casualties and dry weapons. The Nips' will to resist was as inflexible as ever. As American firepower drove them back and back on the eastern half of the island, their snipers scampered up palm trees or lay among their dead comrades, feigning death until they could leap up and attack Marines whose backs were to them. Monday night they launched three vicious counterattacks against the Marine line, which now lay athwart the entire island. Despite naval gunfire and Marine artillery, some Japs penetrated the American perimeter. Hand-to-hand fighting followed, with Kabars and bayonets. A Marine lieutenant sent back word: "We're killing them as fast as they come at us, but we can't hold much longer. We need reinforcements." He was told: "We haven't got them to send you. You've got to hold."

They did; Tuesday morning they counted 325 Jap bodies around their foxholes. At the time it was impolitic to pay the slightest tribute to the enemy, and Nip determination, their refusal to say die, was commonly attributed to "fanaticism." In retrospect it is indistinguishable from heroism. To call it anything less cheapens the victory, for American valor was necessary to defeat it. There were brave Marines, too, men who didn't commit suicide, as Tubby did, but who knew the risk, decided an objective was worth it, and never looked back. There was Jim Crowe, charging and shouting over his shoulder, "You'll never get the Purple Heart a-laying in those foxholes, men!" There was Lieutenant William "Hawk" Hawkins, who knocked out machine guns by standing in full view of the gunners and firing into pillbox slits, then tossing in grenades to finish off the Nips inside. He was wounded by a mortar burst and told a corpsman: "I came here to kill Japs, not to be evacuated." Still erect in the terrible heat, Hawk blew up three more pillboxes before a shell killed him. And there was Lieutenant Alexander Bonnyman, an officer of engineers who could have left the fighting to the infantry but who chose to attack the enemy's huge headquarters fortress bunker with five of his men. They climbed up the tough, stringy weeds of the slope outside to reach the roof, the highest point on the island. A door opened and a horde of Japanese poured out to drive him off. Bonnyman remained standing for thirty seconds, firing a carbine and then a flamethrower before he fell, mortally wounded. He had held the erupting Nips off just long enough for his men to drop grenades into the strongpoint's ventilation system. When the grenades exploded, more Nips swarmed up, shells and small-arms fire drove them back. A bulldozer sealed the entry. Gasoline was poured in vents still open and ignited by TNT. The Marines heard the blasts, then screams, then nothing. Inside were nearly two hundred Japanese corpses.

One of them was that of the Jap admiral commanding Betio's defenses. His faith in Tarawa's impregnability had been based on the assumption that if he were attacked, Tokyo would send him warships, warplanes, and more troops. His superior had assured him that Tarawa would be "a hornet's nest for the Yankees." He couldn't imagine what had gone wrong. We know now. Because of America's twin-pronged drive, the men and equipment which had been earmarked for him had gone to Bougainville, under assault by the Third Marine Division, and to MacArthur's objectives in New Guinea. Shortly before Bonnyman's feat, the doomed admiral had radioed Tokyo: "Our weapons have been destroyed, and from now on everyone is attempting a final charge. . . . May Japan exist for ten thousand years!" Leaderless now, the remaining Nips formed for the first of those suicidal banzai charges or took their lives in a sick ritual which would soon be familiar to American assault troops all over the Pacific: lying down, jamming the muzzle of an Arisaka rifle in the mouth, and squeezing the trigger with the big toe. By Tuesday Japanese resistance had collapsed. Except for seventeen Nips who surrendered, all were dead or fugitives, running across the reef to other islands in Tarawa's atoll, where they were soon pursued and shot. Tokyo's commentators eulogized them as "flowers of the Pacific" and quickly turned to other news, as well they might. Tarawa had been a Nipponese disaster. Already Hellcats were landing on Betio's airstrip, named Hawkins Field for Hawk. At 1:10 p.m. Tuesday the battle was officially ended. It had lasted seventy-six hours, and the only dispute about it now was whether the island's bird-shaped fragment of coral was worth the price the Americans had paid.

CHAPTER TWO

Hell in a Very Small Place—Ia Drang

The Battle That Changed the War in Vietnam
Lt. Gen. Harold G. Moore (Ret.) and Joseph Galloway

When a book has been made into a popular movie—as in the case of Lt. Gen. Harold Moore's We Were Soldiers Once . . . And Young—*it's hard to look back at the original text without feeling that Hollywood has not grasped the full story. Even when it's a damn good film, such as Mel Gibson's portrayal of* We Were Soldiers Once. *The Gibson movie has all the emotion and rat-tat-tat you could possibly expect from a war film, but it is in the print version of the book that we can fully appreciate what the 1st Cav soldiers endured in the defining battle of the early stages of the Vietnam War.*

These were soldiers of the 7th Cavalry, Garry Owen, Custer's old outfit. Trained at Fort Benning, Georgia, to swoop down on enemy positions with helicopters, they were the Army's best in mobility and firepower. But when they landed in the highlands of Ia Drang in November 1965, they had no idea that they were unknowingly taking on a stronghold of the North Vietnamese Peoples Army, three regiments that outnumbered the Americans eight to one. Landing Zone X-Ray and Landing Zone Albany became known as "The Valley of Death." In his book, Moore tells us that exactly 234 young Americans died there, more than were killed in any regiment, North or South, at Gettysburg or the entire Gulf War. Seventy more died in skirmishes before and after the big battles at X-Ray and Albany, Moore reports.

Although Landing Zone X-Ray is where the first Hueys landed, and the battle started, the Albany landing zone was the scene of some of the bloodiest fighting of the Vietnam War. This excerpt from the book focuses on the fighting at Albany on the third day of the Ia Drang battle. Joseph Galloway, the co-author of the book, was with Moore at X-Ray, but his report account of Albany is as well researched and reported as the X-Ray events. Galloway was a civilian war correspondent whose bravery at X-Ray resulted in him being the only civilian awarded the Bronze Star during the Vietnam War.

The fame of LZ X-Ray in the Mel Gibson movie overshadows the events at the nearby LZ Albany. Three Medals of Honor went to helicopter pilots operating at X-Ray, and Col. Moore and Sergeant Ernie Savage were awarded Distinguished Service Crosses. There were numerous other citations, but Col. Moore had problems with all the awards and he says in his book: "Too many men had died bravely and heroically, while the men who had witnessed their deaths had also been killed. Acts of valor that, on other fields, on other days, would have been rewarded with the Medal of Honor or Distinguished Service Cross or Silver Star were recognized only with a telegram saying, 'The Secretary of the Army regrets . . .' The same is true of our sister battalion, the 2nd of the 7th."

Col. Moore's sister battalion was moving into position at Landing Zone Albany just as Moore and his men were evacuating X-Ray after three days of bloody fighting. Now it was the 2nd Battalion's turn, and this excerpt from We Were Soldiers Once *shows something of what they endured at Landing Zone Albany.*

THE NORTH VIETNAMESE BATTLEFIELD COMMANDER, THEN-SENIOR Lieutenant Colonel Nguyen Huu An, had watched the Americans leaving the clearing they called X-Ray. He and his principal subordinate, 66th Regimental commander Lieutenant Colonel La Ngoc Chau, had one thought uppermost in their minds: General Vo Nguyen Giap's dictum "You must win the first battle." As far as Colonel An was concerned, the fight with the Americans that had begun on November 14, in Landing Zone X-Ray, wasn't over. It was simply moving to a new location a short distance away.

An says: "I think this fight of November seventeenth was the most important of the entire campaign. I gave the order to my battalions: When you meet the Americans divide yourself into many groups and attack the column from all directions and divide the column into many pieces. Move inside the column, grab them by the belt, and thus avoid casualties from the artillery and air. We had some advantages: We attacked your column from the sides and, at the moment of the attack, we were waiting for you. This was our reserve battalion and they were just waiting for their turn. The 8th Battalion had not been used in the fighting in this campaign. They were fresh."

Viewed from the American side, the firelight began at the head of the 2nd Battalion column and swiftly spread down the right, or east, side of the American line of march in a full-fledged roar.

Specialist 4 Dick Ackerman was the right-flank point man in the recon platoon, which was itself the point of the battalion. Says Ackerman: "We were going to the left to a clearing. We had gone about 100 feet when we heard some shots, then more shots and finally all hell broke loose. The main brunt of the attack was right where we had been standing just a few minutes before. We hit the dirt. I was laying in the middle of a clearing and bullets were kicking dirt in my eyes and breaking off the grass."

Some of the platoon gathered at a row of trees in front of Ackerman. "I wasn't going to run over there with the bulky pack, so I unhooked it and took off for the trees. We saw NVA sneaking up. We started picking them off and I don't think any of them ever realized we were there. After awhile we could hear someone calling us from a circle of trees. We started running back across the field. I fell behind a small tree. I was on my side with my shoulder against the tree when I heard a big thump and felt the tree shake. It had taken a bullet just opposite my shoulder. I decided to lay down flat."

Ackerman's first sergeant was standing, shouting and giving directions. "His shirt was off and he was in his tee-shirt. He lifted his left arm to point and I could see where a bullet had ripped open the inside of his arm and part of the side of his chest. He was still giving orders. We were then ordered to another part of the circle that was weak. It was facing the main area of attack. There were people running everywhere. We couldn't just open fire in that direction because our guys were there. We were on semi-automatic and picking off whoever we could be sure of as a target."

Ackerman's recon-platoon leader, Lieutenant Payne, had moved most of his men across the second and larger clearing and into the trees on the western or far side of Albany. Alpha Company had split and sent one platoon around the northeast edge and another around the southwest edge of the clearing. Pat Payne was headed across the clearing to join his platoon when, he says, "all hell broke loose up along the north side of the LZ. I turned to my right and observed some American soldiers moving to the northwest to set up positions and they went down in a hail of bullets. Within minutes we were all under heavy attack and my radio operator and I were pinned down in the middle of the LZ with most of the fire coming from the north and northwest."

Lieutenant Payne's radio came alive as the Alpha Company platoon leaders reported heavy fighting. Payne says, "Mortar rounds began falling, which was a new experience for everyone, since we had never had any kind of mortar fire against us. The noise level was unbelievable. I remember pressing my body flatter against the ground than I had ever been in my life and thinking that certainly the highest things sticking up were my heels. Mortars continued to fall and small-arms and machine-gun fire continued at a hectic pace. Finally my mind seemed to adjust and I once again began to think about the situation we were in and what we were going to do."

Payne raised his head and saw that the North Vietnamese weren't actually ambushing Alpha Company so much as they were attacking it. "I told my radio operator to stay put and I jumped up and ran the twenty-five yards back to the command post in the trees between the two clearings, where I found the battalion S-3, Jim Spires. I explained the situation and recommended that I pull the recon platoon back across the LZ and set up positions so that we could have an adequate field of fire. In LZ X-Ray I had seen the advantages of the fields of fire that the 1st Battalion had set up and how they had successfully repelled heavy attacks. The S-3 agreed and I returned to the middle of the LZ to link up with my radio operator."

Payne was able to get all his squad leaders on the radio, "explained to them what we were going to do, and then we coordinated our movement. I counted down to jump-off; then all of us raced back across the open LZ. Miraculously, we had only one man killed: a new recruit who froze. Just as we reached the tree line, we set up a perimeter and turned to face the first of two or three North Vietnamese attacks across the clearing from the west, where we had just come from. I clearly remember that first attack; we stopped them. They were surprised by the amount of firepower we put across the landing zone."

The recon-platoon leader adds: "As they regrouped I saw what must have been a company commander, North Vietnamese, running back and forth along his line of men encouraging them and rallying them. He then led a second attack. I admired his courage, because there were at least twenty of us all trying to stop him. After a third attempt, the NVA didn't try to come across the landing zone again. Rather, they started coming around to the north side."

Alpha Company's commander, Captain Sugdinis, was in the trees, headed to where he had seen the battalion command group disappear. "Just as I noticed a small clearing up ahead I heard one or two shots to my rear, back where my 1st and 2nd Platoons were. I looked back. There was a pause of several seconds and then slowly all hell began to break loose. Since I was somewhat forward of the remainder of my Company and did not draw fire in the initial exchange, I continued to move forward toward Albany. I knew I had to establish a perimeter that would accommodate helicopters, provide fields of fire and be a distinctive piece of terrain for people to maneuver toward."

Albany was not a typical landing zone—the usual single clearing surrounded by trees. In fact, the small clearing that Captain Sugdinis believed to be Albany was actually only the first of two clearings. A lightly wooded island separated it from a larger clearing up ahead. Within that grove of trees there were at least three giant termite hills: one at the edge of the trees, on the north side; another on the western end; and a third in the middle. The copse was not completely surrounded by open area; the east and west ends were connected to the forest by a few trees about twenty feet or so apart.

Captain Sugdinis says, "Larry Gwin and I hit the edge of Albany on the northeast side of the clearing as the column began to receive intense fire. We began to receive sporadic sniper fire. Part of the Recon Platoon had already reached the island. I yelled across the opening for someone to cover us. We ran to the island. At this point I called my 1st and 2nd Platoons on the radio. Almost immediately I lost communication with the 1st Platoon. The platoon sergeant for the 2nd Platoon came on the radio. That was SFC William A. Ferrell, 38, from Stanton, Tennessee. He was a veteran of World War II and Korea, had been a prisoner of war in Korea, and could have chosen to remain in the States. He did not have to deploy to Vietnam with us. Everyone called him Pappy."

Ferrell kept asking Captain Sugdinis where he was, telling him they were mixed up with the North Vietnamese and had several wounded and killed. "I couldn't pinpoint his location. I knew where he should have been—directly east of our island. Pappy then radioed that he was hit; that there were three or four men with him, all hit. I could hear the firing at his location over the radio. I never heard from Pappy again. He did not survive.

"The survivors of my 1st Platoon, with the Recon Platoon, were the initial defenses at Albany. The battalion command group made it safely into the perimeter. Bob McDade and Frank Henry probably owe their lives to those North Vietnamese prisoners. If they hadn't come forward when they did, and stayed forward, they would have been further back in the column and probably would not have survived. At some point at Albany McDade asked what had become of the North Vietnamese prisoners and was told that they had attempted to escape when the shooting started and had been shot."

Lieutenant Colonel McDade himself recalls, "When things began happening I got in with Alpha Company. I know I was trying to figure out what was going on. I moved very fast—let's get over here in these trees and let's all get together. The enemy seemed to be all over the woods. We had good tight control in the immediate area and were trying to figure out where everybody else was. One of the things I was very concerned with was people being trigger-happy and just shooting up the grass. I was telling them: 'Make sure you know what you are shooting at because we are scattered!'"

Sergeant Jim Gooden, the battalion's assistant operations sergeant, was with the headquarters detachment, toward the rear of the column. "We were getting fire from three sides. We were getting it from up in the trees, and from both sides. A guy got hit next to me and I grabbed his machine gun. I braced myself against an anthill. Then we got hit by mortars. It was zeroed in right on us. I looked around and everybody was dead. The commo sergeant, SFC Melvin Gunter, fell over hit in the face, dead. The same mortar round that killed Gunter put shrapnel in my back and shoulder. They were closing in for the final assault. I was shooting, trying to break a hole through them, but didn't know which way to go. I went the wrong way, right into the killing zone. I found stacks of GIs." Gunter, thirty-eight, was from Vincent, Alabama.

The battalion operations officer, Captain Spires, believes that the fact that the commanders were absent from their companies when the fight started contributed to the confusion. "It had the most effect, I think, on Charlie Company. Their commander, Captain Skip Fesmire, was up with us and Don Cornett, the Charlie Company executive officer, was killed early on, so they had no commander and they just disintegrated."

Spires also remembers that the shooting began "at the head of the column; then it moved back down the column. I think the enemy battalion ran head on into the recon and Alpha Company troops, withdrew, hooked around, and ran straight into Charlie Company. They also hit part of Delta Company. The battalion command group was just ahead of Delta Company. I had four men back there, including my operations sergeant, and three of them were killed."

Specialist 4 Jim Epperson, McDade's radio operator, says: "We set our radios down behind an anthill. The artillery guys were on their own radio calling in. We honestly did not know much about the situation in the rest of the column. Some of the radio operators were already killed. We were cut off from everyone. Colonel McDade wasn't getting anything from his people down the line. Charlie, Delta, and Headquarters Company weren't reporting because they were either dead or, in the case of Headquarters, didn't have any radios."

By now it was 1:26 p.m. The recon platoon; the Alpha Company commander, Sugdinis, and his executive officer, Gwin; and Colonel McDade's command group were in the small wooded area between the clearings. Sugdinis and Gwin were near one of the termite hills, Payne's recon platoon was near another, and McDade and his group behind the third hill.

Lieutenant Larry Gwin looked back south at the point where he and Captain Sugdinis had emerged from the jungle just minutes before; the entire area was now alive with North Vietnamese soldiers who had obviously cut through the battalion's line of march, severing the head of the battalion from the body. Gwin saw three GIs coming through the high grass, running from the area swarming with the enemy. "I jumped up and screamed to them, waving my arm. They saw me and headed directly to our position. The first man was a captain, our Air Force forward air controller, who was completely spent. I pointed out the battalion command group, which was huddled to our rear at another anthill, and he crawled toward them. He was followed by the battalion sergeant major, Jim Scott, who dropped down next to me. And Scott was followed by a young, very small PFC who was delirious and holding his guts in with his hands. He kept asking, 'Are the helicopters coming?' I said, 'Yes, hang on.'"

"The battalion commander initially thought that the incoming rounds were all friendly fire. He had been hollering for all of us to cease fire and the word went out over the command net but to no avail, as the troops on the perimeter could see North Vietnamese. The sergeant major and I were looking to the rear when I heard a loud blast. The sergeant major yelled: 'I'm hit, sir!' He had taken a round in the back under his armpit and there was a large hole underneath his right arm. I told him he would be OK, to bandage it himself. This he did, ripping off his shirt. Then he picked up his M-16 and headed back to one of the ant hills. I saw the sergeant major a few times after that and he was fighting like a demon."

Sergeant Major Scott says, "I took a bullet through my chest, not more than fifteen or twenty minutes into the battle. I could see enemy soldiers to our left, right and front in platoon- and company-size elements. They were up in the trees, up on top of the anthills, and in the high grass. We weren't exactly organized. We didn't have time. Everything happened at once. I did not see a hole being dug prior to eight p.m. that night. We did use the trees and anthills for cover. Within half an hour there was an attempt to organize groups into a defensive position in a company area. Individuals did this, no one in particular. I think that is what saved us."

Lieutenant Gwin rejoined the Alpha Company command group on the western edge of the copse of trees. "Joel Sugdinis told me that our 1st Platoon, on our right, was gone, and that the 2nd Platoon, to our rear, was cut off and all wounded or dead. I stood up to get a better view of the woods on the other side of the clearing to the north and saw about twenty North Vietnamese bent over, charging toward our position and only about sixty yards away. I screamed 'Here they come!' and jumped forward firing. I heard the battalion commander yell 'Withdraw!' and I thought that was odd because there didn't seem like anywhere to go.

"Almost everyone jumped up and ran back to the third anthill. First Sergeant Frank Miller; Joel Sugdinis; the artillery FO, Hank Dunn; and PFC Dennis Wilson, the radio operator; and I stayed and killed all the North Vietnamese. I shot about three with my first burst, and then remember sighting in on the lead enemy, who was carrying an AK-47. I got him with my first round, saw him drop to the ground and start to crawl forward. I was afraid he would throw a grenade. I sighted very carefully and squeezed again, and saw him jolted by my second round, but he continued to move and I stepped out from cover and emptied my remaining rounds into him. He was about twenty yards from our anthill.

The rush had been stopped, but we could still see many, many Vietnamese milling around on the other side of the clearing."

The Alpha Company command group now returned to their original position, facing the area where they had first emerged from the forest, to the southwest. Lieutenant Gwin says, "Joel Sugdinis and I had pretty much decided we would make our stand right here. No point in moving. The North Vietnamese were between us and the rest of the battalion column, and that jungle was crawling with bad guys. They were fighting, moving on down the column."

Sugdinis and Gwin agree that it was not long after this that the commander of Alpha Company's missing 2nd Platoon, Lieutenant Gordon Grove, staggered into the American position from the east. Larry Gwin: "I saw Gordy Grove coming across the field along with two wounded men. They were the only ones left of his platoon who could move. Grove was distraught. We got him and his two men in with us, and got our medics working on the wounded. Then Gordy asked for men to go back with him and get his people. Joel Sugdinis said: 'Gordy, I can't send anybody back out there.' It was clear that to leave this perimeter was death. Everywhere you looked you could see North Vietnamese. Gordy asked permission to go talk to the battalion commander. Sugdinis said go ahead. He jogged over, asked McDade for help to go get his men, got a negative response, so he came back to our anthill."

Gwin adds, "There was a tremendous battle going on in the vicinity of where we had come into the clearing and beyond there in the jungle. It was Charlie Company, caught in the killing zone of the ambush, fighting for its life. The mortar fire had ceased—the enemy tubes apparently had been overrun by Charlie Company, because we found them all the next day—but there still were hundreds of North Vietnamese calmly walking around the area we were observing. Now began the sniping phase of our battle. I call it that because for a long period of time all we did was pick off enemy wandering around our perimeter, and this lasted until we started getting air support. Everything that had happened to this point had probably taken less than thirty minutes."

Gwin saw Major Frank Henry, the battalion executive officer, lying on his back using the radio, trying desperately to get some tactical air support and succeeding. "The air was on the way, but there was no artillery or aerial rocket artillery yet. Jim Spires, the S-3, ran over to us and queried Gordy Grove as to the situation outside the perimeter where he had just come from. Grove told him there were still men out there, tightened into a small perimeter, but they were all wounded and dying and the radios had all been knocked out. Captain Spires asked a second time if he thought anyone was still alive and none of us said anything."

Gwin climbed atop the termite hill and began sniping at the North Vietnamese clearly visible across the clearing in the trees to the south with his M-16 rifle. "There were plenty of targets and I remember picking off ten or fifteen NVA from my position. My memories revolve around the way in which each enemy soldier that I hit fell. Some would slump limply to the ground; some reacted as if they had been hit by a truck. Some that I missed on the first and second shots kept on milling around until I finally hit them. What we did not know at the time was that they were wandering around the elephant grass looking for Americans who were still alive, and killing them off one by one."

After an incoming round snapped past his head, Gwin surrendered his vantage point to Lieutenant Grove, who was eager to settle some scores for his lost platoon. Gwin and his boss, Captain Sugdinis, eased behind the hill, leaned back, and smoked their first cigarettes. Gwin says, "That cigarette brought us back to our senses, and we talked the situation over while those around us poured out fire. We knew we had lost our two Alpha Company rifle platoons, about fifty men, during the first half-hour. Joel was despondent."

The survivors in that thinly held grove of trees at the head of the battalion column could hear the noise of a terrible battle continuing in the forest where the rest of the column was caught. Having hit the head of the 2nd Battalion column hard and stopped it, killing most of Sugdinis's two rifle platoons, the North Vietnamese soldiers immediately raced down the side of the American column, with small groups peeling off and attacking.

As the attack began, all of McDade's company commanders were forward, separated from their men. They had brought their radio operators and, in some cases, their first sergeants and artillery forward observers with them. All of them but one would remain in McDade's perimeter for the rest of the battle.

In answer to the radioed summons from Colonel McDade, Captain George Forrest, a high school and college athlete who was in excellent physical condition, had hiked more than five hundred yards from his Alpha Company, 1st Battalion, 5th Cavalry position, at the tail of the American column, to the head. His two radio operators accompanied him.

Just about the time McDade started to talk to them, a couple of mortar rounds came in. Forrest immediately turned and dashed back toward his company. "I didn't wait for him to dismiss us. I just took off. Both of my radio operators were hit and killed during that run. I didn't get a scratch. When I got back to the company I found my executive officer was down, hit in the back with mortar shrapnel. I wasn't sure about the situation, so I pushed my guys off the trail to the east and put them in a perimeter. It appeared for a time that fire was coming from every direction. So we circled the wagons. I think that firing lasted thirty-five or forty minutes. All my platoon leaders were functioning except Second Lieutenant Larry L. Hess. [Hess, age twenty, from Gettysburg, Pennsylvania, was killed in the first minutes.] My weapons sergeant was wounded."

George Forrest's run down that six-hundred-yard-long gauntlet of fire, miraculously unscathed, and the forming of his men into a defensive perimeter, helped keep Alpha Company, 1st Battalion, 5th Cavalry from sharing the fate of Charlie, Delta, and Headquarters companies of the 2nd Battalion in the middle of the column.

North Vietnamese soldiers climbed into the trees and on top of those brush-covered termite hills, and poured fire down on the cavalry troopers trapped in the tall grass below them in the main body of the column. There was furious firing, including mortar fire, from both sides. The strike at the head of the column was followed so quickly by the enemy encircling assaults that the whole business seemed to erupt almost simultaneously.

Without doubt some platoons of McDade's battalion were alert and in as secure a formation as they could achieve in the elephant grass, brush, and thick scrub trees. But the visibility problem made it difficult to maintain formation, and one result was that the American troops were closer to one another than was tactically sound, providing juicy targets for a grenade, a mortar round, or a burst from an AK-47 rifle. All down the column, platoon leaders, sergeants, radio operators, and riflemen by the dozens were killed or wounded in the first ten minutes, rapidly degrading communication, cohesion, and control.

Captain Skip Fesmire was near the Albany clearing when the shooting started. He believed his Charlie Company rifle platoons were close enough to the landing zone to maneuver against the enemy and reach the clearing if he moved them quickly and if he was lucky. Fesmire radioed Jim Spires, the battalion operations officer, reported his location, and told Spires he was returning to his men. He never made it.

Fesmire remembers: "The firing became quite intense. My artillery forward observer [Lieutenant Sidney C. M. Smith, twenty-three, of Manhasset, New York] was hit in the head and killed. I was in radio contact with Lieutenant Cornett [Fesmire's executive officer]. He told me that the fire was very intense, particularly incoming mortar fire that was impacting directly on the company. I instructed him to get the company moving forward along the right flank of Delta Company. This was the direction from which the attack was coming. I felt it was necessary to try to consolidate the battalion; to help protect the flank of Delta Company, and to get Charlie Company out of the mortar killing zone."

Captain Fesmire adds, "As I moved back southeast toward my company, I could see the North Vietnamese in the tree line on the other side of a clearing. They were moving generally in the same direction that I was moving, toward Charlie Company. By this time Lieutenant Cornett had Charlie Company moving; they met the elements of the 66th Regiment's battalion head on and were outnumbered. The result was very intense, individual hand-to-hand combat. In the confusion, I had no idea exactly where the company was located. When Lieutenant Cornett died, it was virtually impossible for me to talk to anyone in my company. The battle had clearly become an individual struggle for life. First Sergeant [Franklin] Hance, my two radio operators and I found our return to the company blocked. We were on the edge of an open area and all we could see were enemy."

Specialist 4 Jack P. Smith, who was in Charlie Company, had been a radio operator until a week or so before this operation, when he was shifted to a supply clerk's job. The events of November 17 are etched on his mind. Smith's company commander, Captain Fesmire, had, like the others, been called to the front by Lieutenant Colonel McDade. "Subsequently, many people pointed to this as a major error, and in light of what happened, it was. The firing began to roll all around us. The executive officer of my company, a man called Don Cornett, a very fine officer, jumped up and in the best style of the Infantry School yelled: 'Follow me!'

"Elements of our 1st and 2nd platoons ran right toward a series of anthills. Within ten feet of them we saw there were machine gunners behind them firing point-blank at us. Men all around me began to fall like mown grass. I had never seen people killed before. They began to drop like flies and die right in front of me. These were the only friends I had, and they were dying all around me."

Charlie Company, 2nd Battalion, 7th Cavalry would suffer the heaviest casualties of any unit that fought at LZ Albany. Before its violent collision with the North Vietnamese, the company had some 112 men in its ranks. By sunrise the next day, November 18, forty-five of those men would be dead and more than fifty wounded; only a dozen would answer "present" at the next roll call.

Captain Henry Thorpe, the Delta Company commander, was a hundred yards forward of his company when the fighting began. He and his first sergeant and radio operator sprinted ahead into the island of trees in the Albany clearing to join the battalion command group and helped organize and control a defensive perimeter. The radio operator, Specialist 4 John C. Bratland, was shot in the leg. They were lucky to be where they were. Delta Company, back down the column, was being torn apart. This day it would lose twenty-six men killed and many others severely wounded.

PFC James H. Shadden was in Thorpe's Delta Company mortar platoon. Shadden says the heavily laden mortarmen, exhausted from the march, had dropped in the trail for a short rest and a smoke. He recalls, "I had carried the base plate a long ways. Sergeant Amodias, true to his word, took the base plate, gave me the sights, and went in front of me. When the enemy sprung the ambush, Amodias was killed instantly. The ones who were not killed in the first volley hit the dirt, with the exception of our radio operator, Duncan Krueger. I saw him still standing a few seconds later, until he was shot down. I have no idea why he didn't get down." PFC Duncan Krueger, eighteen, of West Allis, Wisconsin, was killed where he stood.

The intensity of the fire rapidly increased to the point where Shadden couldn't hear anything but weapons firing. "Tone Johnson came crawling by me, hit in the cheek and back of the hand. The trees were full of North Vietnamese, but spotting one was almost impossible. They blended in so well. I kept raising up to try to detect a good target. Matthews Shelton, who was lying next to me, kept jerking me down. As I raised up again a bullet pierced my helmet straight through, front to back I went down again and as I came back up a bullet struck the tree beside my head from behind.

"I don't know if we were surrounded or it was our own men. They were firing wild—anything that moved, somebody shot at it. One trooper crawled up next to me, shooting through the grass a few inches off the ground toward where our own people lay, never thinking what he was doing. I told him to be sure he knew what he was shooting."

The firing eventually began to slack off. Shadden has no idea how much time elapsed. There was no way to keep track of time in a fight like this. "Men were wounded and dead all in the area. Six were alive that I know of: Sergeant [Earthell] Tyler, [PFC A. C.] Carter, [PFC Tone] Johnson, [PFC Matthews] Shelton, [PFC Lawrence] Cohens, and myself. Tyler gave the only order I heard during the entire fight: 'Try to pull back before they finish us off.' Shelton froze to the ground and would not move. [PFC Matthews Shelton, age twenty, of Cincinnati, Ohio, was killed later that afternoon.] The five of us proceeded to try to pull back, but the snipers were still in the trees. Soon I was hit in the right shoulder, which for a time rendered it useless. Tyler was hit in the neck about the same time; he died an arm's length of me, begging for the medic, Specialist 4 William Pleasant, who was already dead. [Pleasant was twenty-three years old and a native of Jersey City, New Jersey.] The last words Tyler ever spoke were 'I'm dying.'" Sergeant Earthell Tyler, thirty-five, was from Columbia, South Carolina.

The soft-spoken Shadden says, "The helplessness I felt is beyond description. Within a few minutes I was hit again, in the left knee. The pain was unbearable. Cohens was hit in the feet and ankle. We were wounded and trapped. I could see we were getting wiped out. A buddy helped me bandage my leg. He got the bandage off a dead Vietnamese. I got behind a log and there was a Vietnamese there, busted up and dead. This was behind us, so I knew we were surrounded."

Specialist 4 Bob Towles, who was with Delta Company's antitank platoon, heard the firing and mortar blasts forward and could see where the trail disappeared into the brush ahead of him. But he saw no one at all up there. As the front came alive with intense firing, and no information came back to him, Towles's concern redoubled:

"The sound of firing on our right flank got our attention in a hurry. We all faced in that direction. A couple of senior NCOs moved forward and joined the line of enlisted men. We formed a solid battle line about twenty yards long; twelve of us. Bullets whizzed overhead. Still we could see nothing. We waited, expecting to see our men out on flank security break cover and enter the safety of our perimeter. They never did. The sound came closer. Within seconds the wood line changed.

"North Vietnamese troops shattered the foliage and headed straight for us, AK-47 rifles blazing, on the dead run. I selected the closest one and fired twice. I hit him but he refused to go down; he kept coming and shooting. I turned my M-16 on full automatic, fired, and he crumpled. I shifted to another target and squeezed the trigger. Nothing happened. The fear I felt turned to terror. I saw a cartridge jammed in the chamber. I removed it, reloaded, and began firing again. They kept pouring out of the wood line; we kept firing; then finally they stopped coming. On the ground in front of me lay the three magazines I taped together to carry in my rifle plus one other magazine. I had fired eighty rounds."

The lull did not last long. Towles peered beyond the anthill toward the mortar platoon. "It appeared as if the ground was opening up and swallowing the mortarmen, they fell so fast," Shadden recalls. "A brown wave of death rolled over them and on into Charlie Company. Vietnamese intermixed with them. Then reality set in: The enemy held the ground beyond the anthill. The column was cut in half!

"Incoming gunfire drew our attention back to the tree line. The firing rapidly increased. We returned fire at muzzle flashes. I heard an explosion behind me. Turning, I saw ChiCom grenades landing. All flash and smoke, no casualties. The volume of fire became almost unendurable. Bullets peeled bark from trees. Vegetation disintegrated. I looked to Lieutenant James Lawrence for help. Saw his head violently recoil. He hit the ground.

"A second later I was spun around, then slammed into the dirt. I rose to my hands and knees and started down the line. Blood ran everywhere. The mortar-platoon sergeant's .45 pistol had been shot from his hand. His right hand hung limp from his wrist, and blood poured to the ground. Someone tried to dress his wound. Someone raised Lieutenant Lawrence and attempted to steady him. The firing continued."

Towles's tight twelve-man line was shrinking fast. "I turned back toward the wood line and detected movement. I shifted in that direction and spotted North Vietnamese in the underbrush. Enemy turning our flank! Our position was no longer tenable. I turned back with the warning. Sergeant Jerry Baker took charge now; he realized we needed to pull out. He appointed the unwounded and some slightly wounded to help the severely wounded. An instant later he ordered the move.

"I led this retreat because of my position in the battle line. I rose to my feet and headed in the only direction void of enemy fire—toward our left rear—at a run. Thirty or forty yards and I broke out of the trees into a large clearing of waist-deep grass. The sunlight hurt my eyes. Twenty yards into the field I noticed the man running half a step to my rear go down. I dove to the ground and turned to see PFC Marlin Klarenbeek struggling with a leg wound."

Captain George Forrest was now back with his Alpha Company, 1st Battalion, 5th Cavalry soldiers at the rear of the column. "I had lost my radio operators, and when I got back and got another radio I found out McDade's lead elements were in heavy firefights to their front and to their west. I got maybe two transmissions from McDade, then lost contact. We circled up. My parent battalion had come up on my net and I was able to contact Captain Buse Tully, commander of Bravo Company, 1st Battalion, 5th Cav. I have never felt such relief at hearing and recognizing a voice. I knew someone who cared about us was close at hand."

Here's what the Vietnam War looked like in the midafternoon of November 17, through the eyes of two of Captain Forrest's Alpha

Company riflemen, PFC David A. (Purp) Lavender of Murphysboro, Illinois, and Specialist 4 James Young of Steelville, Missouri.

Says Lavender: "My Platoon was bringing up the rear. We started to maneuver and work our way up the column to help those up ahead. Every time we made a move we were hit by mortars. It was something you can't describe. People were dropping like flies. The first blast killed a young soldier named [PFC Vincent] Locatelli. Every time we moved they dropped mortars on us. I know we must have had twelve or fifteen wounded out of our platoon, including our platoon leader.

"These were my buddies I had been in the Army with for two years. [The] majority of our whole battalion had been drafted at age twenty-one [and] had been in service for over eighteen months. All of us were near twenty-three years old. They became my brothers over time. Hearing these fellows scream, hearing them killed, stuck in my heart and mind ever since. The most critical part of this fight was the beginning. It was the surprise. They had us in a U-shaped ambush and they had us cut off with mortars."

Rifleman Jim Young says: "I sat down and took a nap. We had flankers out a hundred yards or so on left and right, so I thought it was safe to grab some sleep. That little bit of shooting up front got a lot worse. That woke me up. Then our 1st Platoon received mortar fire. Five men wounded. I heard them calling for medics. Mortars kept coming in. Heard them order 1st Platoon to pull back out of the area where those rounds were hitting."

Young's platoon was ordered to get on line and move in reaction to the enemy fire. "Everyone had hit the ground when those mortars began coming in. They told us to move ahead toward the enemy. We got on line and we walked right into an enemy ambush. They were behind trees, anthills, and down on the ground. There was waist-high grass and a lot of trees around us. There were enemy soldiers in that grass. They were hard to see and we had to shoot where we thought they were. The medic had his hands full, couldn't take care of all the wounded. One man to my right was hit in the heel. His name was Harold Smith.

"There was a grassy field to my left twenty-five or thirty yards, and a sniper off on my right. I couldn't see him, but I saw a tracer bullet go across my hand. I felt the wind of that bullet. The same bullet passed over the back of Smith's neck. He was lucky he had his head down. Our company commander, Captain Forrest, came running along our line. He was stopping and telling everybody where to go. He acted as though he was immune to the enemy fire. I don't know how he kept from getting hit."

Just ahead of Alpha Company, 1st Battalion, in the hodgepodge of admin and supply staffers, medics, and communications people that constituted Headquarters Company of the 2nd Battalion, 7th Cavalry marched Doc William Shucart, the 2nd Battalion surgeon, Lieutenant John Howard of the medical platoon, and Lieutenant Bud Alley, the communications-platoon leader.

Says Shucart: "Before the fight I remember smelling cigarette smoke. Vietnamese cigarettes. I said: 'I smell the enemy smoking!' The next thing we knew mortars were dropping all around us, then a lot of small-arms fire was coming in, and then everything just dissolved into confusion. We thought that the head of the column had gotten turned and somehow we were getting shot by our own troops. Guys were dropping all around us. It seems like in a very short time I found myself all alone. We had gotten widely dispersed. I was running around with my M-16. I had a .45 pistol, which was useless and I picked up somebody's M-16.

"I was under direct enemy fire all this time. I got one little zinger up my back, nothing serious, just a grazing wound that left me a nice little scar. This was the most scared I've ever been in my life. I was wearing a St. Christopher's medal around my back that somebody had sent me. I thought: *This is the time to make a deal.* Then I thought: *I've never been very religious. He isn't likely to want to deal.* So I got up and started looking for somebody, anybody. I found one of our radio operators, dead, and got on his radio trying to raise somebody. I remember trying to get them to throw some smoke so I could find them."

Lieutenant John Howard remembers: "Soon after the first shots, mortars and grenades started hitting all around us. The small-arms fire picked up to an intense level and soldiers started going down very quickly with gunshot or shrapnel wounds. There was confusion, and some thought they were being fired at by other American soldiers in the area. This confusion cleared up pretty quickly as the North Vietnamese assault wave moved in so close that we could see them and hear them talking.

"They suddenly appeared behind anthills and up in the trees, sniping at anyone who moved, and we found ourselves shooting at them in all directions. As we crawled around in the tall elephant grass it was very difficult to tell where anyone was, or whether they were friendly or enemy. One thing I caught on to very quickly was how the NVA were signaling to each other in the high grass by tapping on the wooden stocks of their AK-47 rifles."

Lieutenant Bud Alley recalls clearly when "word came back that recon had been shot at. Then that recon had hit an ambush. Then orders to Charlie Company, just in front of us, to move on line and roll up the flank of it. John Howard and I were sitting beside each other. All of a sudden a couple of shots rang out twenty-five yards in front of us. By now we're all standing up, scared. The call comes back: 'Medic! Medic!' The first group of medics in front of us takes off and John Howard takes off with them. Now the leaves begin to shake as bullets arc coming in. The infantry in Charlie Company are yelling: 'Get on line!' I pushed my guys up on line, twenty-five yards inside the tree line, and suddenly all hell broke loose. There was lots of shooting and it was difficult to maintain the line.

"A fellow got hit and screamed. My radio operator and I ran up to him and dragged him behind a little tree. He was shot through the wrist and kept screaming. Then he got shot again. I put my M-16 on automatic and fired up high and something fell out of the tree. I crawled down to an anthill where a couple of guys were. I stayed there and found a guy who had a radio. I called in to see what the hell was happening. About then the net went dead; somebody got shot with his finger on the transmit key, or something. The last thing I heard on the net was that Ghost 5 got hit; that was Don Cornett, the Charlie Company executive officer."

Colonel Tim Brown, the 3rd Brigade commander, the man who had the authority to order in reinforcements, was overhead in his command helicopter asking his ground commander, Lieutenant Colonel Bob McDade, for information on the seriousness of the situation. With Brown was the brigade fire-support coordinator, Captain Dudley Tademy, who was eager to unleash all the artillery, air support, and aerial rocket artillery at his command.

Brown and Tademy had just left LZ Columbus where they had been talking to Lieutenant Colonel Tully when the first shots were fired at Albany. Colonel Brown was headed back to brigade headquarters at the tea plantation.

Captain Tademy recalls, "Suddenly I heard Joe Price, the artillery forward observer with McDade's battalion, saying 'We have a problem! I need help!' Price was hollering for everything he could get: air, artillery, ARA. We finally got him to slow down so we could understand what was happening. I notified Colonel Brown that something was going on down there. He tried to get on the command net and talk to McDade. I stayed on the artillery net trying to get some support for them. By then we were overflying their position and we could see puffs of smoke coming out of the woods. When Joe Price would come up on the net I could hear the loud firing over their radio."

Major Roger Bartholomew, commander of the aerial rocket artillery helicopters, was in contact with Captain Tademy and flew a zigzag pattern over the forest trying to get a fix on the location of friendly troops so that his helicopters could support them. He had no luck. Captain Tademy had the artillery fire smoke rounds to try to register defensive fires. No luck there either. "It didn't help because everybody was so mixed up by then on the ground. We had tactical air, ARA, and artillery and still we couldn't do a damned thing. It was the most helpless, hopeless thing I ever witnessed."

Colonel Tim Brown's helicopter was running low on fuel and the chopper had to return to Catecka to refuel. Brown says, "I knew they were in contact. I did not know how severe, or anything else. While I was talking to McDade I could hear the rifle fire, but he didn't know what was happening. I asked: 'What happened to your lead unit?' He didn't know. 'Where's your training units?' He didn't know. And he didn't know what had happened to any of the rest of them. Nobody knew what the hell was going on. We were not in [a] position to shoot a bunch of artillery or air strikes in there because we didn't know where to put them."

Captain John Cash, in the center of the now busy Brigade Headquarters at Catecka, recalls the return of Colonel Brown: "Brown was standing there, on our radio, asking McDade what's going on, yelling,

'Goddammit, what is going on out there?' McDade came back with, 'Got a couple of KIA's [killed in action] here and trying to get a handle on the situation. Let me get back to you later. Out.' Captain Tademy, who was at Brown's side in the tactical operations center [TOC] says, "I heard McDade talking. Brown kept asking him what was going on. The radio speakers were all blaring. What I was hearing was that things were not going very well in McDade's area."

After his command helicopter had refueled, Brown flew back into the valley. "All of a sudden I heard all kinds of firing while I was talking to McDade on the radio. He started yelling: 'They're running! They're running!' I thought for one terrible moment he meant that his battalion was running. What it was, the Air Force had dropped napalm on a company-size North Vietnamese unit and *they* were running, not the Americans. About then I began to figure that McDade was in real trouble."

Only now did Colonel Brown begin rounding up reinforcements to send in to help Bob McDade's 2nd Battalion. Brown ordered Lieutenant Colonel Frederic Ackerson to send a company from his 1st Battalion, 5th Cavalry overland from LZ Columbus toward LZ Albany. Ackerson dispatched Captain Walter B. (Buse) Tully's Bravo Company, 1st Battalion, 5th Cavalry on the two-mile march toward the tail of McDade's embattled column. Meanwhile, Brown radioed orders warning McDade's missing component, Captain Myron Diduryk's Bravo Company, 2nd Battalion, 7th Cav, to prepare to be airlifted from Camp Holloway into Landing Zone Albany.

Brown acknowledges that it was too little, too late. "I've thought a good deal about this action over the years, and I believe that most of the casualties occurred in the first hour of fighting. I think the bulk of it was done right at the very first. They did not have decent security for moving through a jungle."

Lieutenant Colonel McDade for his part confirms that he was unable to provide Colonel Brown with detailed reports of what was happening to three of the four companies in his stalled column—most of which were out of sight and out of reach. Says McDade: "In that first hour or so, the situation was so fluid that I was acting more as a platoon leader than a battalion commander. We were trying to secure a perimeter. I was trying to figure out what the hell was going on, myself. I don't think anybody in the battalion could have told you what the situation really was at that time. I can see where I might have left Tim Brown in the dark about what was going on; I didn't really know myself until things quieted down."

The battalion commander adds, "I could have yelled and screamed that we were in a death trap, and all that crap. But I didn't know it was as bad as it was. I had no way of checking visually or physically, by getting out of that perimeter, so all I could do was hope to get back in touch. I wasn't going to scream that the sky was falling, especially in a situation where nobody could do anything about it anyway."

Lieutenant Colonel John A. Hemphill was the operations officer at Brigadier General Knowles's division forward command post at Pleiku. He recalls that he and Knowles flew over the Ia Drang on November 17 and watched the B-52 bombing strike on the Chu Pong massif. They then flew back to Pleiku. Says Hemphill: "When we got back to Pleiku, here came Tim Brown to see Knowles. I brought him to Knowles and he said, 'I have not heard from or made contact with McDade and I am concerned.' So we went piling out and flew out in late afternoon, and that's when I think was the first time we were aware that anything was amiss."

Although Knowles does not recall the Brown visit to his headquarters described by Hemphill, he does have a vivid memory of how he first learned that McDade's battalion was heavily engaged with the enemy. "I had a warrant officer in the support command at Pleiku. His job was to watch the beans, bullets, fuel, and casualties. He had a direct hotline to me; I wanted to know immediately when things got off track. In the afternoon, around two or three o'clock, he called me and said: 'I got fourteen KIA from McDade's battalion.' All the bells went off. I called my pilot, Wayne Knudsen, and John Stoner, my air liaison officer, and went out to see McDade. I stopped at 3rd Brigade before flying on out to Albany. Tim Brown had nothing to tell me."

Knowles adds, "We got over Albany and McDade was in deep trouble. I wanted to land. McDade said, 'General, I can't handle you. I can't even get medevac in.' I couldn't land. I wanted to get something moving on the ground over there. I told Stoner and Bill Becker, the division artillery commander, 'This guy doesn't know what he's got; put a ring of steel around him.' I could help him with firepower and did. I then went back to see Tim, who still had no information. I was irked. A hell of a mess; no question."

The 2nd Battalion, 7th Cavalry had been reduced from a full battalion in column line of march to a small perimeter defended by a few Alpha Company survivors, the recon platoon, a handful of stragglers from Charlie and Delta Companies, and the battalion command group at the Albany landing-zone clearing—plus one other small perimeter, five hundred to seven hundred yards south, which consisted of Captain George Forrest's Alpha Company, 1st Battalion, 7th Cavalry. In between, dead or wounded or hiding in the tall grass, was the bulk of Bob McDade's command: the fragments of two rifle companies, a weapons company, and Headquarters Company.

Each and every man still alive on that field, American and North Vietnamese, was fighting for his life. In the tall grass it was nearly impossible for the soldiers of either side to identify friend or foe except at extremely close range. Americans in olive-drab and North Vietnamese in mustard-brown were fighting and dying side by side. It may have begun as a meeting engagement, a hasty ambush, a surprise attack, a battle of maneuver—and, in fact, it was all of those things but within minutes the result was a wild melee, a shoot-out, with the gunfighters killing not only the enemy but sometimes their friends just a few feet away.

There would be no cheap victory here this day for either side. There would be no victory at all—just the terrible certainty of death in the tall grass.

Chapter Three

Into the Fire

Ploesti, the Most Fateful Mission of World War II
Duane Schultz

Some of the most savage and memorable battles of World War II were not fought on the ground, or at sea. They were fought in the skies over Nazi targets, with names like Schweinfurt, Berlin, and Hamburg.

On August 1, 1943, four-engine B-24 Liberator bombers of the Ninth Air Force flew a raid to destroy Nazi oil-producing refineries at Ploesti, Romania. Taking off from their base at Benghazi in Northern Africa, 177 B-24s carried out the mission. In that attack, which lasted 27 minutes from the first bomb being dropped to the last, more decorations and awards for bravery under fire went to the pilots and crewmembers than any other mission in the history of

American aerial combat. All received the Distinguished Flying Cross. Five Medals of Honor were awarded, three posthumously.

In his illuminating and graphic account of the Ploesti raid, in his book Into the Fire, Ploesti, the Most Fateful Mission of World War II, *author Duane Schultz describes the historic mission:*

"Of the 177 Liberators assigned to the mission, 54 had been lost by day's end. Only 93 returned to base, and 60 of these were so badly damaged they never flew again. Of the others, 19 landed in Allied airfields such as Cypress 7 in Turkey . . . three crashed into the sea. The remainder crashed in and around Ploesti.

"The casualties were staggering. Of the 1,726 airmen on the mission, 532 were killed, captured, interned, or listed as missing in action. In addition, 440 of those who returned to Benghazi were wounded, some so severely they never returned to active service."

What was it like during those 27 minutes, when the skies over Ploesti were filled with smoke and deadly anti-aircraft fire? When planes on fire and doomed flew on to the target, dropping their bombs? When pilots of burning and doomed aircraft tried desperately to gain altitude, so their crews could bail out? All that, and more, was the stuff of Ploesti, and this excerpt from Duane Schultz's book goes far in helping us share what happened that day.

"WE FLEW THROUGH SHEETS OF FLAME, AND AIRPLANES WERE EVERY-where, some of them on fire and others exploding. It's indescribable to anyone who wasn't there." So wrote Col. Leon Johnson, commanding officer of the Flying Eight Balls, the 44th bombardment group.

Flying as copilot in *Suzy Q,* Johnson was heading toward Ploesti on the right side of the tracks that carried the flak train. Killer Kane's 98th was on the other side, taking the brunt of the train's antiaircraft fire. The 44th was spared the worst of it because their flight path took them closer to the train, which meant that the German guns would have to be elevated higher to hit them.

In addition, the planes of the 44th presented a smaller target; only 16 followed *Suzy Q.* The remainder of the group, led by Lt. Col. James Posey, had already turned south to attack their designated target five miles south of Ploesti.

Colonel Johnson was wrestling with the same dilemma Kane had faced. Should he continue with the mission even though his target had already been attacked, or seek another target in the few seconds left to him to decide? The pilot, Maj. William Brandon, glanced at Johnson, silently asking whether they should turn back. "William," Johnson said, "*you* are on target!" But Johnson could not yet see the target. He recalled:

> *Ahead the target looked like a solid wall of fire and smoke, it appeared that we would have to fly through it. When we got closer to the target we could see that the smoke was staggered a little. Our individual targets were in the center of a clearer spot so we were able to get through.*

The break in the smoke also allowed them to see how many planes from previous waves had been shot down. One crewman reported that "the ground was littered with charred and still burning bodies of fallen comrades, many racing desperately for cover to avoid capture." One of the ships being consumed by raging fires was Addison Baker's plane, *Hell's Wench*.

Johnson led the 44th into the smoke, as though maneuvering his way through an obstacle course. "We found that we could weave around the fires like we weaved over the trees and over the high-tension wires because the fires were not a continuous line across."

They were no higher than 130 feet when they jettisoned their bombs, low enough to see them hit. The tail gunner, William Brady, was snapping pictures and saw one bomb strike an industrial plant. Two others took a couple of bounces and crashed into a boiler house. Then Brady saw a lone German soldier crouched beside a house. He raised his rifle and took aim at the plane. Brady shifted position to put away his camera just as a bullet crashed through the turret's Plexiglas precisely where his head had been. He had escaped death by a fraction of an inch and no more than a second in time.

The planes of the 44th flew on past the target but not yet out of danger. Johnson spied an 88-mm gun aimed directly at *Suzy Q*. He swung the ship left and right and passed over the gun as it fired. A shell went through one wing, leaving a gaping hole. Fortunately it did not explode; had it gone off at that low altitude, no one would have survived.

So it was for many of the bombers, life or death by an inch, a second, a turn to the right, a swing to the left. Perhaps a difference of a few feet in altitude, or because something went wrong with a shell and it did not explode where it was supposed to. The crew of *Suzy Q* was among the lucky ones.

Calaban was lucky too. Piloted by James Hill and Ed Dobson, the ship was in the second three-plane element behind *Suzy Q's* lead element. As they headed into the bomb run, Dobson pushed himself upright when he realized what was in front of them. "Balloon cables!" he shouted, knowing there was no time to take evasive action. Some 50 years later, Dobson's son described what happened.

A cable whipped past Calaban's *nose and sliced into the right wing a foot from the fuselage and Lt. Dobson. It missed the inside propeller, a hit which might have been fatal. It cut the deicer boot and the air speed indicator tube, but the main spar held. The cable snapped instead of the wing, and it snapped before any of the affixed contact bombs hit the wing.*

As the plane approached the target, a huge fireball erupted from the smoke and flames already filling the sky, caused by the delayed action bombs of the 93rd. *Calaban* dropped its bombs and flew clear. Watching from the rear, Hubert Womack, the tail gunner saw a Liberator from another group bearing down on them. Two of its engines were on fire and it was angling downward from the right, apparently out of control. Womack struggled with his throat microphone to try to warn the pilot, but Dobson, the copilot in the right-hand seat, saw it in time to turn *Calaban* out of the way.

Then Womack spotted several German fighters, "at least a hundred fighters everywhere I looked and so many of our own ships behind us that I couldn't shoot at any fighters. Our own ships were being shot down behind us so fast that I didn't think we'd ever make it through."

Dobson added, "*Calaban* got away from Ploesti but the ship was all shot up." Their bomb bay doors were open, waving in the wind. The pilot took the plane down so low that it lopped off the tops of corn stalks, but he was more concerned about burning out the engines by going too fast. The barrage balloon cable had destroyed the air speed indicator, so he had no idea how fast they were going. He told Dobson to watch the engine RPMs and the manifold pressure. "Don't worry about the speed," Dobson answered. "Just drive it."

Years later Dobson recalled dryly that "the irony of driving a B-24 through cornfields took the edge off for the moment."

In the element following *Calaban*, Worden Weaver's plane, *Lil' Abner*, was not so lucky. (There was also a *Lil' Abner* in the 376th Bombardment Group.) The navigator, Walter Sorenson, recalled his thoughts as they flew toward Ploesti. He knew "this would be a day for the history books. If the raid was successful, it would be hailed as a brilliant idea. However, if unsuccessful, it could go down as one of the U.S. Air Force's biggest blunders."

Lil' Abner made it over the target and dropped its bomb load, but the ship had been riddled by ack-ack fire. Three engines were damaged and most of the flight controls destroyed. Barely able to stay airborne, Weaver realized he had no choice but to crash-land in a field some 40 miles from Ploesti.

The impact was so severe that the nose ended up beneath the fuselage. The top turret broke loose (as often occurred in crash landings), crushing to death William Scheltler, the flight engineer. Fire broke out behind the flight deck, trapping both pilots and the navigator in the cockpit. Six other crewmen fled from the rear of the ship before the flames spread.

Weaver managed to break through the windshield to try to escape, with Sorenson, the navigator, pressing close behind him. But Sorenson's parachute snagged on the shattered windshield, leaving him hanging halfway out of the plane and trapping the copilot, Robert Snyder. The fire was spreading forward and there was no other way out.

The bombardier, Lloyd Reese, had escaped from the rear but when he saw what was happening at the cockpit he plunged through the fire to cut Sorenson's parachute free so that he and Snyder could get out. Then, Sorenson recalled, he saw "a German fighter plane circling over our wrecked plane. I guess he was reporting our position. We all ran to a nearby farmhouse where some women treated our burns as best they could before enemy troops showed up and took us away."

Wing Dinger, flown by George Winger, was damaged so badly as it passed over the target area that it was knocked off course and forced to fly under cover of another ship. By the time Winger got the plane beyond the target, it was orange with flames from nose to tail. The fuel tanks in the bomb bay were afire and the flames were spreading rapidly. Winger had already flown 27 missions and was officially finished with combat, but when he learned how important the Ploesti raid was to the war effort, he volunteered to go one last time.

The two waist gunners jumped from the burning *Wing Dinger* and parachuted to safety. Bernard Trout, 17 years old, was so tired from not sleeping the night before the raid that he found some bushes for concealment and promptly fell asleep. He was *Wing Dinger's* only survivor.

John Harmonoski, a bombardier aboard another plane nearby, later said that he "saw Lieutenant Winger salute him just before he pulled his plane upwards." Winger must have known that he was not going to make it but he was trying to gain altitude to give his crew a chance to bail out.

Horse Fly dropped its bombs through the smoke and fire surrounding the target area and headed into the clear. The flight engineer, Leo Spann, recalled:

> We then went down on the deck as low as we could, as those picturesque haystacks opened up and then revealed their guns. And these guns started giving us hell! They shot out the number four engine and a shell exploded between the two waist gun positions, wounding both gunners in the legs.

Horse Fly collided with a balloon cable, snapping it, and the ship flew on, but by then it was on its own. With one engine dead, it could no longer keep up with the formation. German fighter planes pounced on the stricken plane.

> With the two waist gunners out, [the fighters] came in so close to us it seemed we could almost touch them. We figured that we had shot down

four of them, and they finally left us, but the number four engine had frozen up and with a flat propeller, it caused a hell of a drag. The propeller would not feather.

The crew of *Sad Sack II* was in worse shape by the time they dropped their bombs. (There was also a *Sad Sack* in the 98th Bombardment Group.) Henry Lasco was the pilot; the copilot was Joe Kill, "for whom crew members erected a sign in the plane that read 'Kill, the Copilot.'" Kill had been sick with dysentery prior to the raid but found that his severe intestinal cramps miraculously disappeared as the plane made its final turn toward the target. "This proved to me," he joked later, "that one can be 'scared shitless.'"

Before *Sad Sack II* reached the target, however, Charles DeCrevel, a waist gunner, was wounded in the thigh. He strapped on his parachute, ready to bail out, but changed his mind when he realized they were flying level with the treetops rather than above them. Before they could drop their bombs, someone shouted over the intercom that the tail gunner had been killed. Then, as the bombardier yelled "bombs away," the navigator took a fatal hit in the chest. He managed to crawl to the rear of the plane before he collapsed. At the same time, the number two engine was crippled.

When the plane cleared the target area the antiaircraft gunners were waiting. This time they got the radio operator and the top turret gunner, DeCrevel, the wounded waist gunner, recalled that he "began to have grave doubts if anyone was alive on the flight deck. Wherever he looked he could see holes as big as his fist, and the left wing was almost scraping the ground. *Sad Sack II* was vibrating badly and extremely rough to handle."

As many as nine German fighters lined up to attack *Sad Sack II* from the rear. DeCrevel shot down the first one and Al Shaffer, the other waist gunner, scored a few hits even though one of his legs had been nearly torn off by an enemy shell. Lasco and Kill were having great trouble controlling the ship. *Sad Sack* was shaking to pieces. And if that was not enough, some of the ammunition on board had caught fire and was going off in all directions.

DeCrevel took a second hit. He said it felt like fingers were plucking at his clothes. "I received shrapnel wounds in the back, head and knee, and was floored by a 13-mm. in the butt. The parachute pack in that area saved me."

A German fighter circled the crippled B-24 and attacked head on. The American pilot remembered:

We were very low to the ground, probably 50 feet, when an ME-109 circled around us and came in very shallow at ten o'clock on my side. I saw his wing light up and felt a tremendous sock on the jaw. I was shot through both cheeks and upper palate, I had no strength. I couldn't see anything.

Sad Sack II was dropping into a cornfield with Lasco sprawled over the control wheel. Kill, the copilot, was still desperately trying to lower the flaps by hand and level the ship by pushing hard on the right rudder pedal. In back, DeCrevel heard someone scream.

The navigator was kneeling on the catwalk and holding on to the open door to the bomb bay. He looked like he had caught an 88 right in the chest. The flesh was stripped away and I could see the white ribs. I wanted to help him but there wasn't time. We were all dead, anyway.

The next thing DeCrevel remembered was the crash. "I tumbled head over heels in flame and tearing metal and hit the forward bulkhead with a sweet, black thud. [There was] no plane to speak of, just a pile of burning junk."

He hauled himself out of the wreckage and tried to run on his wounded leg. Something made him turn to look at the plane and he saw Shaffer trapped in the burning debris. He went back, pulled the gunner free, and dragged him 50 yards away from the plane.

Both pilots were trapped in the cockpit. Kill later recalled how Lasco, who had been shot in the face,

was blindly thrashing around, pinned in his harness. All I could do was to tell him I couldn't get out. Both of my legs were broken and the right

*foot was out of the socket at the ankle. Lasco somehow got loose and
unfastened my legs from a tangle of wires and cables. He grabbed me
under the arms and dragged me through a hole in the side of the fuselage.*

The four crewmen who survived *Sad Sack*'s mission to Ploesti,
seriously wounded and in great pain, were left sitting in a corn field in
Romania awaiting help, or perhaps to be killed on the spot.

The rest of the 44th, 21 planes led by Lt. Col. James Posey, were
on course for a refinery five miles south of Ploesti. Their portion of the
mission was going flawlessly, just as they had practiced, rehearsed, and
drilled back in Benghazi. They were the first over their target, so it was
free of smoke and flames, but it quickly turned out not to be safe from
antiaircraft fire.

The bulk of the formation roared over the target in four five-plane
waves. Colonel Posey was the copilot for *V For Victory*, second from the
left in the first wave. Its gunners kept up a steady fire as the ship pulled
up to chimney height to drop its bombs. The unrelenting return fire from
the ground was strong and accurate, and a shell that shattered a portion
of the tail also killed one of the waist gunners.

After the first wave dropped its bombs, Posey led them back down,
flying as low as they could get. "People ask me what I mean by low level,"
wrote David Alexander, pilot of *Flak Alley*, on Posey's left. "I point out
that on the antenna on the bottom of my airplane I brought back sun-
flowers and something that looked suspiciously like grass."

Satan's Hellcat bombed its target even though one engine, hit by
flak, was trailing smoke. The pilot, Rowland Houston, was able to keep
up with the rest of the formation, but once they got beyond the target,
they were hit by German fighters. Set ablaze, *Satan's Hellcat* began to
fall, taking with it an enemy plane that had been flying beneath it. The
two planes plummeted to the ground, exploding on impact. The German pilot, Wilhelm Steinman, was thrown clear, but all aboard *Satan's
Hellcat* perished.

Avenger, flown by Bill Hughes and Willie Weant, had brought an
extra passenger, as usual, Rusty, a cocker spaniel, who belonged to Robert
Peterson, the navigator. Rusty enjoyed flying and spent the journey to

Ploesti asleep on the nose wheel doors, but once the action started, he took up his favorite post in the nose to bark at the flak exploding ahead of them. After dropping their bomb load on target, Avenger was pounced on by four German fighters. The American gunners quickly shot down three of them before they could inflict any serious damage.

Timb-A-A-AH, in the third wave over the target, also had a dog on board. Eightball, a black terrier, had been found in an airplane hangar in Ireland two months before. He crept under the pilot's seat when the firing started over Ploesti and remained there, apparently asleep, until the plane and its crew were safely home.

Earthquake McGoon was a band-chested wrestler in the popular comic strip "Li'l Abner." It was also the name of a B-24 in the second wave, flown by Walter Bunker and Dick Butler. As they passed over a large building with a red cross painted on the roof, the recognized symbol of a hospital, no one aboard noticed that an antiaircraft gun was also on the roof until it started firing at them. The plane took a hit in one wing, and another shell struck the fuselage near the bomb bay, destroying electrical and hydraulic lines.

After *Earthquake* dropped its bombs, a shell caught the number three engine. As Butler, the copilot, reached for the button to feather that engine, the ship snagged a steel cable from a bar rage balloon. The cable snapped, but in the confusion, Butler pressed the control for the number four engine. With both engines suddenly gone, *Earthquake McGoon* tipped sharply to the right. Loy Neeper in the top turret "glanced sideways and watched the right wingtip barely clearing the cornstalks while the other wingtip pointed towards the clear blue sky." Bunker struggled to level the ship while Butler corrected his mistake. He unfeathered number four and feathered number three.

On the run to the target, Dale Lee, a waist gunner in *Southern Comfort*, saw on the ground "a German sergeant [who] had three rows of troops all lined up in formation. I just wanted to even the score for them having wiped out so many of my good buddies. In my anger and frustration I opened my 50-caliber guns and mowed right down their lines. At the time it seemed so justifiable and right."

As they got closer to the target, Lee saw something else, a sight that stayed with him for a long time. "An old lady stood right out in the middle of all this commotion. She was calmly pumping water into a bucket." After the plane passed over her, Lee spotted some oxcarts in the middle of a cornfield. "Those poor oxen went berserk from all the noise and the excited farmers were in hot pursuit, trying to bring them under control."

Glen Hickerson, *Southern Comfort*'s tail gunner, opened fire at a gun partially concealed in a haystack, but he did not notice, until it was too late, that several civilians were standing nearby. Everyone disappeared in a cloud of dust and smoke as his stream of bullets tore them apart.

Southern Comfort bombed its target but was seriously damaged in return. One shell knocked down a waist gunner. The impact sent the small incendiaries bouncing out of their box. The gunners picked them up as fast as they could, before they could catch fire. They tossed the explosives out the window, adding to the devastation on the ground. Another shell exploded beneath one wing. The plane pitched over on its side, with one wing high and the other about to scrape a furrow in the ground before the pilot brought it under control.

In the last wave of B-24s, *Old Crow*, piloted by James McAtee and Harold Lautig, flew over a B-24 that had crash-landed. Beyond it they saw an old shed. Suddenly the walls tumbled down to reveal an antiaircraft gun, but there was no one around to fire it. A German soldier appeared from across the field and raced toward it, but *Old Crow*'s gunners were faster. They directed a withering fire at the man, raining bullets all around him. He fell to the ground, either wounded or pretending to be.

One of the waist gunners, Mack Morris, saw several civilians waving at the planes.

I saw dogs, and I swear even some chicken running. In one picnic group the women even waved aprons. At one point a group of civilians were in an area between two gun emplacements that were concealed in grain shocks. Suddenly some of them fell as our gunners swung from firing at one gun emplacement to the other.

Colonel Posey's group lost no planes over the target, and only two after the bombs were dropped, both casualties of enemy fighters. Compared with the groups that had already attacked the Ploesti refineries, Posey's men had the fewest losses and the greatest success. For them, the mission went much the way Colonel Smart had planned. The refinery that was their designated target was destroyed so completely that it could not be brought back into production for the rest of the war.

The 389th Bombardment Group, led by Col. Jack Wood, was assigned a target 18 miles northwest of Ploesti. When word of their target became known back in Benghazi, the men of the 389th took considerable kidding from the other groups about having such an easy mark, one far removed from the concentration of defenses in the Ploesti area.

The crews of the 389th were the freshest to arrive in England and had no combat experience prior to their departure for North Africa to prepare for the Ploesti raid. Because they were so green, they were out to prove that they could accomplish their task as well as their more battle-seasoned counterparts.

But as they approached the target, they were off to a shaky start. Colonel Wood, in *The Scorpion,* sat behind pilots Kenneth Caldwell and Otis Hamilton. Wood was acting as his own navigator. When *The Scorpion* crossed over a ridge and he spotted a valley seeming to lead in the direction of the target, he ordered Caldwell to turn right.

And as Caldwell executed the turn, all 28 ships in the flight behind him followed in synchrony, even though some of the other navigators immediately recognized that they were turning too soon. Colonel Wood had just repeated the mistake made earlier by Colonel Compton of the 376th. "Too soon!" shouted Stell Meador, Wood's navigator, into the intercom. "You're turning too early!" Navigators in other planes yelled the same warning to their pilots. Aboard the ship called *I-For-Item,* in the second wave, navigator Herbert Solomon told pilot Edward Fowble, "They've turned too soon. We are not in the right valley."

Although no one dared break radio silence to inform Colonel Wood of his mistake, Meador was soon able to convince him of the error. Wood then made a course correction to the left, leading the formation into almost a 180-degree turn, until they were back on their original heading for the town of Campina.

Once again they were approaching their refinery precisely as planned. The crews observed scenes of ordinary domestic life on the ground as they flew over—people having picnics, farmers in their fields, women waving, a little boy who tossed a stone in the air in their direction. As they neared the target, Wood led their descent to 30 feet, just as they had practiced over the desert. Now that they were on course, everything seemed as smooth as a practice run above the sand, except that this time people started shooting at them.

Maj. Philip Ardery, a command pilot occupying the copilot's seat in *I-For-Item* in the second wave, wrote:

> *We found ourselves at that moment running a gauntlet of tracers and cannon fire of all types that made me despair of ever covering those last few hundred yards to the point where we could let the bombs go. The antiaircraft defenses were literally throwing up a curtain of steel. From the target grew the column of flames, smoke, and explosions, and we were headed straight into it.*

In the first wave, Colonel Wood in *The Scorpion* spied the gun emplacements firing at them. As they roared toward the refinery assigned to them, Wood's ship dropped its four 1,000-pound bombs squarely on the boiler house, which exploded in a mixture of scalding steam and flaming gases. *I-For-Item* flew past with no casualties or major damage.

Chattanooga Choo Choo, flown by Robert O'Reilly, was also in the first wave. Up front in the nose, navigator Richard Britt grabbed the 50-caliber machine gun and fired into the trees. "We were on target," Britt wrote. "The noise was deafening with the bursting of the antiaircraft shells, machine gun fire and the *carumping* of some of the bombs. Thick black smoke was rising in tall columns of brilliant yellow-red colors of burning oil."

Britt watched in fascination as the bombs dropped from the plane beside his. He followed one as it broke through high-voltage wires, setting off sparks, leaving a 15-foot gap in the side wall of a brick building.

He felt his plane lurch as the bombs fell and then jolt as it sustained several hits from ground fire. Control cables snapped and one engine was damaged, forcing the right wing toward the ground.

The pilot yelled through the intercom for the crew to prepare for a crash. At almost the same instant, someone else shouted that there was still a bomb aboard. Alfred Romano, the bombardier, rushed to the bomb bay to try to break it loose. If they crash-landed with it still on board, no one would get out alive.

Britt tore his navigation charts and maps into tiny pieces and tossed them out through the slits around the nose wheel door. He made his way to the bomb bay to help and saw Romano and Frank Kees, the top turret gunner, perched on the narrow catwalk, working to pry the bomb loose with a screwdriver. Finally, it dropped through the open bomb bay door. Britt remembered:

Roof tops and trees were blurring below us. Our speed was still 220 miles per hour. People were scurrying to get away from this huge monster dropping destruction on them. You could almost touch the houses. One had a porch swing like the one on my grandmother's front porch in Illinois.

Britt scrambled up to the flight deck as fast as he could, with Romano right behind him. Kees remained on the catwalk in the middle of the open bomb bay doors, fascinated by the sight of the trees and houses appearing to whiz by beneath his feet. Britt said, "Looking down at the housetops below, he knew he couldn't jump. He looked at us, then down below, and finally started to climb."

Chattanooga Choo Choo plunged toward a dry river bed. "The next few seconds seemed to last for hours." Britt wrote,

The terrible crunching, grinding, scraping and buckling of metal against metal was deafening as we slid along the ground. It seemed we would never stop. I was braced between the radio desk and the wall between the flight deck and the bomb bay. Two pieces of metal began to squeeze my head in a vice-tight grip. Tighter and tighter they pressed as I slipped into darkness. For one brief moment, a mental picture of my father flashed before me. I felt no pain, just a numb feeling of weightlessness, making me giddy. "This isn't such a bad way to die," I thought.

By the time the second wave of the 389th Bombardment Group approached the target, the burning refinery was shooting up huge columns of flame higher than the planes. The ships bore into the inferno with bomb bay doors open and bombardiers zeroing in on their portion of the target. Just before *I-For-Item* plunged into the smoke, Philip Ardery glanced to his right at *Eager Eagle,* piloted by Lloyd H. "Pete" Hughes.

Gasoline was pouring from *Eager Eagle's* left wing in a stream so thick that no one in neighboring planes could see the waist gunners in their open windows. "Poor Pete!" Ardery thought. "Fine, religious, conscientious boy with a young wife waiting for him back in Texas."

Hughes kept his place in the formation, aware that by staying on that flight path he would fly directly into the flames with all that raw fuel drenching his ship. He had only a few seconds to make a decision: try to save himself and his crew by pulling up and riding above the flames or stay steady on course to bomb the target. He flew straight ahead.

A moment later we were in the inferno, dropping our bombs, Hughes along with the rest of us. Next I remember heat coming up into our bomb bay as the flames enveloped us.

Emerging from the flames, I looked again at Hughes' aircraft. It was now a huge, flying torch. Hughes apparently cut the throttles to attempt a crash landing. For a moment, it seemed as though he might make it. He was headed toward a stream bed on our right. Then, just as the flaming B-24 was about to touch down, the whole left wing came off and a big ball of fire appeared where the aircraft had been.

The only survivors were two of the gunners.*

When *Scheherazade* approached the refinery in the second wave, Milton Nelson, the bombardier, told John Blackis, the pilot, that the

---

*Six months after the raid, in February 1944, Hughes was approved for a Medal of Honor.

bomb bay doors were stuck. The extra fuel tanks in the bomb bay had jammed them shut. Blackis ordered the flight engineer, Joseph Landry, to climb down into the bomb bay and pry open the doors, but they would not budge. Blackis made his decision quickly: if the doors would not open, then *Scheherazade* would drop the bombs right through them. The bombs struck their target. The damaged doors trailed low beneath the plane, snagging cornstalks and other debris, but the ship was fine. While Landry was at work in the bomb bay, David Rosenthal, the radioman, climbed in the top turret and shot down an ME-109. He had never fired the guns before.

For a variety of reasons, a few of the planes in the bombardment group had not been given names; one was 42-406-19-N. The tail gunner, George Fulton, habitually got airsick every time they practiced low-level flying in North Africa. Sure enough, he got sick again on the long flight to Romania. Another gunner, Brandon Healy, volunteered to take his place in the rail until they got close to the target. Fulton threw up in the bomb bay and settled down to sleep. He slept soundly throughout the raid and did not wake up until his plane was on its way home.

Aboard *Sandwitch,* in the fourth wave, no one fell asleep. A gunner one plane over, *The Little Gramper,* saw what happened. Some crewmen from *Sandwitch* were waving at him when an antiaircraft shell struck the bomb bay fuel tank. In an instant, gas poured out of *Sandwitch* and the plane caught on fire. The pilot, Robert Horton, took the plane up to bombing altitude and dropped their bomb load squarely on the target, but *Sandwitch* was finished. It took several more hits. The gunner watching from *The Little Gramper* said, "It was a horrible sight watching the burning plane and knowing that the men in there were fighting for their lives and there was nothing we could do to help."

One of *Sandwitch's* wings hit a tree and broke off. The fuselage plowed on through the woods and disintegrated into several flaming pieces. The top turret was thrown clear; the gunner Zerril Steen, although badly burned, managed to crawl to safety.

Vagabond King, in the last wave of the 389th, became the last plane to bomb Ploesti. By the time it reached the target, all of the German guns were trained on it. The flames and smoke from the burning refinery were so thick that the crew could hardly see anything. John McCormick, the pilot, remembered, "Tracers, red, white, streaming up at the boys ahead and hitting them too. Then our cockpit exploded with sparks, noise and concussion. Tracers spat over my head. Wham! More bullets through the cockpit. The emergency windows blew open, giving us a 225 mph blast of air in the cockpit."

They dropped their bombs and McCormick brought *Vagabond King* as close to the ground as he dared and raced away from the burning refinery. Three minutes later, he said, "the boys told me we had been hit pretty hard, that Van [Martin Van Buren, the radioman] was bleeding badly. An antiaircraft shell had hit as he was turning on the automatic camera. [Paul] Millet; in the tail turret, called to say that the bombs we dropped had exploded, and our target was burning fiercely."

The crewmen of the 389th had done their job well. Four of the 29 planes in the group were shot down in the raid, but their bombs inflicted such extensive damage that the refinery did not resume production until after the war was over.

As the planes set course for Benghazi, "The sky was a bedlam of bombers flying in all directions," remembered Philip Ardery.

Some (of them were) actually on fire, many with smoking engines, some with great gaping holes in them or huge chunks of wing or rudder gone. Many were so riddled it was obvious their insides must have presented starkly tragic pictures of dead and dying, of men grievously wounded who would bleed to death before they could be brought any aid; pilots facing the horrible decision about what to do, whether to make a quick sacrifice of the unhurt in order to save the life of a dying man, or to fly a ship home and let some crew member pay with his life for the freedom to the rest.

The mission to Ploesti was over. Now began the mission to survive.

CHAPTER FOUR

Sergeant York and His People

Sam K. Cowan

For many Americans, there is no doubt that the face of Gary Cooper on the movie screen as Sergeant York will always be the memory of the most remarkable soldier of World War I. In 1918 when the bravery of the modest backwoodsman from Tennessee earned the Medal of Honor, U.S. troops had only been on the battlefields for a short time, about five months when the Armistice was signed. The story of Alvin York is an epic one, and the best re-telling is in the book Sergeant York and His People, *by Sam K. Cowan. Cowan's own introduction to the story cannot be topped in this editor's opinion.*

From a cabin back in the mountains of Tennessee, forty-eight miles from the railroad, a young man went to the World War. He was untutored in the ways of the world.

Caught by the enemy in the cove of a hill in the Forest of Argonne, he did not run; but sank into the bushes and single-handed fought a battalion of German machine gunners until he made them come down that hill to him with their hands in air. There were one hundred and thirty-two of them left, and he marched them, prisoners, into the American line.

Marshal Foch, in decorating him, said, "What you did was the greatest thing accomplished by any private soldier of all of the armies of Europe."

His ancestors were cane-cutters and Indian fighters. Their lives were rich in the romance of adventure. They were men of strong hate and gentle love. His people have lived in the simplicity of the pioneer.

This is not a war-story, but the tale of the making of a man. His ancestors were able to leave him but one legacy—an idea of American manhood.

In the period that has elapsed since he came down from the mountains he has done three things—and any one of them would have marked him for distinction.

—◡—

Just to the north of Chatel Chehery, in the Argonne Forest in France, is a hill which was known to the American soldiers as "Hill No. 223." Fronting its high wooded knoll, on the way to Germany, are three more hills. The one in the center is rugged. Those to the right and left are more sloping, and the one to the left—which the people of France have named "York's Hill"—turns a shoulder toward Hill No. 223. The valley which they form is only from two to three hundred yards wide.

Early in the morning of the eighth of October, 1918, as a floating gray mist relaxed its last hold on the tops of the trees on the sides of those hills, the "All America" Division—the Eighty-Second—poured over the crest of No. 223. Prussian Guards were on the ridge-tops across the valley, and behind the Germans ran the Decauville Railroad—the artery for supplies to a salient still further to the north which the Germans were striving desperately to hold. The second phase of the Battle of the Meuse-Argonne was on.

As the fog rose the American "jumped off" down the wooded slope and the Germans opened fire from three directions. With artillery they pounded the hillside. Machine guns savagely sprayed the trees under which the Americans were moving. At one point, where the hill makes a steep descent, the American line seemed to fade away as it attempted to pass.

This slope, it was found, was being swept by machine guns on the crest of the hill to the left which faced down the valley. The Germans were hastily "planting" other machine guns there.

The Americans showered that hill top with bullets, but the Germans were entrenched.

The sun had now melted the mist and the sky was cloudless. From the pits the Germans could see the Americans working their way through the timber.

To find a place from which the Boche could be knocked away from those death-dealing machine guns and to stop the digging of "fox holes" for new nests, a non-commissioned officer and sixteen men went out from the American line. All of them were expert rifle shots who came from the support platoon of the assault troops on the left.

Using the forest's undergrowth to shield them, they passed unharmed through the bullet-swept belt which the Germans were throwing around Hill No. 223, and reached the valley. Above them was a canopy of lead. To the north they heard the heavy cannonading of that part of the battle.

When they passed into the valley they found they were within the range of another battalion of German machine guns. The Germans on the hill at the far end of the valley were lashing the base of No. 223.

For their own protection against the bullets that came with the whip of a wasp through the tree-tops, the detachment went boldly up the enemy's hill before them. On the hillside they came to an old trench, which had been used in an earlier battle of the war. They dropped into it.

Moving cautiously, stopping to get their bearings from the sounds of the guns above them, they walked the trench in Indian file. It led to the left, around the shoulder of the hill, and into the deep dip of a valley in the rear.

Germans were on the hilltop across that valley. But the daring of the Americans protected them. The Germans were guarding the valleys and the passes and they were not looking for enemy in the shadow of the barrels of German guns.

As the trench now led down the hill, carrying the Americans away from the gunners they sought, the detachment came out of it and took skirmish formation in the dense and tangled bushes.

They had gone but a short distance when they stepped upon a forest path. Just below them were two Germans, with Red Cross bands upon their arms. At the sight of the Americans, the Germans dropped their stretcher, turned and fled around a curve.

The sound of the shots fired after them was lost in the clatter of the machine guns above. One of the Germans fell, but regained his feet, and both disappeared in the shrubs to the right.

It was kill or capture those Germans to prevent exposure of the position of the invaders, and the Americans went after them.

They turned off the path where they saw the stretcher-bearers leave it, darted through the underbrush, dodged trees and stumps and brushes. Jumping through the shrubs and reeds on the bank of a small stream, the Americans in the lead landed in a group of about twenty of the enemy.

The Germans sprang to their feet in surprise. They were behind their own line of battle. Officers were holding a conference with a major. Private soldiers, in groups, were chatting and eating. They were before a little shack that was the German major's headquarters, and from it stretched telephone wires. The Germans were not set for a fight.

Out from the brushwood and off the bank across the stream, one after another, came the Americans.

It bewildered the Germans. They did not know the number of the enemy that had come upon them. As each of the "Buddies" landed, he sensed the situation, and prepared for an attack from any angle. Some of them fired at German soldiers whom they saw reaching for their guns.

All threw up their hands, with the cry "Kamerad!" when the Americans opened fire.

About their prisoners the Americans formed in a semicircle as they forced them to disarm. At the left end of this crescent was Alvin York—a young six-foot mountaineer, who had come to the war from "The Knobs of Tennessee." He knew nothing of military tactics beyond the simple evolutions of the drill. Only a few days before had he first seen the flash of a hostile gun. But a rifle was as familiar to his hands as one of the fingers upon them. His body was ridged and laced with muscles that had grown to seasoned sinews from swinging a sledge in a blacksmith-shop. He had never seen the man or crowd of men of whom he was afraid. He had hunted in the mountains while forked lightning flashed around him. He had heard the thunder crash in mountain coves as loud as the burst of any German shell. He was of that type into whose brain and heart the qualm of fear never comes.

The Americans were on the downstep of the hill with their prisoners on the higher ground. The major's headquarters had been hidden away in a thicket of young undergrowth, and the Americans could see but a short distance ahead.

As the semicircle formed with Alvin York on the left end, he stepped beyond the edge of the thicket—and what he saw up the hill surprised him.

Just forty yards away was the crest, and along it was a row of machine guns—a battalion of them!

The German gunners had heard the shots fired by the Americans in front of the major's shack, or they had been warned by the fleeing stretcher-bearers that the enemy was behind them. They were jerking at their guns, rapidly turning them around, for the nests had been masked and the muzzles of the guns pointed down into the valley at the foot of Hill No. 223, to sweep it when the Eighty-Second Division came out into the open.

Some of the Germans in the gun-pits, using rifles, shot at York. The bullets "burned his face as they passed." He cried a warning to his comrades which evidently was not heard, for when he began to shoot up the hill they called to him to stop as the Germans had surrendered. They saw only the prisoners before them.

There was no time for parley. York's second cry, "Look out!" could carry no explanation of the danger to those whose view was blinded by the thicket. The Germans had their guns turned. Hell and death were being belched down the hillside upon the Americans.

At the opening rattle of these guns the German prisoners as if through a prearranged signal, fell flat to the ground, and the streams of lead passed over them. Some of the Americans prevented by the thicket from seeing that an attack was to be made upon them, hearing the guns, instinctively followed the lead of the Germans. But the onslaught came with such suddenness that those in the line of fire had no chance.

The first sweep of the guns killed six and wounded three of the Americans. Death leaped through the bushes and claimed Corporal Murray Savage, Privates Maryan Dymowski, Ralph Weiler, Fred Wareing, William Wine and Carl Swanson. Crumpled to the ground, wounded, were Sergeant Bernard Early, who had been in command, Corporal William B. Cutting and Private Mario Muzzi.

York, to escape the guns he saw sweeping toward him, had dived to the ground between two shrubs.

The fire of other machine guns was added to those already in action and streams of lead continued to pour through the thicket. But the toll of the dead and wounded of the Americans had been taken.

The Germans kept their line of fire about waist-high so they would not kill their own men, some of whom they could see groveling on the ground.

York had seen the murder of his pals in the first onset. He had heard someone say, "Let's get out of here; we are in the German line!" Then all had been silence on the American side.

German prisoners lay on the ground before him, in view of the gunners on the hilltop. York edged around until he had a clear view of the gun-pits above him. The stalks of weeds and undergrowth were about him.

There came a lull in the machine gun fire. Several Germans arose as though to come out of their pits and down the hill to see the battle's result.

But on the American side the battle was just begun. York, from the brushes at the end of the thicket, "let fly."

One of the Germans sprang upward, waved his arms above him as he began his flight into eternity.

The others dropped back into their holes, and there was another clatter of machine guns and again the bullets slashed across the thicket.

But there was silence on the American side. York waited.

More cautiously, German heads began to rise above their pits. York moved his rifle deliberately along the line knocking back those heads that were the more venturesome. The American rifle shoots five times, and a clip was gone before the Germans realized that the fire upon them was coming from one point.

They centered on that point.

Around York the ground was torn up. Mud from the plowing bullets besmirched him. The brush was mowed away above and on either side of him, and leaves and twigs were falling over him.

But they could only shoot at him. They were given no chance to take deliberate aim. As they turned the clumsy barrel of a machine gun down at the fire-sparking point on the hillside a German would raise his head above his pit to sight it. Instantly backward along that German machine gun barrel would come an American bullet—crashing into the head of the Boche who manned the gun.

The prisoners on the ground squirmed under the fire that was passing over them. Their bodies were in a tortuous motion. But York held them there; it made the gunners keep their fire high.

Every shot York made was carefully placed. As a hunter stops in the forest and gazes straight ahead, his mind, receptive to the slightest movement of a squirrel or the rustle of leaves in any of the trees before him, so this Tennessee mountaineer faced and fought that line of blazing machine guns on the ridge of the hill before him. His mind was sensitive to the point in the line that at that instant threatened a real danger, and instinctively he turned to it.

Down the row of prisoners on the ground he saw the German major with a pistol in his hand, and he made the officer throw the gun to him. Later its magazine was found to have been emptied.

He noted that after he shot at a gun-pit, there was a break in the line of flame at that point, and an interval would pass before that gun would again be manned and become a source of danger to him. He also realized that where there was a sudden break of ten or fifteen feet in the line of flame, and the trunk of a tree rose within that space, that soon a German gun and helmet would be peeking around the tree's trunk. A rifleman would try for him where the machine guns failed.

In the mountains of Tennessee Alvin York had won fame as one of the best shots with both rifle and revolver that those mountains had ever held, and his imperturbability was as noted as the keenness of his sight.

In mountain shooting-matches at a range of forty yards—just the distance the row of German guns were from him—he would put ten rifle bullets into a space no larger than a man's thumb-nail. Since a small boy he had been shooting with a rifle at the bobbing heads of turkeys that had been tethered behind a log so that only their heads would show. German heads and German helmets loomed large before him.

A battalion of machine guns is a military unit organized to give battle to a regiment of infantry. Yet, one man, a representative of America on that hillside on that October morning, broke the morale of a battalion of machine gunners made up from members of Germany's famous Prussian Guards. Down in the brush below the Prussians was a human machine gun they could not hit, and the penalty was death to try to locate him.

As York fought, there was prayer upon his lips. He was an elder in a little church back in the "Valley of the Three Forks o' the Wolf" in the mountains of Tennessee. He prayed to God to spare him and to have mercy on those he was compelled to kill. When York shot, and a German soldier fell backward or pitched forward and remained motionless, York would call to them:

"Well! Come on down!"

It was an earnest command in which there was no spirit of exultation or braggadocio. He was praying for their surrender, so that he might stop killing them.

His command, "Come down!" at times, above the firing, was heard in the German pits. They realized they were fighting one man, and could not understand the strange demand.

When the fight began York was lying on the ground. But as the entire line of German guns came into the fight, he raised himself to a sitting position so that his gun would have the sweep of all of them.

When the Germans found they could not "get him" with bullets, they tried other tactics.

Off to his left, seven Germans, led by a lieutenant, crept through the bushes. When about twenty yards away, they broke for him with lowered bayonets.

The clip of York's rifle was nearly empty. He dropped it and took his automatic pistol. So calmly was he master of himself and so complete his vision of the situation that he selected as his first mark among the oncoming Germans the one farthest away. He knew he would not miss the form of a man at that distance. He wanted the rear men to fall first so the others would keep coming at him and not stop in panic when they saw their companions falling, and fire a volley at him. He felt that in such a volley his only danger lay. They kept coming, and fell as he shot. The foremost man, and the last to topple, did not get ten yards from where he started. Their bodies formed a line down the hillside.

York resumed the battle with the machine guns. The German fire had "eased up" while the bayonet charge was on. The gunners paused to watch the grim struggle below them.

The major, from among the prisoners crawled to York with an offer to order the surrender of the machine gunners.

"Do it!" was his laconic acceptance. But his vigilance did not lessen.

To the right a German had crawled nearby. He arose and hurled a hand-grenade. It missed its objective and wounded one of the prisoners. The American rifle swung quickly and the grenade-thrower pitched forward with the grunt of a man struck heavily in the stomach pit.

The German major blew his whistle.

Out of their gun-pits the Germans came—around from behind trees—up from the brush on either side. They were unbuckling cartridge belts and throwing them and their side-arms away.

York did not move from his position in the brush. About halfway down the hill as they came to him, he halted them, and he watched the gun-pits for the movement of anyone left skulking there. His eye went cautiously over the new prisoners to see that all side-arms had been thrown away.

The surrender was genuine.

There were about ninety Germans before him with their hands in air. This gave him over a hundred prisoners.

He arose and called to his comrades, and several answered him. Some of the responses came from wounded men.

All of the Americans had been on York's right throughout the fight. The thicket had prevented them from taking any effective part. They were forced to protect themselves from the whining bullets that came through the brush from unseen guns. They had constantly guarded the prisoners and shielded York from treachery.

Seven Americans—Percy Beardsley, Joe Konotski, Thomas G. Johnson, Feodor Sak, Michael A. Sacina, Patrick Donahue and George W. Wills—came to him. Sergeant Early, Corporal Cutting and Private Muzzi, tho wounded, were still alive.

He lined the prisoners up "by twos."

His own wounded he put at the rear of the column, and forced the Germans to carry those who could not walk. The other Americans he stationed along the column to hold the prisoners in line.

Sergeant Early, shot through the body, was too severely wounded to continue in command. York was a corporal, but there was no question of rank for all turned to him for instructions. The Germans could not take their eyes off of him, and instantly complied with all his orders, given through the major, who spoke English.

Stray bullets kept plugging through the branches of the trees around them. For the first time the Americans realized they were under fire from the Germans on the hill back of them, whom they had seen when they came out of the deserted trench. The Germans stationed there could not visualize the strange fight that was taking place behind a line of German machine guns, and they were withholding their fire to protect their own men. They were plugging into the woods with rifles, hoping to draw a return volley, and thus establish the American's position.

To all who doubted the possibility of carrying so many prisoners through the forest, or spoke of reprisal attacks to release them, York's reply was:

"Let's get 'em out of here!"

The German major looking down the long line of Germans, possibly planning some recoup from the shame and ignominy of the surrender of so many of them, stepped up to York and asked:

"How many men have you got?"

The big mountaineer wheeled on him:

"I got a-plenty!"

And the major seemed convinced that the number of the Americans was immaterial as York thrust his automatic into the major's face and stepped him up to the head of the column.

Among the captives were three officers.

These York placed around him to lead the prisoners—one on either side and the major immediately before him. In York's right hand swung the automatic pistol, with which he had made an impressive demonstration in the fight up the hill. The officers were told that at the first sign of treachery, or for a failure of the men behind to obey a command, the penalty would be their lives; and the major was informed that he would be the first to go.

With this formation no German skulking on the hill or in the bushes could fire upon York without endangering the officers. Similar protection was given all of the Americans acting as escort.

Up the hill York started the column. From the topography of the land he knew there were machine guns over the crest that had had no part in the fight.

Straight to these nests he marched them. As the column approached, the major was forced by York to command the gunners to surrender.

Only one shot was fired after the march began. At one of the nests, a German, seeing so many Germans as prisoners and so few of the enemy to guard them—all of them on the German firing-line with machine gun nests around them—refused to throw down his gun, and showed fight.

York did not hesitate.

The remainder of that gun's crew took their place in line, and the major promised York there would be no more delays in the surrenders if he would kill no more of them.

As a great serpent the column wound among the trees on the hilltop swallowing the crews of German machine guns.

After the ridge had been cleared, four machine gun-nests were found down the hillside.

It took all the woodcraft the young mountaineer knew to get to his own command. They had come back over the hilltop and were on the slope of the valley in which the Eighty-Second Division was fighting. They were now in danger from both German and American guns.

York listened to the firing, and knew the Americans had reached the valley—and that some of them had crossed it. Where their line was running he could not determine.

He knew if the Americans saw his column of German uniforms they were in danger—captors and captives alike—of being annihilated. At any moment the Germans from the two hilltops down the valley—to check the Eighty-Second Division's advance—might lay a belt of bullets across the course they traveled.

Winding around the cleared places and keeping in the thickly timbered section of the hillslope whenever it was possible, Sergeant York worked his way toward the American line.

In the dense woods the German major made suggestions of a path to take. As York was undecided which one to choose, the major's suggestion made him go the other one. Frequently the muzzle of York's automatic dimpled the major's back and he quickened his step, slowed up, or led the column in the direction indicated to him without turning his head and without inquiry as to the motive back of York's commands.

Down near the foot of the hill, near the trench they had traveled a short while before, York answered the challenge to "Halt!"

He stepped out so his uniform could be seen, and called to the Americans challenging him, and about to fire on the Germans, that he was "bringing in prisoners."

The American line opened for him to pass, and a wild cheer went up from the Doughboys when they saw the column of prisoners. Some of them "called to him to know" if he had the "whole damned German army."

At the foot of the hill in an old dugout an American P. C. had been located, and York turned in his prisoners.

The prisoners were officially counted by Lieut. Joseph A. Woods, Assistant Division Inspector, and there were 132 of them, three of the number were officers and one with the rank of major.

When the Eighty-Second Division passed on, officers of York's regiment visited the scene of the fight and they counted 25 Germans that he had killed and 35 machine guns that York had not only silenced but had unmanned, carrying the men back with him as prisoners.

———❧———

In pinning the Congressional Medal of Honor upon him—the highest award for valor the United States Government bestows—General John J. Pershing called York the greatest civilian soldier of the war.

Marshal Foch, bestowing the Croix de Guerre with Palm upon him, said his feat was the World War's most remarkable individual achievement.

At his home in the "Valley of the Three Forks o' the Wolf," after the war was over, I asked Alvin York how he came to be "Sergeant York."

"Well," he said, as he looked earnestly at me, "you know we were in the Argonne Forest twenty-eight days, and had some mighty hard fighting in there. A lot of our boys were killed off. Every company has to have so many sergeants. They needed a sergeant; and they jes' took me."

In the summer of 1917 when Alvin York was called to war, he was working on the farm for $25 a month and his midday meal, walking to and from his work. He was helping to support his widowed mother with her family of eleven. When he returned to this country to be mustered out of service he had traveled among the soldiers of France the guest of the American Expeditionary Force, so the men in the lines could see the man who single-handed had captured a battalion of machine guns, and he bore the emblems of the highest military honors conferred for valor by the governments composing the Allies.

At New York he was taken from the troop-ship when it reached harbor and the spontaneous welcome given him there and at Washington was not surpassed by the prearranged demonstrations for the Nation's distinguished foreign visitors.

The streets of those cities were lined with people to await his coming and police patrols made way for him. The flaming red of his hair, his young, sunburned, weather-ridged face with its smile and its strength, the worn service cap and uniform, all marked him to the crowds as the man they sought.

Many business propositions were made to him. Some were substantial and others strange, the whimsical offerings of enthused admirers.

Among them were cool fortunes he could never earn at labor.

Taking as a basis the money he was paid for three months on the farm in the summer before he went to France, he would have had to work fifty years to earn the amount he was offered for a six-weeks' theatrical engagement. For the rights to the story of his life a single newspaper was willing to give him the equivalent of thirty-three years. He would have to live to be over three hundred years of age to earn at the old farm wage the sum motion picture companies offered, as a guarantee.

He turned all down, and went back to the little worried mother who was waiting for him in a hut in the mountains, to the gazelle-like mountain girl whose blue eyes had haunted the shades of night and the shadows of trees, to the old seventy-five acre farm that clings to one of the sloping sides of a sun-kissed valley in Tennessee. He refused to capitalize his fame, his achievements that were crowded into a few months in the army of his country.

The "Valley of the Three Forks o' the Wolf," where Alvin York was born and lives, which has been the home of his ancestors for more than a hundred years, is a level fertile valley that is almost a rectangle in form. Three mountains rising on the north and south and west enclose it, while to the east four mountains jumble together, forming the fourth side. It seems that each of these is striving for a place by the valley.

Across the spring branch, up the mountainside in a clump of honeysuckle and roses and apple trees is the home to which Sergeant York returned.

It is a two-room cabin. The boxing is of rough boards as are the unplaned narrow strips of batting covering the cracks. There is a chimney at one end and in one room is a fireplace. The kitchen is a "lean-to" and the only porch is on the rear, the width of the kitchen-dining room. The porch is for service and work, railed partly with a board for a shelf, which holds the water-bucket, the tin wash basin and burdens brought in from the farm.

His friends and neighbors at Pall Mall waited eagerly for his return. They wanted to hear from his own lips the story of his fight.

No man of the mountains was ever given the home-coming that was his. It was made the reunion of the people, with the neighbors the component parts of one great family.

When home again, Alvin wanted no especial deference shown him. He wished to be again just one of them, to swing himself upon the counter at the general store and talk with them as of old. He had much to tell from his experience, but always it was of other incidents than the one that made him famous.

Months passed. He lived in that mountain cabin with his little mother, whose counsel has ever influenced him, and yet not once did he mention to her that he had a fight in the Forest of Argonne.

His consent was gained for the publication of the story of his people, but it was with the pronounced stipulation that "it be told right."

I asked the meaning of his statement that he would not "mind the publication if the story were done right."

"Well," he said with his mountain drawl, "I don't want you bearing down too much on that killing part. Tell it without so much of that!"

Down by the spring I met the little mother bringing a tin bucket to the stone milk-house which nature had built. Her slender, drooping figure, capped by the sunbonnet she always wore, reached just to the shoulder of her son, as he placed his arm protectingly about her.

I asked if she were not proud of that boy of hers.

"Yes," she answered, with pride in every line of her sweet though wrinkled face, "I am proud of all of them—all of my eight boys!"

Chapter Five

Long Rifle

Joe LeBleu

Because sniper weapons and activities did not reach books, movies, and TV until U.S. operations in Iraq, many Americans did not realize that snipers have been in action for decades—making impossible shots over distances their unsuspecting targets foolishly thought protected them. Take Union Maj. Gen. John Sedgwick during the Civil War in 1864. He stood in full view of the distant Confederate lines and shunned his companions urging him to take cover, saying, "They couldn't hit an elephant at that distance." He then fell dead, struck by a bullet under his left eye.

In World War II, women specially trained as snipers played a significant role in the Russian Army defense of Stalingrad. Since then, in every conflict, snipers have gone about their deadly business with varying degrees of effective-ness, with little public attention.

In Iraq and Afghanistan, the cloaks over sniper activities were thrown aside. Many stories have gained national attention, and even have become award-winning movies. This account by former U.S. Army Ranger and Sniper Team Leader Joe LeBleu is from his book Long Rifle, *and takes us deep into a sniper mission in the mountains of Afghanistan. For actions on that night, Sergeant John Howerton received the Bronze Star.*

WE FLEW INTO BAGRAM AIR FORCE BASE NEAR KABUL IN EARLY SEP-tember 2004. It seemed way too early to be putting on desert battle dress uniforms again. I felt like I'd just taken them off. Walking off the World Airways 747, I could see snowcapped mountains of the Hindu Kush sur-rounding us at all points of the compass. I immediately felt that this loca-tion—being in this depression with mountains all around us—made for an easy target. It was quite sunny, but not hot, with cool breezes flowing off the mountains. It felt like springtime, even though it was September. It was nowhere near the extreme temperatures we'd endured in Iraq.

The air in Afghanistan was much thinner than in Iraq, with Kabul and the valley there at 5,000 feet and the nearby mountains ranging from 8,000 to 10,000 feet. The ridgelines and ranges were incredibly dry, much like the mountains in Nevada: treeless, sandy, and very rocky and rugged. As in Iraq, the air was thick with the stench of raw sewage, diesel fumes, and other pungent aromas. (I noticed that body odor in Afghanistan was much worse than in Iraq—as if they hadn't bathed in years.)

I always tell people now, "If you ever want to know what the earth looked like when Jesus walked the earth, go to Afghanistan." Clear, cobalt-blue skies flooded the horizons, with very few clouds floating over the rocky peaks. I remember thinking that if the skies stayed cloudless like that, it was going to be a very cold night—and it always was. Afghan-istan was unbearable at night, stark, freezing cold, the type of cold where you just don't want to move, or even breathe.

Lopez had picked up his First Sergeant (E-8) before we'd swooped for Afghanistan, and he'd requested that I be attached to Charlie Com-pany. He knew I was getting out of the army in June of 2005, and he'd said to me, "Look, since you're getting out, why don't you join us at Charlie Company and be our sniper—help our paratroopers out with tactics and all your Special Ops knowledge."

"Sure, I've got no problem with that," I replied.

So Charlie Company, 1st Platoon, became my new family. To tell you the truth, I don't think I had much of a choice in the matter. I was used to getting adopted, being attached to everybody and their mother, because of my background and experience in Special Operations. Now I was among folks like Sergeant First Class Mike Lahoda, platoon sergeant for Charlie Company 1st Platoon, also a school-qualified sniper. We would often lean on each other for opinions and advice. I had the pleasure of meeting Lahoda when I first arrived at Fort Bragg, and also in Iraq, where our paths crossed on occasion. The platoon leader was 1st Lieutenant Jason Dumpser; fairly new to combat, he listened well (most of the time) and was a pretty good lieutenant.

These days, I carried a wooden-stocked M14 with a Leupold 10x scope, a decent sniper rifle, lethal and accurate out to 800 meters in mountain terrain such as that found in Afghanistan. With a match-grade barrel, it's solid out to 1,000 meters. The M14 fires the NATO round, 7.62x51, same as the M24 sniper rifle. A rifle with great stopping power, it was favored by Marine infantry and many U.S. Army infantry in Vietnam, and it's still used by many people in Special Operations.

Carrying our rifles slung barrel down over our shoulders, we moved to an open-bay tent and set up our gear. Having lived through many cold desert nights in Western Iraq, we were familiar with the routine. I pulled out all my cold-weather gear first, and lined my cot with my thick, black, cold-weather sleeping bag, and rearranged my ruck so that all my cold-weather gear was on top, for easy access during night missions.

In Afghanistan, three years after Al-Qaeda's attacks on the American homeland, I was first and foremost concerned with staying alive and keeping the paratroopers around me alive. Even though I was now in the place where the war against the U.S. had been planned, and where it had started, I was even more aware that I was back on the ground where the blood of my brothers had been spilled. This alone had me focused and enraged, ready to return the favor. At this point it had become personal to me. I wanted to avenge my brothers because I know they would have done the same for me. Every time I would gear up for a mission or patrol through the lovely mountains and valleys of Afghanistan, I always had Crose, Anderson, and Commons in mind. Each time I went out the wire, I would say to myself, "Now it's my turn."

I'd completed countless combat missions in Special Operations, and now, I was a combat sniper veteran. I remember thinking in Afghanistan, *It's not so surreal anymore; it's just another day at the office.* I knew we were in Afghanistan for a historic mission: to secure the first national elections ever held in that country. President Hamid Karzai's personal security had been at grave risk since the spring of 2002, with some of his most trusted and closest advisors assassinated in Kabul. Karzai, of course, was one of the leading candidates in the running to rule Afghanistan during that fall of 2004. Our mission, then, to ensure that the national elections went off without a hitch, came at one more difficult fork in the road for Afghanistan, a country whose people had known little but war for the last thirty years.

Night and day, we patrolled through Afghan villages, talking with the village elders, handing out flyers, and trying to get field intelligence on Al-Qaeda and the Taliban. Of course, elders and villagers alike were scared to speak due to the threat of being beheaded by the Taliban and Al-Qaeda if they were in any way deemed to be informants, so we really got nowhere on our village patrols.

In that short tour, three missions stand out in my mind from Afghanistan.

The first was an early-morning mission, rolling out the gate in the gray predawn darkness. Afghans crowded around the gate—it looked like a swap meet—very crowded, with Afghan men, some in turbans, wearing long, baggy *dishdashas* over trousers and battered, torn leather vests, bunching up around the gates and clamoring for work on the base. Going outside the wire was like fighting traffic in downtown New York.

Once free of the crowd, we rolled into our first city, a village roughly a mile from the base. We stopped in the middle of the road to let Afghans cross. Looking to my left, an eerie feeling came over me as I saw four Afghan men holding AK-47 Kalashnikovs with banana magazines jacked in. They stared at me, grinning in a hateful manner—what we call in America a "smartass grin"—only 10 meters away from me. They wore green camouflage uniforms with multicolored badges sewn on their sleeves. Once again, nobody had given us any field intelligence before we'd gone out the wire on any Afghans dressed like these men, carrying AK-47s. Sitting in the back of the Humvee without doors, I stared into the eyes of the four men, with my rifle laid across my lap, barrel pointed toward them. I suddenly pushed forward my safety lever inside the trigger well of my M14. My rifle was set live now, and I laid my finger on the stock, above the trigger, so it wasn't obvious.

I started to picture in my mind who to take out first if anything went down, but I knew not to fire right away, as we were third in the convoy. If they were enemy, they would've likely fired on the first vehicle. As I watched them, I could tell by the way they were talking with the locals, at ease among their fellow Afghans, that they were obviously welcome. But being stared at by four guys with AK-47s just 10 meters away still didn't sit easy with me. I made mental notes, and as I'd done in Iraq, I stored away a photographic memory recon of the village.

We continued our staring contest, like we hated each other. I said to the driver of our Humvee, without taking my eyes off of them, "How much longer are we going to sit here?"

"Not long. We'll be moving in a second," he replied.

"Good. Because I've got four guys with AKs staring at me, and I have no idea who they are."

A paratrooper riding shotgun said, "Those are the village police, the local security."

"Don't you think that's something everybody should have known before we rolled out the wire?"

"Oh, so nobody told you?" he said, sarcastically.

"Well, if somebody *had* told me then I would've known, wouldn't I?" I immediately found out that Charlie Company had no communication whatsoever, and this was just one of many problems to come. *I'm really starting to regret my transfer*, I thought at the time.

The convoy started to move now, and as we slowly pulled forward, I waved at the four village cops, and smiled at them. They just kept staring at me, eyeing my rifle. I could still feel their eyes on my back as we rolled on through the village, and I knew that the word would spread that American snipers were in the area. I made a mental note to be prepared, and base my actions on the fact that the enemy was aware of my presence.

As we drove on toward the next village, I remember thinking to myself how close that had been to the situation with the red ninja in the Iraq desert. Now, at first glance, it may not appear to some folks that it was in the same league as my brush with death in Western Iraq. However, that same eerie feeling was present. I had no cover, I was in a naked Humvee, and for those four Afghans, armed AK-47s, killing me would've been like shooting fish in a barrel. So all I could do was smile because yet again, I'd cheated death.

We arrived at our second village, and poverty was everywhere—kids without shoes or even rags to wrap around their feet, sunken, weathered faces all around us, and mud huts the most-common residences. Mud was the only sealant available for the Afghans to lay between roof beams (actually, sticks and scavenged wood), and plants and wild grass were growing out of many of the roofs. Just like any village that we came to, the streets suddenly filled with Afghans, children playing in the dirt, their faces marred with dried mud, as the boys offered us hash: "Five bucks, *hasheesh,* hash, five bucks, *hasheesh,*" the dark, oily hashish rolled up in torpedo cigarette form. We pushed these boys away, focusing on the mission at hand, which was to gain field intelligence on Taliban and Al-Qaeda, and pass out flyers for the elections that November.

The sun was really bright now as it neared high noon. We all had to wear dark sunglasses, not only to protect our eyes from the harsh glare of the sun but also, from the constant stream of dust all around us. As in all Afghan villages, goats and sheep clogged the streets, and you could smell the god-awful scent of raw sewage in the air. It was clear this country had focused on little else but war. The total lack of investment in schools, health clinics, sanitation, and social welfare could not be ignored.

As I did in every village, I would always distance myself from the rest of 1st Platoon so that I could have eyes on the surrounding areas. Not being surrounded by paratroopers gave me the ability to scan the crowds and sense any potential danger to my fellow paratroopers, while simultaneously eyeballing the dirt roads leading in and out of the village.

"LeBleu!" Lahoda yelled now, and I ran over to him. He was kneeling next to a berm that overlooked farm fields, the furrows bare. *This is all too familiar*, I thought as I ran to him. It felt like the ambush in Fallujah a year earlier when I'd made the 1,100-meter shot. Everything felt the same. Closing on him, I slowed down my breathing to prepare for a shot.

"Five hundred meters out, two men in a field," he said to me as he eyeballed the field with naked-eye vision.

I took a knee and raised my rifle, looking through my scope. I could see no mortar tubes, no rifles, no munitions of any kind, nor vehicle to escape with. It was odd that they'd chosen the middle of a field in plain sight to hold their conversation. They kept glancing at the village and gesturing as they talked. I remember thinking it could have been two farmers discussing a poor harvest, or what we were doing in the village— or it could have been some kind of reconnaissance. Either way—as with any such activity in a war zone—it was nothing to take lightly.

I said to Lahoda, "Two guys talking, no weapons. But we should still check it out. Could be reconnaissance for a mortar attack, or an IED ambush."

"Yeah, all right," he said, nodding.

By now, 1st Platoon had finished talking with folks in the village and the flyers had all been handed out. Everyone moved back to the convoy of Humvees to load up and return inside the wire. We couldn't get to the two men because there were no roads leading to the field, and in Afghanistan, there were unmarked mines every five feet. It wasn't worth the risk, especially if they were simply farmers.

Afghanistan is plagued by land mines like nowhere else in the world. In the fall of 2004, land mines were as endemic to Afghanistan as the poverty I saw there. They have mines left from the Russian occupation, as well as Italian and other European mines laid by the Taliban and various Afghan warlords. On patrol in Afghanistan, you have to be especially watchful for land mines. The phrase *Take real care* comes to mind. On our patrols there, paratroopers took small baby steps, which would slow us down and make us a prominent target in the open fields. So we'd yell at the paratroopers, "Just walk—if you step on a mine, you won't feel it anyway."

After a while, we just got used to being around land mines, and learned where—and where not—to walk. For instance, we'd be on the lookout for mines on any trails that led to the villages, and aware that basically anything off of a main road would be mined. The only potentially safe places for us on patrol were the main roads, but even there, we were still dealing with IEDs and antitank mines.

Heading slowly back toward our forward operating base, we took our time, doing a convoy patrol; this was a hasty reconnaissance to get our bearings locked on the routines and activities of the Afghans in the villages near us. We got back in the wire an hour before sundown. The early dusk was coming on, and you could feel that the dramatic drop in temperature was not far away.

A few days later, we got the word to check out another village, due to suspected Taliban and Al-Qaeda activity, and to pass out more flyers. We moved out on Humvees in the late afternoon, a few hours before the sun went down, and halted five miles from the mud huts of the village. A tremendous sandstorm hit the entire platoon as we approached the village on foot. We had to keep our heads down as we walked against the wind, the sand slamming into us. The very loose sand on the ground made it hard to walk, and while we were fighting our way through the storm, I remember thinking, *This is a prime opportunity for the enemy to hit us, because we can't see anything.*

I did my best to hold my helmet down with my left hand and to keep my right hand tight around the wooden barrel guards of my M14, well in front of the magazine. I had a 20-round magazine jacked in my sniper rifle. I looked over to Lahoda and said, "What was the point of this walk again?" and he looked back at me, aggravated, and muttered, "So we can pass out flyers." Both of us were laughing and shaking our heads now. I couldn't help but think, *So this is how we are going to win wars against the evil, radical Islamists—by passing out flyers. Sure, why not.*

Walking on, a few paratroopers behind us started to fall back, so I kept turning around and keeping my eye on them, until eventually, I walked back and took over the rear for 1st Platoon. It was clear that the paratroopers were not pulling rear security effectively, and I needed to make sure that nobody would come up behind us. You're only as fast as your slowest man. By the time we reached the village, the sandstorm had died down a little bit—enough for us to pick up our heads, glance around, and talk with each other. We were now completely covered in sand, including our gear and weapons. *Great, this is all we need—sand-covered weapons.* Everybody knows that in a gunfight, if your weapon jams, you die, and that is just what the desert sand is best at.

As 1st Platoon went into the village and began interviewing Afghans and passing out flyers, I stayed at the entrance to the village. As usual, I separated from the paratroopers to gain a better overview of the entire situation. On that day, I leaned up against the side of a house on my left shoulder, scanning the village and terrain without my scope. I could see the snowcapped mountains off in the distance, near Kabul. As the sun settled in the west, 1st Platoon finished handing out flyers. We started to move out on a different route back to our Humvees. Although the sandstorm was over, sand still coated our weapons and gear. With darkness falling, we put on our night-vision goggles and patrolled back in a staggered formation on opposite sides of a dirt road, with the lights of distant villages glowing faintly in the early evening.

An Afghan wearing a camouflage uniform and a sidearm on his hip was with us. I presumed that he was an officer, since he was similar in appearance to the four Afghan policemen I'd seen in the other village a few days earlier. He gestured to Lieutenant Dumpser, indicating that he'd show us a quicker route. Dumpser agreed to follow him, and I said out loud, "Yeah, right—that's the oldest trick in the book for an ambush." Dumpser said, "He knows a quicker way out of here, so we've got to follow him." I turned around to all of 1st Platoon and said, "All right, men, prepare for an ambush."

The paratroopers, some of whom had not seen action with Task Force 1Panther in Western Iraq and were in their first war zone in Afghanistan, looked at me, confused and unsure of what was going on. We'd been on foot for well over five hours, walking through a sandstorm and humping rifles, water, ammo, and combat gear, and we were tired. After warning the paratroopers of an ambush, I took point for the platoon, right next to the Afghan. Watching his every move, I said to the lieutenant, "Hey, sir, if this goes down, I'm taking him out first."

The lieutenant said nothing.

"I don't know if you can understand me," I said to the Afghan, leaning over and talking right into his ear, "but if you set us up, I'm taking you out first." He looked back at me, his face blank. I was puzzled by his lack of expression. Usually when someone has no expression in a combat situation, they are ready for something to go down. We moved out, taking a bend in the road to the right, still staggered. In the middle of the bend, on the left side of the road, a two-story house appeared in the shadows. *This has got to be the ambush site*, I thought.

Not caring about noise discipline anymore, I said, "Put every single laser on that door, those windows, the rooftops, the corners—I want that house covered with lasers. And don't worry about the right side; I've got security right." Infrared lasers flooded the house as we walked by it. With the house all lit up by our lasers—which are unseen to the naked eye—I stared at the Afghan now, reading his body language. His eyes showed nothing. He just kept walking, leading us on. As the platoon cleared the bend, past the house now, we patrolled on until we reached where the Humvees were located for our exfil.

The lieutenant thanked the Afghan, as our platoon loaded up in the convoy. As I walked away from the man, I said, "You did good; you're still alive."

Rolling back toward our fire base, our temporary base for quarters, food and re-supply, and ammunition, I remember thinking, *That had to be the stupidest thing I've ever been a part of; we were just asking to get hit.*

We were also extremely lucky.

Lieutenant Dumpser had just proven a long-known adage of war to be true: People new to combat make amateur mistakes that can likely get many people under them killed. Anyone with two brain cells who has picked up a rifle at war knows that not only do you *never* let someone lead you to your death, but also, *You never trust anyone in combat except for the guy to the left and right of you. And you never trust anything in combat but your instincts.* Both of those ancient laws of war go back to the Spartans. And even those two real and distinct truths about combat are a gamble, half the time.

We rolled back in the wire that night like living ghosts, our lives spared. The Afghan cold was in effect, and our teeth were chattering and we rubbed our hands together as we slowly got out of the Humvees. Nothing was said as we moved into our open tents. Everyone started to realize what I already knew in the field—what a stupid mistake the lieutenant had made. The paratroopers laid on their cots, bone-tired, and wrapped in our sleeping bags, we all fell quickly to sleep.

———

As the days and nights went by that autumn, the icy cold winds carrying winter on them, we continued our operations in support of the upcoming elections. We went from village to village, passing out flyers to encourage people to vote, and at the same time, carrying out field intelligence missions on Taliban and Al-Qaeda activities close to Kabul. When the elections were a week away, we entered one of the few villages that was still new to us near Kabul. Walking into the village at about nine in the morning, I immediately noticed much larger crowds of people, almost all males, more than in any other village we'd been in. Right off the bat, this kept us on edge, knowing that with their long, baggy clothes, the Afghans could've been carrying knives, rifles, submachine guns, grenades, or suicide vests under their garments.

I separated from the paratroopers according to my usual habit, walking about 20 meters north of them. I kept eyes-on for the most likely enemy attack route, the sun bright and warm now in the mid-morning sky over Kabul. As 1st Platoon handed out flyers and talked with the village elders, they also cleared a few houses in the village and discovered weapons caches: AK-47s, RPGs and launchers, and 7.62x39mm bullets. We knew that the village elders and the villagers had lied to us, having earlier told us that there was no Taliban or Al-Qaeda presence in the village. This discovery definitely put us on edge, and we were now expecting to be attacked. We started clearing all the mud huts and ramshackle houses in the village. I stayed on the street, on overwatch, and kept carrying out reconnaissance and surveillance on the village. We'd already pulled out the men from all the buildings in the village so we could keep an eye on them while our squads searched the huts.

As I took a knee to watch the men, I noticed that a camel was walking down the street. A blanket covered the camel's hump, but it didn't have a saddle. Close enough for me to touch it, the camel ambled on down the dirt street, eventually disappearing down the road. I went back to scanning the crowd, saying out loud, "Now there's something you don't see every day."

The paratroopers found nothing in the other huts. I could see an Afghan man on a roof, fairly young—I reckoned he was about eighteen or nineteen—watching our paratroopers from a two-story house with antennas on it. It was the same house where we'd found the first cache of AK-47s and RPGs. I yelled across the street to Lahoda, "You've got a guy on a rooftop with antennas, and it's the same house that has the weapons. He's got no weapon on him, but he's scoping you guys out. Don't worry; if he makes a move, it'll be his last."

Lahoda was upset, as all Afghans in the village were supposed to be in the streets. Paratroopers quickly moved to the house and detained the young man, flex-cuffing him while Lahoda yelled at the owner, "You told me everyone was out of this house! You lied to me twice: You lied about the weapons and now, you lied again. You've got antennas on your house, and weapons, and this guy hiding up there. We'll be back to pay you a visit."

A call came over the radio right then that one of our paratrooper checkpoints up the road from us, about 200 meters, had just stopped a gas tanker. We knew that the gas tanker, quite possibly, was a suicide bomb, with the elections only a week away. The paratroopers at the checkpoint told us over the radio that they'd stopped the tanker 100 meters before it got up to the checkpoint, aiming raised M4s and M4/M203s at it and yelling for it to stop. Which it did.

As everyone moved out, I stayed in place, scanning the crowd with my M14 raised near shoulder level. Lahoda grabbed the flex-cuffed detainee and said, "You're coming with us," as the paratroopers ran and jumped on the Humvees. With everyone clear now, I kept tail-end Charlie and jumped on the last Humvee. "We're good," I shouted, latching the tow strap, and our Humvees moved as one, pulled a U-turn, and sped down the road, coming up to the rear of the gas tanker.

We all jumped out as the Humvees stopped, half of us peeling off left on the tight road, ditches on both sides of the road preventing our drivers from getting any farther away from the gas tanker. The rest of us peeled off right and ran up to where we had eyes on the cab of the truck.

A driver sat in the cab, alone.

Lahoda was yelling now to our interpreter, "Tell the driver to open his door, and get out with his hands up."

You could tell the driver was local—threadbare clothes, disheveled hair, dust all over his face, and torn-up sandals. Lahoda held his M4 on the driver as he got out of the cab—in truth, we all had a bead on him—and he stepped away from the gas tanker with his hands held high in the air. He seemed uneasy and really nervous, his hands and arms shaking as he walked slowly away from the tanker. Lahoda moved swiftly, grabbed him, and put him facedown on the ground.

"Search him," Lahoda said to our paratroopers. They patted him down and checked him thoroughly, but found nothing. Lahoda picked the guy back up and told the interpreter, "Ask him, why is he driving this gas truck, and why is he so nervous?"

The interpreter quickly asked him in Pashto and the driver replied, close to tears, "I must do this for my family, so they won't be harmed."

The interpreter's eyes lit up now, real excited, and Lahoda asked, "What's going on?"

The interpreter said, "That truck is probably rigged as a suicide bomb, and he's said that he must do this for his family so they won't be hurt." We were very fortunate that Lahoda had been around the block before, a seasoned combat veteran, and he knew immediately what that meant. Lahoda yelled at everyone, "Get back in the Humvees—*now!*"

The whole time this was going on, I had the feeling that something wasn't right. As I scanned with my scope, back and forth over the truck, I saw wires hanging underneath the belly of the gas tank, some red, others black. I told all the paratroopers near me, "Move, move, move," and ran behind them, all of us dashing back to our Humvees. Lahoda detained the driver, so now we had two flex-cuffed detainees. We rolled back to the village with Lahoda telling everyone not to use their radios. He knew that any radio frequency from our Motorolas could set off and detonate a suicide bomb.

Once we were back at the village, Lahoda used the platoon radio—which had a closed, secure frequency and was safe to communicate on—to let our checkpoint know, "If you guys haven't figured it out yet, that truck is rigged to explode."

"Roger," they replied.

Within minutes, the paratroopers moved their checkpoint some 300 meters back, closer to another mud-hut village. The checkpoint called in EOD specialists, and we held in the place in the village. People filled the streets, going to and from the village market. I pulled out a Snickers I had been saving in my ammo pouch, opened it, and said, "Not going anywhere for a while." Lahoda just shook his head and smiled.

Within a couple of hours, by late afternoon, EOD came out and set a mobile robot with a camera on it near the gas tanker. The suicide bomb was rigged with C-4 plastic explosives and the red and black wires I'd scoped. It turned out that the wires were not attached correctly, and EOD realized they could move in and disable the suicide bomb, so they got under the tanker and cut the wires. After disassembling the suicide bomb, they gave the all-clear and we moved up to the vehicle. An EOD specialist got in the cab and drove the truck slowly off the road. The rest of the EOD team secured all of the plastic explosives and wire. Strangely, like the EOD specialists in Iraq, they never said "Thank you." I guess when you're playing with bombs all day, there's not much that needs to be said.

With our two detainees sitting in the back of a Humvee, we sped off, rolling back toward the fire base. Dusk rolled in, the sun a far distant fire falling behind the ridgelines west of us. Entering our base, we halted quickly and Lahoda dropped off the detainees at our MPs' shack to be interrogated and processed. We rolled on back to our open tents, the temperature dropping swiftly in the early dark, and dropped our gear under our cots. Lahoda and Dumpser met Lopez and gave him a quick after-action report on stopping the suicide bomber and the weapons caches found in the village.

One of the things that blew my mind over there was when we'd patrol through the mountain terrain during the day. We would mostly find abandoned fighting bunkers; while some looked freshly used, with expended 7.62 brass left behind from their AK-47s, others looked like they'd been there for quite some time. I'm assuming those older bunkers were from the days when they were fighting Russia, which, ironically, the U.S. had helped to fund. We'd also found caves, which, to my surprise, went pretty deep into the mountains. Some of the caves ran so deep that you would come up to a split to either go left or go right, which meant they continued even deeper. The others were what we called "dry holes"; in other words, a short cave. Just like any other room or hut, we cleared the caves with anxious anticipation of disturbing the Taliban's Monday-night poker game.

Inside the cave, we would switch to our night vision because of how dark the caves were. It was pure blackness; you couldn't even see your hand in front of your face. The stench of the cave was toxic. We could never figure out what the smell was or where it originated from, but the suffocating stench was bad enough to interrupt our noise discipline by making us cough. It smelled like the worst body odor mixed in with a little bit of death. I could also hear bats hovering above us at times.

Once we'd cleared the cave, we would search around for any intelligence left behind, such as maps, weapons caches, even clothing. It wasn't easy to spot a cave or bunker because they were so well camouflaged, as if they were a natural part of the mountainside. As we would exit the caves and begin our descent back to base, I would stop on a ridgeline, scouting the path ahead for any potential ambushes. While the platoon kept moving I would just sit there and look out over the mountains into the distant horizon, thinking to myself, *Funny how hell can look so beautiful.*

Afghanistan sunrises and sunsets over the many snowcapped mountains literally looked like paintings, and for those few seconds, time would stop and allow me to embrace the beauty around me. In all of combat, I found dusk to be my favorite. It seemed to be the only time of day when you could take in a fresh breath, relax, and hear your thoughts. I would always refer to it as "the calm before the storm."

Back inside the wire with the cold night setting in, I would stand outside by the tents and just scan all the mountains in a slow circle, looking for any lights or flashes—anything to indicate that there was still activity around us. Then I would do the same motion with night vision on. What I saw made me cringe inside. When I donned my night vision and scanned the surrounding mountains, I could see campfires literally all around us. I assumed many of them might be near caves. I couldn't help but think of how many of those caves we didn't see and probably walked right by.

I definitely had the feeling that we were outnumbered. Talk about "the hills have eyes"! I guess in the end, we *were* in their backyard, so I'm sure there were many trails, caves, bunkers, and key Taliban leaders we missed by not seeing what was really in front of us. Then again, we didn't have the best intelligence to work with—if we had any at all. From that point on I had a running joke at night when I'd see any campfires or lights up in the mountains. I'd say, "Hey, there goes Osama bin Laden. Do you think I'll get the reward for finding him?"

Since we had pretty much pushed most of the Taliban out of Afghanistan, there wasn't much combat going down in our immediate area—Bagram, Kabul, and the villages close to Kabul—other than IEDs placed by Taliban and Al-Qaeda. All the action at that time was on the Pakistan border—especially since there were travel tunnels that ran underneath both borders used by Taliban and Osama bin Laden as a way to escape and hide. The whole time we were dealing with the villages, our Scouts were patrolling the Pakistan border, which is just four days' forced march, on foot, from Kabul.

One night, Howerton and his sniper team were patrolling on the Pakistan border and had set up a hide site, looking for any Taliban and Al-Qaeda crossing from Pakistan into Afghanistan. Howerton had set in trip flares in his surrounding area, the flares laid in at 50 and 100 meters from his hide site in the mountains, to ensure no one could sneak up on him in the night. He also placed a Claymore mine, winding the wire back to his hide site and camouflaging it. He held the trigger for the Claymore himself. As they lay there, they heard rocks falling, scattering down the ridgelines, as if someone had disturbed the terrain.

Within moments, the trip flares went off, white flashes shooting up in the sky. The flares exposed a squad-sized element of Taliban, about six enemy in long robes and turbans, carrying weapons. Howerton set his Claymores and his team emptied two magazines rapidly at the Taliban, sixty rounds. The flares started to go out—you've only got about six seconds once a flare is tripped until the light dies—and the team changed magazines as the flares went out completely. Howerton ordered his team to break contact, which is exactly what Scouts and snipers are trained to do in that situation, and they hustled back through the mountains to a safe location, communicating to Scout platoon the contact they'd been through and their movement.

Waiting through the night, they carried out reconnaissance and surveillance in the mountains near the Pakistan border. With dawn's arrival, they moved back to their forward operating base. For his actions on that night, Sergeant John Howerton of San Antonio, Texas, received a Bronze Star. Within a week, for the first time in history, Afghanistan held its first-ever elections. Thanks in no small part to our presence, the elections went off without any disturbance or delay. It really seemed to me that we'd pushed many insurgents toward the Pakistan border during the fall of 2004.

Soon after the elections, we got orders to return home. We flew from Bagram to Pope Air Force Base at Fayetteville, via Germany, landing back in North Carolina in time for a real Thanksgiving dinner stateside—not like the lone meatball we'd enjoyed at the Rad Site just one year before.

Now back in Fayetteville, which I liked to refer to as "FayetteNam," because there wasn't much to do in that town and it was purely military, I remember saying to myself, *If I ever put these desert BDUs on again, it will be too soon.*

It was very calming and relaxing to be back from Afghanistan, and to be able to really enjoy all of the holidays in America for the first time in eight years. *I wish I could've spent all my holidays like this*, I remember thinking.

As my ETS (expiration term of service) date neared, I decided not to reenlist. My decision had nothing to do with my duty. I loved being a sniper more than anything else, because it ran through my veins. If there was anything that I was good at, it was being a sniper.

It was the political bullshit that had burned me out, and I wanted nothing more to do with this war. I could no longer stand to watch our leadership bed the same enemy we were fighting. As much as I wanted to stay in, I fundamentally disapproved of the new direction our military was being forced to follow. Along with many of my comrades who remain on active duty today, I object to our being forced to become friends with Al-Qaeda and the Taliban, the enemy we'd started out to kill in this war.

One thing you need to understand about a soldier: From day one in boot camp, we are being taught to kill, kill, kill. When the leadership starts to tell the soldier in combat to *stop* killing and to start rebuilding what he has just destroyed, and that he now has to become *friends* with the enemy, it really messes with his state of mind. In the long run, that causes mental problems, such as post-traumatic stress disorder (PTSD) and depression. It can also spark the blame game, making the soldier feel guilty for killing people that his leadership is now telling him to befriend. It's like having two bosses telling you two different things, pulling you in two opposite directions.

What really bothers me to this day, and no doubt will bother me until the day I die, is that we have lost our foothold in Afghanistan. Basically, we have to start back at square one, because since the autumn of 2004, we've lost one-third of the country back to the Taliban and Al-Qaeda. That tells me that the brothers I lost in Afghanistan in March of 2002, and all of the men and women who are still dying there, have died in vain. We don't even have the foothold that we won on the battlefields of Afghanistan in 2001 and 2002. Crose, Anderson, and Commons died to gain the foothold that Bush has lost.

You can't start two wars and think that you'll win either of them without even committing fully to one. The war started in Afghanistan and never ended because Bush was so anxious to retaliate against Iraq and finish what his dad had started. That whole time, we should have focused on Afghanistan, ensuring that we'd strike and kill all Taliban and Al-Qaeda where they sleep. Now, we're on a never-ending chase for Al-Qaeda terrorists worldwide, and Taliban in Pakistan and Afghanistan, because Bush failed to focus on one war.

Feeling frustrated and downhearted in the fall of 2004, I decided that I'd had enough of our leadership failing us and leading us blindly to the slaughter. As my last months in the military flew by at Fort Bragg, North Carolina, I knew it was time for me to check out. I told all my guys, "Good luck, and keep your head down."

CHAPTER SIX

Capturing a Locomotive

William Pittenger

During America's great Civil War in 1862, a military clash took place that was so exciting, so dramatic and action-packed, that over a hundred years later Hollywood would turn the event into a major feature film. The courage of the event's Union heroes was so profound that a grateful nation had to come up with some new and distinct way to honor such bravery: The Medal of Honor was created. One of the first recipients was William Pittenger, who eventually became Rev. William Pittenger and penned the book Capturing a Locomotive, *the detailed account of how a band of Union soldiers, led by civilians J.J. Andrews and William Campbell, penetrated the Confederate rail complex, captured a train, and raced it toward glory. A furious chase resulted in the capture of the raiders. The citation includes this description of Pittenger:*

"one of the 19 of 22 men who penetrated nearly 200 miles south into enemy territory and captured a railroad train at Big Shanty, Georgia, in an attempt to destroy the bridges and track between Chattanooga and Atlanta." Tried as spies, Andrews and seven of the Union soldiers were hanged. The soldiers were later awarded the Medal of Honor posthumously (as a civilian Andrews did not qualify), after some of the surviving soldiers were honored with the medal by Secretary of War Edwin Stanton. Some had escaped the Confederate prisons, others, including Pittenger, had been freed in prisoner-of-war exchanges. The movie was The Great Locomotive Chase, *released by Walt Disney Studios in 1956.*

Editor's Note: In the first part of this excerpt, Pittenger describes meeting Andrews and hearing the details of the audacious raid he and fellow members of the Union Army had volunteered to undertake.

WE FORMED A CLOSE CIRCLE AROUND MR. ANDREWS WHILE HE revealed to us his daring plans. In a voice as soft and low as a woman's, but tremulous with suppressed enthusiasm, he painted the greatness of the project we were to attempt, the sublimity of rushing through a hostile country at the full speed of steam, leaving flaming bridges and raging but powerless foes behind. But he did not disguise the dangers to be encountered.

"Soldiers," he said, "if you are detected while engaged in this business, the great probability is that you will be put to death,—hung as spies, or massacred by a mob. I want you to clearly understand this, and if you are not willing to take the risk, return to camp, and keep perfectly quiet about it."

A murmur all around the circle conveyed the assurance that we would follow him to the last extremity.

"Our plan," he continued, "is simply this: you are to travel on foot, or by any conveyance you can hire, either to Chattanooga or some station not far from that point on the Memphis and Charleston Railroad; then you can take passage on the cars down to Marietta; that will be our next place of assembling, and not Atlanta. You must be there by Thursday evening, ready to take passage on the cars northward again by Friday morning. I will be there as soon as you, and tell you what more is to be done."

One of the soldiers asked, "If any of us are suspected, and find we can't get away, what would you advise us to do?"

"Enlist without hesitation in the rebel army," was the response. "You are fully authorized to do that, and no one of this party will be accused of desertion, even if captured among the rebels. I would be sorry to lose any one of you, but it will be far better that you should serve awhile with the enemy than to acknowledge who you are, and thus risk the disclosure of the enterprise."

"But is it likely that we could get the chance thus to enlist?" it was further asked.

"Most certainly," said Andrews. "They are taking all the prisoners out of the jails and enlisting them. They are picking up men who have run away from the conscription wherever they can find them, and serving them in the same manner. If you tell your story and stick to it, even if they are not satisfied that you are telling the truth, they will put you into the service. You can stay until some dark night on picket. But I hope you will escape all trouble, and all meet me at Marietta safely. Break this party up into squads of three or four, and don't recognize each other on the way. I will ride along the same country you are travelling, and give you any help or direction in my power. But you must not recognize me unless sure that we are not observed."

There was but one subject on which I cared to ask any questions, and that related to a distant contingency. I was well informed as to the first part of the intended enterprise.

"Suppose we succeed in capturing the train," I said, "and in burning the bridges, are we then to leave the train, and try to steal back to our lines in the same way we are now going South?"

"By no means," replied Mr. Andrews. "We will run the train right through Chattanooga, and westward until we meet Mitchel, who by that time will be coming eastward on the road from Memphis. If we should not quite reach him, we will get so close that we can dash through in a body."

This was satisfactory as far as it went, but there was still another contingency. More than anything else I dreaded being left alone in an unknown country.

"If we fail to run the captured train through Chattanooga, will we then disperse or stick together?"

"After we meet at Marietta, we will keep together, and, if necessary, cut our way back to our own lines. Form your squads now, and I will give out the money."

Swiftly we selected our companions. There was little time for choice. Most of the men were strangers. The darkness was intense, and the thunder-peals almost overhead. In a moment we formed six or seven little groups. My former comrade, Ross, stood with another man or two beside Andrews. Two men from Captain Mitchel's company and one from the next company to that in the regimental line stood by my side. Andrews went from group to group, giving out the money freely, and answering questions that were still asked. When this was accomplished, he addressed himself once more to the whole number, and we crowded around to listen to his parting words. They gave us the fullest insight into the whole plan we had yet received.

Editor's Note: Now Pettinger's text, excerpted from the book, shifts to his description of what happened on the fateful day of The Great Locomotive Chase.

War has a secret as well as a public story. Marches and battles are open to the popular gaze; but enterprises of another class are in their very nature secret, and these are scarcely less important and often much more interesting than the former. The work of spies and scouts, the enterprises that reach beyond the lines of an army for the purpose of surprise, the councils of officers, the intrigues by means of which great results often flow from apparently insignificant causes, and all the experiences of hospitals and prisons—these usually fill but a small place on the historian's page, though they are often of romantic interest, and not infrequently decide the course and fate of armies.

The enterprise described in these pages possesses all the unity of a drama, from the first plunge of the actors into the heart of the enemy's country, through all their adventures and changing fortunes, until the few survivors stood once more under the old flag! No single story of the war combines so many of the hidden, underground elements of the contest against rebellion as this. Disguise and secrecy, the perils of a forlorn hope, the exultation of almost miraculous success, the sufferings of prisoners, and the gloom of despair are all mingled in a varied and instructive war-picture.

In telling the story all fictitious embellishments have been rejected. No pains have been spared to ascertain the exact truth, and the reader will find names, dates, and localities so fully given that it will be easy to verify the prominent features of the account.

In narrating those events which fell under his own eye, the writer has waived all scruples of delicacy, and used the first personal pronoun. This is far more simple and direct, while an opposite course would have savored of affectation.

This is not a revision or new edition of the little volume published by the present writer during the rebellion. *Daring and Suffering*, like a number of similar sketches published in newspapers, magazines, and pamphlets, was a hasty narrative of personal adventure, and made no pretense of completeness. *Capturing a Locomotive* is broader and more historic; a large amount of valuable material is now employed for the first time; and the story is approached in an entirely different manner. No paragraph of the old book is copied into the new.

—Woodbury, New Jersey, January 1882

THE CAPTURE

The greater number of us arranged to pass the night at a small hotel adjoining the Marietta depot. Before retiring we left orders with the hotel clerk to rouse us in time for the northward-bound train, due not long after daylight. Notwithstanding our novel situation, I never slept more soundly. Good health, extreme fatigue, and the feeling that the die was now cast and further thought useless, made me sink into slumber almost as soon as I touched the bed. Others equally brave and determined were affected in a different way. Alfred Wilson says:

No man knows what a day may bring forth, and the very uncertainty of what that day's sun would bring forth in our particular cases was the reason that some of us, myself at least of the number, did not sleep very much. Our doom might be fixed before the setting of another sun. We might be hanging to the limbs of some of the trees along the railroad, with an enraged populace jeering and shouting vengeance because we had no more lives to give up; or we might leave a trail of fire and destruction behind us, and come triumphantly rolling into Chattanooga and Huntsville, within the Federal lines, to receive the welcome plaudits of comrades left behind, and the thanks of our general, and the praises of a grateful people. Such thoughts as these passed in swift review, and were not calculated to make one sleep soundly.

As the hotel was much crowded, we obtained a few rooms in close proximity, and crowded them to their utmost capacity. Andrews noted our rooms before retiring, that he might, if necessary, seek any one of us out for consultation before we rose. Porter and Hawkins were unfortunately overlooked; they had arrived on an earlier train and obtained lodging at some distance from the depot. The clerk failed to have them called in time for the morning train, as they had ordered, and, greatly to their regret and chagrin, they were left behind. This was a serious loss, as they were both cool, brave men, and Hawkins was the most experienced railway engineer of our company. W. F. Brown, who took his place in this work, was, however, fully competent, though possibly somewhat less cautious.

Long before the train was due, Andrews, who had slept little, if at all, that night, glided from room to room silently as a ghost, the doors being purposely left unfastened, and aroused the slumberers. It seemed to some of us scarcely a moment from the time of retiring until he came thus to the bedside of each sleeper in turn, and cautiously wakening him, asked his name, to prevent the possibility of mistake, and then told each one exactly the part he was expected to take in the enterprise of the day. There was hasty dressing, and afterwards an informal meeting held in Andrews's room, at which nearly one-half of the whole number were present, and plans were more fully discussed.

Then Marion A. Ross, one of the most determined of the whole number, took the bold step of advising and even urging the abandonment, for the present, of the whole enterprise. He reasoned with great force that under present circumstances, with the Rebel vigilance fully aroused by Mitchel's rapid advance, with guards stationed around the train we were to capture, as we had learned would be the case at Big Shanty, and with the road itself obstructed by numerous trains, the enterprise was sure to fail, and would cost the life of every man engaged in it. Andrews very gently answered his arguments and strove to show that the objections urged really weighed in favor of the original plan. No such attempt as we purposed had ever been made, and consequently would not be guarded against; the presence of a line of sentinels and of so many troops at Big Shanty would only tend to relax vigilance still further; and the great amount of business done on the road, with the running of many unscheduled trains, would screen us from too close inquiry when we ran our train ahead of time.

This reasoning was not altogether satisfactory, and some of the others joined Ross in a respectful but firm protest against persisting in such a hopeless undertaking. But Andrews, speaking very low, as was his wont when thoroughly in earnest, declared that he had once before postponed the attempt, and returned to camp disgraced. "Now," he continued, "I will accomplish my purpose or leave my bones to bleach in Dixie. But I do not wish to control any one against his own judgment. If any of you think it too hazardous, you are perfectly at liberty to take the train in the opposite direction and work your way back to camp as you can."

This inflexible determination closed the discussion, and as no man was willing to desert his leader, we all assured him of our willingness to obey his orders to the death. I had taken no part in the discussion, as I was not in possession of sufficient facts to judge of the chance of success, and I wished the responsibility to rest upon the leader, where it properly belonged.

The train was now nearly due, and we proceeded to the station for the purchase of tickets. By the time they had been procured—not all for one place, as we wished to lessen the risk of suspicion—the train swept up to the platform. Hastily glancing at it in the early morning light, and seeing only that it was very long and apparently well filled, the twenty adventurers entered by different doors, but finally took their places in one car.

From Marietta to Big Shanty the railroad sweeps in a long bend of eight miles around the foot of Kennesaw Mountain, which lies directly between the two stations. This elevation is now scarred all over with Rebel entrenchments, and was the scene of one of the severest contests of the war. This, however, as well as the whole of the three months' struggle from Chattanooga to Atlanta, came a year and a half later. At this time the nearest Federal soldiers were more than two hundred miles away.

When the train moved on and the conductor came to take our tickets, we observed him carefully, as we knew not how closely his fate and ours might be linked together in the approaching struggle. The most vivid anticipation fell far short of the reality. Upon the qualities of that one man our success or failure hinged. He was quite young—not more than twenty-three or -four—and looked like a man of resolution and energy. We noticed that he was also scrutinizing us and the other passengers very closely, and naturally feared that he had in some manner been put on his guard. In fact, as we learned long afterwards, he had been warned that some of the new conscripts who were reluctant to fight for the Confederacy were contemplating an escape, and might try to get a ride on the cars. His orders were to watch for all such and arrest them at once. But he did not think that any of the men who got on at Marietta looked in the least like conscripts or deserters.

The train ran slowly, stopping at several intervening points, and did not reach Big Shanty until it was fully daylight. This station had been selected for the seizure, because the train breakfasted there, and it was probable that many of the employees and passengers would leave it for their meal, thus diminishing the opposition we might expect. Another most important reason for the selection was the absence of any telegraph office. But, on the other hand, Camp McDonald had been lately located here, and a large body of soldiers—some accounts said as many as ten thousand men—were already assembled. Their camp included the station within the guard-line. When Andrews and the first party had been at Atlanta, three weeks earlier, few troops had yet arrived at this point. The capture of a train in the midst of a camp of the enemy was not a part of the original plan, but subsequently became necessary. It was certainly a great additional element of danger, but it was not now possible to substitute any other point.

The decisive hour had arrived. It is scarcely boastful to say that the annals of history record few enterprises more bold and novel than that witnessed by the rising sun of Saturday morning, April 12, 1862. Here was a train, with several hundred passengers, with a full complement of hands, lying inside a line of sentinels, who were distinctly seen pacing back and forth in close proximity, to be seized by a mere score of men, and to be carried away before the track could be obstructed, or the intruding engineer shot down at his post. Only the most careful calculation and prompt execution, concentrating the power of the whole band into a single lightning-like stroke, could afford the slightest prospect of success.

In the bedroom conference every action was predetermined with the nicest accuracy. Our engineer and his assistant knew the signal at which to start; the brakesmen had their work assigned; the man who was to uncouple the cars knew just the place at which to make the separation; the remainder of the number constituted a guard, in two divisions, who were to stand with ready revolvers abreast of the cars to be seized, and shoot down without hesitation anyone who attempted to interfere with the work. Andrews was to command the whole, and do any part of the work not otherwise provided for. Should there be any unexpected hindrance, we were to fight until we either overcame all opposition and captured the train or perished in a body. If we failed to carry off our prize we were inevitably lost; if any man failed to be on board when the signal was given, his fate also was sealed. A delay of thirty seconds after our designs became clearly known would have resulted in the slaughter of the whole party.

When our train rolled up to the platform, the usual announcement was shouted: "Big Shanty; twenty minutes for breakfast!" Most fortunately for us, the conductor, engineer, firemen, and train-hands generally, with many of the passengers, poured out, and hurried to the long, low eating-room which gave its name to the station. The engine was utterly unguarded. This uncommon carelessness was the result of perfect security, and greatly favored our design. Yet it was a thrilling moment! Victory or death hung on the next minute! There was no chance for drawing back, and I do not think any of us had the disposition. A little while before, a sense of shrinking came over the writer like that preceding a plunge into ice-water; but with the next breath it passed away, and left me as calm and quiet as if no enemy had been within a hundred miles. Still, for a moment, we kept our seats. Andrews went forward to examine the track and see if there was any hindrance to a rapid rush ahead. Almost immediately he returned, and said, very quietly, "All right, boys; let us go now." There was nothing in this to attract special observation; but whether it did or not was now a matter of indifference. The time of concealment was past.

We rose, left the cars, and walked briskly to the head of the train. With the precision of machinery, every man took his appointed place. Three cars back from the tender the coupling-pin was drawn out, as the load of passenger-cars would only have been an encumbrance. Wilson W. Brown, who acted as engineer, William Knight as assistant, Alfred Wilson as fireman, together with Andrews, mounted the engine, Knight grasping the lever, and waiting the word for starting. The appointed brakesmen threw themselves flat on the top of the cars. At a signal from Andrews, the remainder of the band, who had kept watch, climbed with surprising quickness into a boxcar which stood open. All was well! Knight, at Andrews's orders, jerked open the steam-valve, and we were off! Before the camp-guards or the bystanders could do more than turn a curious eye upon our proceedings, the train was under way, and we were safe from interruption.

The writer was stationed in the boxcar, and as soon as all were in, we pulled the door shut to guard against any stray musket-balls. For a moment of most intense suspense after we were thus shut in, all was still. In that moment a thousand conflicting thoughts swept through our minds. Then came a pull, a jar, a clang, and we were flying away on our perilous journey. Those who were on the engine caught a glimpse of the excited crowd, soldiers and citizens, swarming and running about in the wildest confusion. It has been said that a number of shots were fired after us, but those in the boxcar knew nothing of it, and it is certain that no one was injured. A widely circulated picture represented us as waving our hats and shouting in triumph. Nothing so melodramatic took place. The moment was too deep and earnest, and we had too many perils still to encounter for any such childish demonstration.

Yet it was a grand triumph, and having nothing of a more practical character for the moment to do, I realized it to the fullest extent. There are times in life when whole years of enjoyment are condensed into a single experience. It was so with me then. I could comprehend the emotion of Columbus when he first beheld through the dim dawn the long-dreamed-of shores of America, or the less innocent but no less fervent joy of Cortez when he planted the Cross of Spain on the halls of Montezuma. My breast throbbed fast with emotions of joy and gladness that words labor in vain to express. A sense of ethereal lightness ran through my veins, and I seemed [to be] ascending higher, higher, with each pulsation of the engine. Remember, I was but twenty-two then, full of hope and ambition. Not a dream of failure shadowed my rapture. We had always been told that the greatest difficulty was to reach and take possession of the engine, after which success was certain. But for unforeseen contingencies it would have been.

Away we rushed, scouring past field and village and woodland. At each leap of the engine our hearts rose higher, and we talked merrily of the welcome that would greet us when we dashed into Huntsville a few hours later, our enterprise done, and the brightest laurels of the war eclipsed!

We found the railroad, however, to be of the roughest and most difficult character. The grades were very heavy and the curves numerous and sharp. We seemed to be running toward every point of the compass. The deep valleys and steep hills of this part of the country had rendered the building of the road difficult and costly. There were numerous high embankments where an accident would be of deadly character. The track was also uneven and in generally bad condition, for the war had rendered railroad iron scarce and high-priced, besides diverting all attention and resources into other channels. This unfavorable character of the road very greatly increased the difficulty experienced by an engineer unfamiliar with the route in making rapid time, or in avoiding the varied difficulties incident to our progress. But we trusted implicitly that the farsighted plans of Andrews, the skill of our engineers, and our own willing efforts would overcome all hindrances.

Our first run was short. There was a sudden checking of speed and a halt. When those of us who were in the boxcar pushed open our door and asked the reason for stopping so soon, we were told that the fire was low and the steam exhausted. This was startling intelligence, and caused a moment of consternation. If our "General"—the name of the locomotive we had captured—failed us at the beginning of the race, we too well knew what the end would be. For hundreds of miles on every side of us were desperate and daring foes. A hundred times our number on horse and on foot could be gathered against us in a few hours. The most timid bird pursued by hounds feels safe, for its wings can bear it above their jaws. But if those wings should be broken! This engine gave us wings; but if it should be disabled, no valor of ours could beat back the hosts about us, no skill elude their rage.

But we found a less threatening explanation of our premature halt. The schedule time of our train was very slow—only about sixteen miles an hour—and the fires had been allowed to run down because of the expected stop of twenty minutes for breakfast at Big Shanty—a stop that we had reduced to less than two minutes. Then the valve being thrown wide open, the little steam in the boiler was soon exhausted. But this difficulty was of short duration. A rest of three minutes, with plenty of wood thrown into the furnace, wrought a change, and we again glided rapidly forward.

But when viewed soberly, and in the light of all the facts since developed, what were the chances of success and escape possessed by the flying party? Was the whole attempt, as has been frequently asserted, rash and foolhardy? Or had it that character of practicability which is ever the stamp of true genius? Historical accuracy, as well as justice to the memory of a brave but unfortunate man, compels me to pronounce the scheme almost faultless. In this estimate I have the full concurrence of all who were engaged on the opposite side. It is hard to see how the plan could have been improved without allowing its projector to have had a knowledge of the precise condition of the enemy such as no commander at the beginning of an important enterprise ever has. No one of the plans by which Generals Grant and Sherman finally overthrew the Rebellion presented a clearer prospect of success.

These are the elements of the problem upon which Andrews based his hopes. Big Shanty is twenty-eight miles north of Atlanta and thirty-two south of Kingston. Short of these places he was convinced that no engine could be obtained for pursuit. He could obstruct the road so that no train would reach Big Shanty for hours. Pinch-bars and other instruments for lifting track might be found on the captured engine, or obtained from some station or working-party. His force of twenty men was counted ample to overcome resistance at any switch or passing train. One irregular train only was expected to be on the road, and that would soon be met—certainly at Kingston or before—after which it would be safe to run at the highest speed to the first bridge, burn it, and pass on to the next, which, with all other large bridges, could be served in the same manner. Each bridge burnt would be an insuperable barrier to pursuit by an engine beyond that point. Thus, every part of the scheme was fair and promising. Only those critics who are wise after the event can pronounce the attempt rash and hopeless. The destruction of the telegraph would also be necessary; but this was not difficult. It seemed as if every contingency was provided for, and then there was the additional fighting power of twenty chosen men to guard against any possible emergency. We were now embarked on this most perilous but hopeful voyage. Coolness, precision of work, and calm effort could scarcely fail to sever the chief military communications of the enemy before the setting of the sun, and convince him that no enterprise was too audacious for the Union arms.

After the fire had been made to burn briskly Andrews jumped off the engine, ran back to the boxcar, about the door of which we were standing, and clasped our hands in an ecstasy of congratulation. He declared that all our really hard work was done and that our difficulties were nearly passed; that we had the enemy at such a disadvantage that he could not harm us; and exhibited every sign of joy. Said he, "Only one train to meet, and then we will put our engine to full speed, burn the bridges that I have marked out, dash through Chattanooga, and on to Mitchel at Huntsville. We've got the upper hand of the Rebels now, and they can't help themselves!" How glad we all were! When, three years later, the capture of Richmond set all the bells of the North ringing out peals of triumph, the sensation of joy was more diffused but less intense than we then experienced. Almost everything mankind values seemed within our grasp. Oh, if we had met but one unscheduled train!

This reference of Andrews to one train which he expected to meet before we began to burn bridges has been quoted in many public sketches, and has led to some misapprehension. He did expect to meet three trains before reaching Chattanooga; but two of these were regular trains, and being also farther up the road, were not supposed to present any serious difficulty. Their position at any given time could be definitely ascertained, and we could avoid collision with them, no matter how far we ran ahead of time. But so long as there were any irregular trains on the road before us, our only safety was in keeping the regular time of the captured train. This was, unfortunately, very slow; but if we exceeded it we lost the right-of-way, and were liable to a collision at any moment.

This risk was greatly increased by our inability to send ahead telegraphic notifications of our position. The order of southward-bound trains, according to the information we then had, was as follows: First, a way-freight, which was very uncertain as to time, but which we expected to meet early in the morning, and felt sure that it would be at Kingston or south of that point. This was the only real hindrance according to our program, and it was to this train that Andrews referred. Behind this were the regular freight train, and still farther north, the regular passenger train. As a matter of fact, we did meet these trains at Adairsville and Calhoun, the latter being somewhat behind time; but we might have met them farther north had it not been for unforeseen hindrances.

There is considerable discrepancy in the many published accounts of the following chase, which the writer has not in every case been able to perfectly reconcile. In the intense excitement and novel situations involved men were not likely to observe or remember every event accurately. But no pains have been spared to combine fullness and completeness in the following account. Using the best of my own recollections, consulting my comrades, reading carefully all published accounts, and especially going over the whole route years after, with Fuller and Murphy, two of the pursuing party, who kindly gave me all the information in their power, it is hoped that substantial accuracy has been obtained. Some of the incidents of the chase, such as the number of times the track was torn up, and whether we were fired upon by pursuing soldiers, allow some room for a conflict of memory. But the variations are not material.

Side by side with the road ran the telegraph-wires, which were able, by the flashing of a single lightning message ahead, to arrest our progress and dissipate our fondest hopes. There was no telegraph station where we had captured the train, but we knew not how soon our enemies might reach one, or whether they might not have a portable battery at command. Therefore we ran but a short distance, after replenishing the furnace, before again stopping to cut the wire.

John Scott, an active young man of the Twenty-first Ohio, scrambled up the pole with the agility of a cat, and tried to break the wire by swinging upon it; but failing in this, he knocked off the insulating box at the top of the pole and swung with it down to the ground. Fortunately, a small saw was found on the engine, with which the wire was severed in two places, and the included portion, many yards in length, was taken away with us, in order that the ends might not be readily joined.

While one or two of the party were thus engaged, others worked with equal diligence in taking up a rail from the track. No good track-raising instruments had been found on the train, and we had not yet procured them from any other source. A smooth iron bar, about four feet long, was the only instrument yet found, and with this some of the spikes were slowly and painfully battered out. After a few had thus been extracted, a lever was got under the rail and the remainder were pried loose. This occupied much more time than cutting the wire, and it required no prophet to foretell that if we did not procure better tools, rail-lifting would have to be used very sparingly in our program. In the present instance, however, the loss of time was no misfortune, as we were ahead of the schedule time, which we still felt bound to observe.

After another rapid but brief run, we paused long enough to chop down a telegraph-pole, cut the wire again, and place the pole, with many other obstructions, on the track. We did not here try to lift a rail; indeed, we had little serious fear of any pursuit at this time, and merely threw on these obstructions because of having spare time to employ.

We thus continued—running a little ahead of time, then stopping to obstruct the track and cut the wire—until Cass Station was reached, where we took on a good supply of wood and water. At this place we also obtained a complete time schedule of the road. Andrews told the tank-tender that we were running a powder-train through to the army of General Beauregard at Corinth, which was almost out of ammunition, and that the greatest haste was necessary. He further claimed to be a Confederate officer of high rank, and said that he had impressed this train for the purpose in hand, and that Fuller, with the regular passenger train, would be along shortly. The whole story was none too plausible, as General Mitchel was now interposed between our present position and Beauregard, and we would never have been able to get a train to the army of the latter on this route; but the tender was not critical and gave us his schedule, adding that he would willingly send his shirt to Beauregard if that general needed it. When this man was afterwards asked if he did not suspect the character of the enemy he thus aided, he answered that he would as soon have suspected the President of the Confederacy himself as one who talked so coolly and confidently as Andrews did!

Keeping exactly on regular time, we proceeded without any striking adventures until Kingston was reached. This place—thirty-two miles from Big Shanty—we regarded as marking the first stage of our journey. Two hours had elapsed since the capture of the train, and hitherto we had been fairly prosperous. No track-lifting instruments had yet been obtained, notwithstanding inquiries for them at several stations. We had secured no inflammable materials for more readily firing the bridges, and the road was not yet clear before us. But, on the other hand, no serious hindrance had yet occurred, and we believed ourselves far ahead of any possible pursuit.

But at Kingston we had some grounds for apprehending difficulty. This little town is at the junction with the road to Rome, Georgia. Cars and engines were standing on the side track. Here we fully expected to meet our first train, and it would be necessary for us to get the switches properly adjusted before we could pass it to go on our way. When we drew up at the station there was handed to Andrews our first and last communication from the management of the road, in the shape of a telegram, ordering Fuller's train—now ours—to wait at Kingston for the local freight, which was considerably behind time. The order was not very welcome, but we drew out on the side track, and watched eagerly for the train. Many persons gathered around Andrews, who here, as always, personated the conductor of our train, and showered upon him many curious and somewhat suspicious questions. Ours was an irregular train, but the engine was recognized as Fuller's. The best answers possible were given. A red flag had been placed on our engine, and the announcement was made that Fuller, with another engine, was but a short way behind. The powder story was emphasized, and every means employed to avoid suspicion. Andrews only, and the usual complement of train-hands, were visible, the remainder of the party being tightly shut up in the car, which was designated as containing Beauregard's ammunition. The striking personal appearance of Andrews greatly aided him in carrying through his deception, which was never more difficult than at this station. His commanding presence, and firm but graceful address, marked him as a Southern gentleman—a member of the class from which a great propor-tion of the Rebel officers were drawn. His declarations and orders were therefore received with the greater respect on this account. But all these resources were here strained to the utmost.

At length the anxiously expected local freight train arrived, and took its place on another side track. We were about to start on our way, with the glad consciousness that our greatest obstacle was safely passed, when a red flag was noticed on the hindmost freight-car. This elicited imme-diate inquiry, and we were informed that another very long freight train was just behind, and that we would be obliged to wait its arrival also. This was most unfortunate, as we had been already detained at Kingston much longer than was pleasant.

There were many disagreeable elements in the situation. A crowd of persons was rapidly assembling. The train from Rome was also nearly due, and though it only came to the station and returned on its own branch, yet it was not agreeable to notice the constant increase of force that our enemies were gaining. If any word from the southward arrived, or if our true character was revealed in any other way, the peril would be imminent. But we trusted that this second delay would be brief. Slowly the minutes passed by. To us, who were shut up in the boxcar, it appeared as if they would never be gone. Our soldier comrades on the outside kept in the background as much as possible, remaining at their posts on the engine and the cars, while Andrews occupied attention by complaining of the delay, and declaring that the road ought to be kept clear of freight trains when so much was needed for the transportation of army supplies, and when the fate of the whole army of the West might depend upon the celerity with which it received its ammunition.

There was plausibility enough in his words to lull suspicion in all minds except that of the old switch-tender of the place, who grumbled out his conviction "that something was wrong with that stylish-looking fellow, who ordered everybody around as if the whole road belonged to him." But no one paid any attention to this man's complaints, and not many minutes after a distant whistle sounded from the northward, and we felt that the crisis had passed. As there was no more room on the side track, Andrews ordered the switch-tender to let this train run by on the main track. That worthy was still grumbling, but he reluctantly obeyed, and the long succession of cars soon glided by us.

This meant release from a suspense more intolerable than the most perilous action. To calmly wait where we could do nothing, while our destiny was being wrought out by forces operating in the darkness, was a terrible trial of nerve. But it was well borne. Brown, Knight, and Wilson, who were exposed to view, exhibited no more impatience than was to be expected of men in their assumed situation. Those of us in the boxcar talked in whispers only, and examined the priming of our pistols. We understood that we were waiting for a delayed train, and well knew the fearful possibilities of an obstructed track, with the speedy detection, and fight against overwhelming odds that would follow, if the train for which we waited did not arrive sooner than pursuers from Big Shanty. When we recognized the whistle of the coming train it was almost as welcome as the boom of Mitchel's cannon, which we expected to hear that evening after all our work was done. As it rumbled by us we fully expected an instant start, a swift run of a few miles, and then the hard work but pleasant excitement of bridge-burning. Alas!

Swift and frequent are the mutations of war. Success can never be assured to any enterprise in advance. The train for which we had waited with so much anxiety had no sooner stopped than we beheld on it an emblem more terrible than any comet that ever frightened a superstitious continent. Another red flag! Another train close behind! This was terrible, but what could be done?

With admirable presence of mind Andrews moderated his impatience, and asked the conductor of the newly arrived train the meaning of such an unusual obstruction of the road. His tone was commanding, and without reserve the conductor gave the full explanation. To Andrews it had a thrilling interest. The commander at Chattanooga had received information that the Yankee general Mitchel was coming by forced marches and in full strength against that town; therefore all the rolling-stock of the road had been ordered to Atlanta. This train was the first installment, but another and still longer section was behind. It was to start a few minutes after he did, and would probably not be more than ten or fifteen minutes behind.

In turn, the conductor asked Andrews who he was, and received the information that he was an agent of General Beauregard, and that he had impressed a train into military service in Atlanta, which he was running through with powder, of which Beauregard was in extreme need. Under such circumstances he greatly regretted this unfortunate detention. The conductor did not suspect the falsity of these pretenses, but told Andrews that it was very doubtful if he could get to Beauregard at Corinth by going through Chattanooga, as it was certain that Mitchel had captured Huntsville, directly on the line between them.

Andrews replied that this made no difference, as he had his orders, and should press on until they were countermanded, adding that Mitchel was probably only paying a flying visit to Huntsville, and would have to be gone soon, or find Beauregard upon him. Andrews also ordered the conductor to run far enough down the main track to allow the next train to draw in behind him, and for both trains there to wait the coming of Fuller with the regular mail. His orders were implicitly obeyed; and then to our party recommenced the awful trial of quiet waiting. One of the men outside was directed to give notice to those in the boxcar of the nature of the detention, and warn them to be ready for any emergency. Either Brown or Knight, I think, executed this commission. Leaning against our car, but without turning his eyes toward it, and speaking in a low voice, he said, "We are waiting for one of the trains the Rebels are running off from Mitchel. If we are detected before it comes, we will have to fight. Be ready." We *were* ready; and so intolerable is suspense that most of us would have felt as a welcome relief the command to throw open our door and spring into deadly conflict.

Slowly the leaden moments dragged themselves away. It seems scarcely creditable, but it is literally true, that for twenty-five minutes more we lay on that side track and waited—waited with minds absorbed, pulses leaping, and ears strained for the faintest sound which might give a hint as to our destiny. One precious hour had we wasted at Kingston—time enough to have burned every bridge between that place and Dalton! The whole margin of time on which we had allowed ourselves to count was two hours; now half of that was thrown away at one station, and nothing accomplished. We dared wait no longer. Andrews decided to rush ahead with the intention of meeting this extra train wherever it might be found, and forcing it to back before him to the next siding, where he could pass it. The resolution was in every way dangerous, but the danger would at least be of an active character. Just at this moment the long-expected whistle was heard, and soon the train came into plain view, bringing with it an almost interminable string of cars. The weight and length of its train had caused the long delay. Obedient to direction, it followed the first extra down the main track, and its locomotive was a long way removed from the depot when the last car cleared the upper end of the side track on which we lay. At length it had got far enough down, and it was possible for us to push on. Andrews instantly ordered the switch-tender to arrange the track so as to let us out.

But here a new difficulty presented itself. This man had been in an ill humor from the first, and was now fully convinced that something was wrong. Possibly the tone in which he was addressed irritated him still more. He therefore responded to Andrews's order by a surly refusal, and hung up the keys in the station-house. When we in the boxcar overheard his denial, we were sure that the time for fighting had come. There was no more reason for dreading the issue of a conflict at this station than at any other point, and we waited the signal with the confident expectation of victory.

But even a victory at that moment would have been most undesirable. We had no wish to shed blood unnecessarily. A telegraph office was at hand, and it was possible that before the wire could be cut a message might be flashed ahead. There were also engines in readiness for prompt pursuit, and while we might have overcome immediate opposition by the use of our firearms, our triumph would have been the signal for a close and terrible chase.

The daring coolness of Andrews removed all embarrassments. While men are hesitating and in doubt, boldness and promptness on the part of an opponent are almost sure to carry the day. Ceasing to address the switch-tender, Andrews walked hurriedly into the station, and with the truthful remark that he had no more time to waste, took down the key and began to unlock the switch. The tender cursed him terribly, and called for someone to arrest him. The crowd around also disliked the action, and began to hoot and yell; but before anyone had decided as to what ought to be done Andrews had unlocked and changed the switch, and waved his hand for the engineer to come on. It was an inexpressible relief when the cars moved forward and the sounds of strife died out. As soon as the locomotive passed to the main track, Andrews tossed the keys to the ruffled owner of them, saying, in his blandest manner, "Pardon me, sir, for being in such a hurry, but the Confederacy can't wait for every man's notions. You'll find it is all right," and stepped on board his engine. The excitement gradually ceased, and no thought of pursuit was entertained until startling intelligence was received a few moments later from Big Shanty.

Before describing the terrible struggle above Kingston, it will be well to narrate the operations of the persons whose train had been so unceremoniously snatched from them at Big Shanty. From printed accounts published contemporaneously by several of those engaged in the pursuit, as well as from personal responses to inquiries made regarding the most material points, the writer is confident that he can tell the strange story without essential error. It is a striking commentary on the promptness of the seizure, that the bystanders generally reported that only eight men, instead of twenty, had been observed to mount the train.

William A. Fuller, conductor, Anthony Murphy, manager of the State railroad shops at Atlanta, and Jefferson Cain, engineer, stepped off their locomotive, leaving it unguarded save by the surrounding sentinels, and in perfect confidence took their seats at the breakfast-table at Big Shanty. But before they had tasted a morsel of food the quick ear of Murphy, who was seated with his back toward the window, caught the sound of escaping steam, and he exclaimed, "Fuller, who's moving your train?" Almost simultaneously the latter, who was somewhat of a ladies' man, and was bestowing polite attentions upon two or three fair passengers, saw the same movement, and sprang up, shouting, "Somebody's running off with our train!" No breakfast was eaten then. Everybody rushed through the door to the platform. The train was then fully under way, just sweeping out of sight around the first curve. With quick decision Fuller shouted to Murphy and Cain, "Come on!" and started at a full run after the flying train! This attempt to run down and catch a locomotive by a foot-race seemed so absurd that as the three, at the top of their speed, passed around the same curve, they were greeted with loud laughter and ironical cheers by the excited multitude. To all appearances it was a foolish and hopeless chase.

Yet, paradoxical as the statement may seem, this chase on foot was the wisest course possible for Fuller and his companions. What else could they do? Had they remained quietly in camp, with no show of zeal, they would have been reproached with negligence in not guarding their train more carefully, even if they were not accused with being in league with its captors. As they ran, Fuller explained the situation and his purposes to his companions. They had neither electric battery nor engine. Had they obtained horses, they would necessarily have followed the common road, instead of the railroad, and if they thought of that expedient at all, it would be as distasteful to railroad men as abandoning their ship to sailors, and they preferred leaving that course for others. It would have been wise for those who could think of nothing else to do to ride as mounted couriers to the stations ahead; but whether this was done or not I have never learned. Certainly it was not done so promptly as to influence the fortunes of the day.

But the truth is that Fuller and Murphy were at first completely deceived as to the nature of the event which had taken place. They had been warned to guard against the escape of conscript deserters from that very camp; and although they would never have suspected an attempt on the part of the conscripts to escape by capturing their engine, yet when it was seen to dash off, the thought of this warning was naturally uppermost. Even then Fuller conjectured that they would use his engine only to get a mile or two beyond the guard-line, and then abandon it. He was therefore anxious to follow closely in order to find the engine and return for his passengers at the earliest moment possible. Little did he anticipate the full magnitude of the work and the danger before him. That any Federal soldiers were within a hundred miles of Big Shanty never entered his mind or that of any other person.

For a mile or two the three footmen ran at the top of their speed, straining their eyes forward for any trace of the lost engine which they expected to see halted and abandoned at almost any point on the road. But they were soon partially undeceived as to the character of their enemies. About two miles from the place of starting they found the telegraph wire severed and a portion of it carried away. The fugitives were also reported as quietly oiling and inspecting their engine. No mere deserters would be likely to think of this. The two actions combined clearly indicated the intention of making a long run, but who the men were still remained a mystery. A few hundred yards from this place a party of workmen with a handcar was found, and these most welcome reinforcements were at once pressed into service.

Fuller's plans now became more definite and determined. He had a good handcar and abundance of willing muscle to work it. By desperate exertions, by running behind the car and pushing it up the steep grades, and then mounting and driving it furiously downhill and on the levels, it was possible to make seven or eight miles an hour; at the same time, Fuller knew that the captive engine, if held back to run on schedule time, as the reports of the workmen indicated, would make but sixteen miles per hour. Fuller bent all his thoughts and energies toward Kingston, thirty miles distant. He had been informed of the extra trains to be met at that point, and was justified in supposing that the adventurers would be greatly perplexed and hindered by them, even if they were not totally stopped. Had the seizure taken place on the preceding day, as originally planned, he might well have despaired, for then the road would have been clear. Yet he had one other resource, as will appear in due time, of which his enemies knew nothing.

Fuller did not pause to consider how he should defeat the fugitives when he had overtaken them, and he might have paid dearly for this rashness. But he could rely on help at any station, and when he had obtained the means of conveyance, as he would be sure to do at Kingston, he could easily find an overwhelming force to take with him. This Saturday was appointed as a general muster of volunteers, State militia, and conscripts, and armed soldiers were abundant in every village. But Fuller's dominant thought was that his property—the property with which he had been entrusted—was wrested from his grasp, and it was his duty to recover it, at whatever personal hazard. That any serious harm was intended to the railroad itself he probably did not yet suspect.

Talking and wearying themselves with idle conjectures, but never ceasing to work, Fuller and his party pressed swiftly on. But suddenly there was a crash, a sense of falling, and when the shock allowed them to realize what had happened, they found themselves floundering in a ditch half filled with water, and their handcar embedded in the mud beside them! They had reached the place where the first rail had been torn from the track, and had suffered accordingly. But the bank was, fortunately for them, not very high at that spot, and a few bruises were all the damage they sustained. Their handcar, which was also uninjured, was lifted on the track and driven on again. This incident increased both their caution and their respect for the men before them.

Without further mishap they reached Etowah Station, on the northern bank of the river of the same name. Here was a large bridge, which the Andrews party might have burned without loss of time had they foreseen the long detention at Kingston; but its destruction was not a part of their plan, and it was suffered to stand. The mind of Fuller grew very anxious as he approached this station. What he should find there depended, in all probability, on his power to overtake the fugitives, whose intentions seemed more formidable with each report he received of their actions. Andrews had firmly believed that no engine for pursuit could be found south of Kingston; but Fuller had a different expectation.

Extensive iron-furnaces were located on the Etowah River, about five miles above the station. These works were connected with the railroad by a private track, which was the property of Major Cooper, as well as the works themselves. Murphy knew that Major Cooper had also bought an engine called the "Yonah." It had been built in the shop over which Murphy presided, and was one of the best locomotives in the State. "But where," Fuller and Murphy asked themselves, "is this engine now?" If it was in view of the adventurers as they passed, they had doubtless destroyed it, run it off the track, or carried it away with them. They could not afford to neglect such an element in the terrible game they were playing. But if it was now at the upper end of the branch at the mines, as was most probable, it would take the pursuers five miles out of their way to go for it, and even then it might not be ready to start. This diversion could not be afforded. Fuller and Murphy had come nineteen miles, and had already consumed two hours and three-quarters. The adventurers were reported as passing each station on time, and if this continued they must have reached Kingston forty-five minutes before Fuller and his companions arrived at Etowah, thirteen miles behind them. One hour and a half more to Kingston—this was the very best that could be done with the handcar. It was clear that if the "Yonah" did not come to their assistance, they were as effectually out of the race as if on the other side of the ocean. Everything now hinged on the position of that one engine.

Here we may pause to note how all coincidences, we might almost say providences, seemed to work against the bridge-burning enterprise. We were at Kingston three-quarters of an hour before our pursuers reached Etowah, thirteen miles distant. If there had been no extra trains, or if they had been sharply on time, so that we could have passed the three with a delay not exceeding fifteen or twenty minutes, which ought to have been an abundant allowance, every bridge above Kingston would have been in ashes before sundown! Or if the delay had been as great as it actually was, even then, if the locomotive "Yonah" had occupied any position excepting one, the same result would have followed.

But Fuller, Murphy, and Cain, with the several armed men they had picked up at the stations passed, could not repress shouts of exultation when they saw the old "Yonah" standing on the main track, already fired up, and headed toward Kingston. It had just arrived from the mines, and in a short time would have returned again. Thus a new element of tremendous importance, which had been ignored in all our calculations, was introduced into the contest.

The pursuers seized their inestimable prize, called for all the volunteers who could snatch guns at a moment's notice, and were soon swiftly but cautiously rushing with the power of steam toward Kingston. The speed of nearly a mile a minute was in refreshing contrast to the slow and laborious progress of the handcar, and they were naturally jubilant. But what lay before them at Kingston? The frequent obstructions of the track, the continued cutting of the telegraph, and especially the cool assumption of the leader of the adventurers in calling himself a Confederate officer of high rank in charge of an impressed powder train, all conspired to deepen their conviction that some desperate scheme was on foot.

But they did not pause long to listen to reports. Their eyes and their thoughts were bent toward Kingston. Had the adventurers been stopped there, or had they surprised and destroyed the trains met? The pursuers could scarcely form a conjecture as to what was before them; but the speed with which they were flying past station after station would soon end their suspense. Even the number of men on the flying train was a matter of uncertainty. At the stations passed observers reported that only four or five were seen; but the track-layers and others who had observed them at work were confident of a much larger number—twenty-five or thirty at the least.

Besides, it was by no means sure that they had not confederates in large numbers to cooperate with them at the various stations along the road. Fuller knew about how many persons had entered the train at Marietta; but it was not sure that these were all. A hundred more might be scattered along the way, at various points, ready to join in whatever strange plan was now being worked out. No conjecture of this kind that could be formed was a particle more improbable than the startling events that had already taken place. The cool courage of these pursuers, who determined to press forward and do their own duty at whatever risk, cannot be too highly rated. If they arrived at Kingston in time to unmask the pretension of the mysterious "Confederate officer," there would doubtless be a desperate fight; but the pursuers could count on assistance there, and all along the line.

Fuller reached Kingston at least an hour earlier than would have been possible with the handcar, and a single glance showed that the adventurers were gone, and his hopes of arresting them at that point were ended. They were, however, barely out of sight, and all their start had been reduced to minutes. But here again the pursuit was checked. The foresight of Andrews had blockaded the road as much as possible with the trains which had so long hindered his own movements. Two large and heavy trains stood on the main road; one of the two side tracks was occupied by the third freight, and the other by the engine of the Rome branch. There was no ready means for the passage of the "Yonah." Some precious time was employed in giving and receiving information, in telling of the seizure at Big Shanty, and hearing of the deportment of Andrews and his men at Kingston.

Then a dispute arose as to the best means of continuing the pursuit, which threatened to disunite Fuller and Murphy. The latter wished to continue the chase with the "Yonah," which was a fine engine, with large wheels; but Fuller would not wait to get the freights out of the way, and, jumping on the Rome engine, he called on all who were willing to assist him to come on. A large, enthusiastic, and well-armed company instantly volunteered; the new engine, the "Shorter," pulled out, and Murphy had only time to save himself from the disgrace of being left behind by jumping on the hindmost car as it swept past. With all the time lost in making this transfer, and in mutual explanations, the pursuers left Kingston just twenty minutes behind the Federals.

What Fuller and his friends learned at Kingston left no doubt in their minds that some deliberate and far-reaching military movement was on foot. While its precise nature was yet concealed, the probability that the road itself, and possibly Confederate towns and stores, were to be destroyed, was freely conceded. All agreed that the one thing to be done was to follow their enemies closely, and thus compel them to turn and fight or abandon their enterprise. A large force—one or two hundred well-armed men—was taken on board, and instructions left that as soon as the track could be cleared, another armed train was to follow for the purpose of rendering any needed assistance.

CHAPTER SEVEN

The Boys from Shangri-La

In Which Jimmie Doolittle Visits Tokyo Uninvited

Lt. Col. Robert Barr Smith (Ret.)
and Laurence J. Yadon

In the Spring of 1942, five months or so after Pearl Harbor, there was little to smile about in the White House, much less laugh about and crack jokes. Yet, President Franklin Delano Roosevelt did exactly that when he described the raid on Tokyo that had just been carried out by American B-25s. "The planes took off from our secret base at "Shangri-La," the President said, referring to the fictional setting of James Hilton's Last Horizon. *Led by Lt. Col. Jimmie Doolittle, launched from the aircraft carrier* Hornet, *the 16 B-25 twin-engine bombers did little overall damage, but they struck a blow the Japanese never*

expected and sent a signal of the guts and capabilities of America's growing military forces. Doolittle was promoted two ranks to Brig. Gen. and awarded the Medal of Honor.

THE SPRING OF 1942 WAS NOT A HAPPY TIME FOR THE UNITED STATES and her allies. America had lost the Philippines; Britain had lost Malaya and was falling back in Burma; Holland had lost her possessions in the Dutch East Indies. Naval losses for all three nations had been heavy, and many people were deeply concerned with the vital short-term need to salvage whatever could be saved from the ruin. And all of these nations had Hitler's rampant Germany to contend with, plus her arrogant ally, Italy, in addition to Japan.

But some of those same people already had their thoughts and dreams focused on something else, something far more satisfying: revenge. Admiral Yamamoto, the able architect of Japan's aggression in the Pacific, had put it perfectly in responding to congratulations on Japan's successful attack on the Hawaiian Islands. "I fear," he said, "that all we have done is awaken a sleeping giant." He was, as most Americans would say, right on the money.

President Roosevelt was one of those intent on striking back, and the sooner the better. And so, just two weeks after the sneak attack on Pearl Harbor, in a meeting with the Joint Chiefs of Staff at the White House, he voiced his notion that the United States should bomb Japan as soon as possible, in order to boost American morale. Planning began immediately.

Since there was no base close enough to Japan from which to fly off bombers against the home islands of Imperial Japan, it became obvious that the raiders would have to come by sea. Taking off from one of the Navy's carriers might just be possible, with some modifications of the bombers and a lot of luck. The raiders would have to be multi-engined bombers, and those belonged to the Army Air Corps. The Navy's aircraft carriers would have to sail deep into the Pacific, dangerously close to Japan's home waters, if the Army's bombers were to carry a decent bomb load and have any chance of flying from their targets on to some place of reasonable safety where the crews might survive.

For the bombers could not return to the carrier from which they had been launched, even if they could manage a carrier landing, a problematical possibility itself. The carriers would have to clear out at high speed once they had launched the strike. Waters that close to Japan were far too dangerous, and America's small carrier force was far too precious to risk by loitering for most of a day so near Japan. In order to reach Japan from any distance with a decent load of bombs—a half ton per plane was the goal—the multi-engined Army aircraft had to be capable of taking off from a carrier flight deck.

No four-engined bomber would even fit on a carrier flight deck, let alone take off from one. So it would have to be a medium bomber, and the planners carefully looked over the available aircraft. Two types were rejected because their wingspan was too broad for the carrier; in the end the planners settled on the B-25 Mitchell. It was twice tested, and both times took off successfully from USS *Hornet*.

Work began immediately on major modifications. The interior changes to the plane were mostly to accommodate extra gas tanks to almost double the bomber's regular fuel capacity, but there were more. The treasured Norden bombsight was replaced by a crude device dreamed up by one of the pilots, called the "Mark Twain" and costing a whole twenty cents. The belly turret and one radio were removed to save weight, and a pair of dummy guns were added to the stern of each B-25.

Starting on the first of March, the crews began rehearsals in Florida, flying at night and over water, practicing low-altitude bombing and take-offs from a section of runway painted in the shape and size of a carrier deck. And on the 1st of April, 1942, sixteen modified bombers were loaded on *Hornet* at Alameda Naval Air Station on San Francisco Bay. Each aircraft had a crew of five, and a two-hundred-man maintenance and support detachment went to sea with them.

Next day the task force sailed, out into the broad Pacific: *Hornet*, sister-ship *Enterprise*—providing fighter cover for the little task force— and three heavy and one light cruisers, eight destroyers, and two fleet oilers. On the 17th the oilers refueled everybody, and then they and the destroyers turned for home. The carriers and cruisers pushed on at high speed for their launching point in the dangerous seas east of Japan.

They were unobserved most of the way, but on the morning of April 18, the little fleet ran into a Japanese picketboat, *Nitto Maru*. Light cruiser *Nashville* promptly sent *Nitto Maru* to the bottom, but she had gotten off a radio signal before she sank. On the correct assumption that the presence of American ships was now known by the Japanese naval command, Capt. (later Admiral) Mark Mitscher of *Hornet* made a hard but wise decision. He would launch the strike immediately, although the task force was still some 170 nautical miles short of the planned launch point, and ten hours ahead of schedule.

All sixteen B-25s got into the air in everybody's first real carrier takeoff. Each bomber carried three 250-pound bombs and a bundle of incendiaries, rigged to break apart and scatter over a broad area once it was dropped. Several bombs had medals attached to them, Japanese "friendship medals" given to Americans in a less hostile time. Now they would be returned . . . with interest.

Flying in at "zero feet," Doolittle's men arrived over Japan and split up, their coming apparently a complete surprise to the Japanese defenders in spite of the little picketboat's radio warning. There was some light anti-aircraft fire and attacks by a few fighters, as the bombers struck at ten targets in Tokyo, two more in Yokohoma, and one each in Nagoya, Kobe, Yokosuka, and Osaka. Only one B-25 was damaged, and gunners on *Hara Karier* got two Japanese fighters; *Whirling Dervish* shot down another one. The bombers' nose gunners sprayed everything in sight, and the force was gone into the west, as suddenly as it had come.

The raid's planners had laid out a course southwest across the East China Sea that would bring the aircraft over China in about twelve hours. There were bases there that could receive them, primarily at a place called Zhuzhou, for which fifteen of the bombers headed. The sixteenth aircraft was gobbling gasoline at a frightening rate, and its commander wisely elected to turn for the closer Soviet Union, landing near Vladivostok. The Russians had a problem: At the time they had a non-aggression pact with Japan, so they decided they could not honor a request from the United States to release the crew. The American crew was therefore interned; well-treated, but still not free. That is, until they were moved to a town near the Iranian border.

There the plane commander managed to bribe a man he thought was a smuggler, who got the Americans across the border into sanctuary at a British consulate. It much later developed that the providential "smuggling" was in fact the work of the Soviets' NKVD law enforcement agency, achieving clandestinely what their government could not legally do in the cold light of day.

The other crews either bailed out or crash-landed in China. They got much unselfish help from the Chinese, soldiers and civilians alike, and also from an American missionary. Sixty-nine men escaped the Japanese; three were killed in action when their B-25 crashed and a fourth died when he fell from a cliff after bailing out. Two crews were missing and unaccounted for, until, in August, the Swiss consul in Shanghai advised that two crew members had drowned after their aircraft landed at sea, and the other eight were prisoners of the Japanese.

In August the Japanese announced that all eight had been "tried" and sentenced to death, although several sentences had been commuted, they said, to life in prison. In fact, three Americans were shot by firing squad. The rest were imprisoned on starvation rations. One man died; the remaining emaciated aircrew were freed by American troops in August 1945. Remarkably, one of those four, Corp. Jacob DeShazer, later returned to Japan as a missionary, and served there for more than thirty years. Greater love hath no man.

The raid was a tremendous psychological blow to Japan, although as predicted, the material damage was relatively light. Until now the holy home islands were thought to be safe from the inferior westerners. By contrast, the delight in America overflowed, a bright ray of sunshine for a country deeply angry at the nation that smiled and talked peace even while its carriers were steaming into position to strike at Pearl Harbor. One of the authors still remembers his father's comment when the news of the raid on Japan broke: "Take that, you bastards!"

Not only in Japan, but all across America, people asked, "Where did the American bombers come from?"

Why, from Shangri-La, said President Roosevelt, using the name of the hidden mountain paradise created in James Hilton's classic novel *Lost Horizon*. The Japanese navy tried hard to find the American ships from which they knew the raid was launched, but they only managed to add to their embarrassment. Even though they used five carriers and a multitude of other ships, they still failed to find the American task force, let alone attack it, adding to the great shame of allowing the enemy to penetrate so deeply into the holy waters of Imperial Japan in the first place.

The dark side of the raid was the predictable Japanese reaction in China, especially in the eastern coastal provinces that could harbor American airmen as they did the Doolittle raiders. Operation *Seigo* did its evil best to ensure that no Chinese who helped the American raiders would ever do so again. The generally accepted civilian death toll from Japanese reprisals was ten thousand. Other estimates run as high as a quarter of a million.

There was an unexpected consequence, too. There is a suggestion that the strike on Japan may have reinforced Adm. Isoroku Yamamoto's decision to strike at Midway Island, or at least forced his hand on timing, setting the stage for the US Navy's decisive whipping of the Japanese in June of 1942. Midway was a startling, massive American victory, gutting Japan's carrier force and, maybe more importantly, destroying much of her cadre of experienced carrier pilots.

America rejoiced at the daring raid on the Japanese homeland. Jimmie Doolittle, who thought he might be court-martialed for losing his entire command, instead received the Congressional Medal of Honor and was promoted two grades to brigadier general.

The bombs didn't do much damage; nobody expected them to. But while Japan was deeply ashamed and could never feel secure again, America smiled. And one small step had been taken toward the far-off day of complete retribution. Japan had sowed the wind at Pearl Harbor. Four years later a big, sleek bomber named *Enola Gay* would bring the very fires of hell to the islands of Japan.

CHAPTER EIGHT

Belleau Wood

"Retreat Hell! We Just Got Here!"
Alan Axelrod

For years, as an "Army brat" I enjoyed hearing snips of gossip about something an NCO was alleged to have said to his men when America entered WWI in 1918. Seeing how nervous his men were, the sergeant said, calmly, and with great force, "What'd you men expect to do? Live forever?"

Like many other war stories, this one is not precisely true, but it's close enough. When the Marines fought our first WWI battle at Belleau Wood in June 1918, the "Live Forever" comment actually happened. Along with the expression "Retreat hell! We just got here!"

Capt. Lloyd Williams spat out the "Retreat Hell!" remark when a French major reported that his lines had been overrun and ordered, in writing, in English, Williams' outfit to withdraw. The "Live Forever" comment was reported by none other than famous correspondent Floyd Gibbons, who heard a sergeant shout above the din of battle, "Come on , you ____! Do you want to live forever?" Gibbons reported the comment with the blank spacing to avoid censorship problems, but you can add whatever expletive you wish.

These quotes from history stand out in the book Miracle at Belleau Wood, *by Alan Axelrod. This chapter, excerpted from that book, is a graphic illustration of the fierce fighting for Hill 142, a strategic position creating a link with Marines on the right flank on Hill 133. The German forces knew the Marines were coming and were determined to make the U.S. wish it had stayed out of the war.*

The fighting at Belleau Wood resulted in the first Medal of Honor of WWI going to Gunnery Sergeant Ernest A. Janson, who was serving under the name Charles Hoffman. Marine Gunnery Sergeant Henry Hulbert was awarded the Distinguished Service Cross.

FIVE IN THE AFTERNOON, BELLEAU WOOD, FRANCE, JUNE 6, 1918. No bugles, *Tribune* correspondent Floyd Gibbons would write. No flashing swords. Just a general advance through fields of wheat toward a former hunting preserve, tangled, overgrown, and now transformed into one big machine-gun nest. Gibbons, as well as the 6th Regiment's Colonel Albertus Catlin, remarked on the beauty of the marines advancing toward the woods in perfect rank and file, as if on parade, a gloriously doomed march into "a veritable hell of hissing bullets," a "death-dealing torrent," against which the marines bent their heads "as though facing a March gale."

That is how many of the marines began the attack, in the orthodox "advance in line of sections" they had learned so painstakingly under French tutelage. It was a style of advance born of a very human desire to impose order on chaos, to ward off confusion with method. It did not work for long.

Against Benjamin Berry's 3rd Battalion, 5th Marines, who had to advance across the most extensive stretch of open wheat field—some four hundred yards of it—the German fire was longest and hottest. "The headed wheat bowed and waved in that metal cloud-burst like meadow grass in a summer breeze. The advancing lines wavered, and the voice of a Sergeant was heard above the uproar: 'Come on, you ____! Do you want to live forever?'"

Correspondent Gibbons had heard this cry, too, or so he reported. In his 1918 memoir, "*And They Thought We Wouldn't Fight*," Gibbons wrote of how, when he was a boy, he read "Hugo's chapters on the Battle of Waterloo in 'Les Misérables'" and conceived his "ideal of fighting capacity and the military spirit of sacrifice." In Hugo's classic, an old sergeant of Napoléon's Old Guard, facing annihilation at the hands of the English, refuses the call of his enemy to surrender. 'Into the very muzzles of the British cannon the sergeant hurled back the offer of his life with one word. That word was the vilest epithet in the French language. The cannons roared and the old sergeant and his survivors died with the word on their lips. Hugo wisely devoted an entire chapter to that single word." Today, Gibbons continued, "I have a new ideal . . . I found it in the Bois de Belleau."

A small platoon line of Marines lay on their faces and bellies under the trees at the edge of a wheat field. Two hundred yards across that flat field the enemy was located in trees. I peered into the trees but could see nothing, yet I knew that every leaf in the foliage screened scores of German machine guns that swept the field with lead. The bullets nipped the tops of the young wheat and ripped the bark from the trunks of the trees three feet from the ground on which the Marines lay. The minute for the Marine advance was approaching. An old gunnery sergeant commanded the platoon in the absence of the lieutenant, who had been shot and was out of the fight. The old sergeant was a Marine veteran. His cheeks were bronzed with the wind and sun of the seven seas. The service bar across his left breast showed that he had fought in the Philippines, in Santo Domingo, at the walls of Pekin, and in the streets of Vera Cruz. I make no apologies for his language. Even if Hugo were not my precedent, I would make no apologies. To me his words were classic, if not sacred.

As the minute for the advance arrived, he arose from the trees first and jumped out onto the exposed edge of that field that ran with lead, across which he and his men were to charge. Then he turned to give the charge order to the men of his platoon—his mates—the men he loved. He said:

"Come on, you sons-o'-bitches! Do you want to live forever?"

The Battle of Bunker Hill gave us "Don't fire until you see the whites of their eyes"; the seagoing duel between John Paul Jones's *Bon Homme Richard* and HMS *Serapis*, "I have not yet begun to fight"; the siege of a San Antonio mission turned fortress, "Remember the Alamo"; and the Battle of Belleau Wood, "Come on, you sons of bitches! Do you want to live forever?" Along with Captain Lloyd Williams's earlier "Retreat, hell! We just got here," they were the most celebrated utterances to emerge from marine throats in World War I, and they became hallowed words in the annals and lore of the Corps. The declaration was universally attributed to Gunnery Sergeant Dan Daly, but nobody has been found who actually heard him say it. Catlin's memoir implied that the sergeant (Catlin does not name him) was attached to Berry's battalion, and Gibbons, who accompanied elements of that unit in its attack on Belleau Wood, implies that he was even within earshot. But Daly, forty-four years old, had shipped out to France as first sergeant (a full rank above gunnery sergeant) of the 73rd Machine Gun Company, and at Belleau Wood was attached not to Berry's battalion but to Sibley's, which attacked Belleau Wood south of Berry's position and formed part of the American center along this entire front. Daly's platoon was on the outskirts of Lucy-le-Bocage when it was either completely pinned down by fire from Belleau Wood or wavered in its advance—sources vary on this—whereupon Daly hefted over his head a bayonet-tipped Springfield and made his deathless declaration. Daly later told a Marine historian that "What I really yelled was: For Christ's sake, men—COME ON! Do you want to live forever?" But, accurately or not, the lore of the Corps has chosen to remember it as "Come on, you sons of bitches!"

Dan Daly was a real marine, who really did fight at Belleau Wood, coming to that battlefield already having received the Medal of Honor twice, once for single-handedly defending the Tartar Wall in the Boxer Rebellion of 1900 and again for defeating four hundred Caco bandits with just thirty-five marines in the Haitian campaign of 1915. John A. Lejeune, who would succeed George Barnett as Marine Corps commandant after World War I, pronounced Daly the "outstanding Marine of all time." Short and slight, standing five foot six and weighing 132 pounds, Daly repeatedly refused offers of a commission throughout his career, protesting that he would rather be "an outstanding sergeant than just another officer." Unassuming, he remained single his entire life and retired from the Corps on February 6, 1929, with the rank of sergeant major. In civilian life, he became a guard in a Wall Street bank and died quietly at sixty-five on April 28, 1937, in his Long Island home.

A real marine in a real battle, Daly really did say something that ended with the rhetorical question, "Do you want to live forever?" That the versions of the legend surrounding Daly and his battle cry vary in the details does not diminish the reality the legend is based on. Both Catlin and Gibbons seized on the phrase, changing its location a bit, and in Gibbons's case even claiming to have heard it personally, for much the same reason that the marines marched against Belleau Wood in the elaborately choreographed line of sections formation: to impose order on chaos, to make sense of it, to extract some greater meaning from it. Even the minor error that all versions of the story share—"demoting" Daly from first sergeant to gunnery sergeant—is significant in the effort to mythologize this aspect of the battle. For while the first sergeant outranks the gunnery sergeant, it is the "gunny" who is the archetypal marine noncom, perceived as the rugged, tough-love layer of command closest to the grunts.

Without such patterns and stories, the Battle of Belleau Wood threatened to emerge into posterity as what Catlin admitted "it has been called"—nothing but "an exaggerated riot," a slaughter, full of sound and fury, signifying—just what?

Even under fire, legends endure far longer than a line of sections. "The ripping fire grew hotter," Catlin wrote. "The machine guns at the edge of the woods were now a bare hundred yards away, and the enemy gunners could scarcely miss their targets. It was more than flesh and blood could stand." Berry's "men were forced to throw themselves flat on the ground or be annihilated, and there they remained in that terrible hail till darkness made it possible for them to withdraw to their original position." Henry Larsen, Berry's adjutant, reported to the brigade after the battle: "three platoons 45th Company went over. Only a few returned," and Catlin wrote: "Berry's men did not win that first encounter in the attack on Belleau Wood," which was another way of saying that not a single one of Berry's marines even reached the edge of the woods, and 60 percent of the battalion became casualties. Among these was Major Benjamin Berry himself. Floyd Gibbons was there when it happened—and he was more than a witness.

Gibbons, with Berry and many of his men, was making his way down a wooded slope, where midway down was a sunken road, littered with French bodies and "several of our men who had been brought down but five minutes before. We crossed that road hurriedly knowing that it was covered from the left by German machine guns." Gibbons, Berry, and the marines came to a V-shaped field, "perfectly flat and . . . covered with a young crop of oats between ten and fifteen inches high." On all sides of the field were dense clusters of trees. Gibbons and the others could hear the machine guns. "We could not see them but we knew that every leaf and piece of greenery there vibrated from their fire and the tops of the young oats waved and swayed with the streams of lead that swept across." After giving orders to follow him at ten- to fifteen-yard intervals, Berry "started across the field alone at the head of the party. [Gibbons] followed." The woods around the field "began to rattle fiercely," and Gibbons could see "the dust puffs that the bullets kicked up in the dirt around our feet." Berry was well beyond the center of the field when he turned toward Gibbons and the other men: "Get down everybody."

He did not have to repeat the order. "We all fell on our faces. And then it began to come hot and fast," the volleys of lead sweeping the "tops of the oats just over us." As Gibbons "busily engaged [in] flattening [himself] on the ground," he heard a shout. "It came from Major Berry. I lifted my head cautiously and looked forward. The Major was making an effort to get to his feet. With his right hand he was savagely grasping his left wrist. 'My hand's gone,' he shouted."

In some ways what really had happened to him was worse. Berry's hand had not been shot off, but a bullet had entered his left arm at the elbow, passing down alongside the bone, "tearing away muscles and nerves to the forearm and lodging itself in the palm of his hand. His pain was excruciating," causing him to stand up as he gripped his arm. Gibbons called to Berry: "Get down. Flatten out, Major," knowing that "he was courting death every minute he stood up." Berry in turn called over to Gibbons: "We've got to get out of here. We've got to get forward. They'll start shelling this open field in a few minutes." Gibbons replied that he was crawling over to him. "Wait until I get there and I'll help you. Then we'll get up and make a dash for it."

Gibbons crawled, pushing "forward by digging in with my toes and elbows extended in front of me. It was my object to make as little movement in the oats as possible."

And then it happened. The lighted end of a cigarette touched me in the fleshy part of my upper left arm. That was all. It just felt like a sudden burn and nothing worse. The burned part did not seem to be any larger in area than that part which could be burned by the lighted end of a cigarette.

A bullet had gone through the biceps of the upper arm and come out the other side. Gibbons looked down at his sleeve and could not even see the hole where the bullet had entered.

Then the second one hit. It nicked the top of my left shoulder. And again came the burning sensation, only this time the area affected seemed larger.

Feeling surprisingly little pain, Gibbons continued to crawl toward Berry.

And then the third one struck me. In order to keep as close to the ground as possible, I had swung my chin to the right so that I was pushing forward with my left cheek flat against the ground and in order to accommodate this position of the head, I had moved my steel helmet over so that it covered part of my face on the right.

Then there came a crash. It sounded to me like someone had dropped a glass bottle into a porcelain bathtub. A barrel of whitewash tipped over and it seemed that everything in the world turned white. That was the sensation. I did not recognize it because I have often been led to believe and often heard it said that when one receives a blow on the head everything turns black.

Gibbons asked himself, "'Am I dead?' . . . I wanted to know. . . . How was I to find out if I was dead? . . . I decided to try and move my fingers on my left hand. I did so and they moved. I next moved my left foot. Then I knew I was alive."

Floyd Gibbons's left eye had just been shot out of his head, along with part of his skull. With his remaining eye, he watched Major Berry "rise to his feet and in a perfect hail of lead rush forward and out of my line of vision." Despite his wound, Berry continued to command, led his men in destroying a German machine-gun nest, and later received the Distinguished Service Cross from General Pershing. Gibbons, with his fellow journalist Hartzell (who was unwounded), remained in the oat field for three hours, until 9:00 p.m., not daring to move until they judged it was sufficiently dark to risk crawling back to the American position. After a series of agonizing stops at various forward dressing stations, Gibbons was loaded into an ambulance and evacuated to a hospital. Astoundingly, he was on his feet and once again covering the war within ten days of having been wounded.

If the line of sections advance in all its archaic formality failed to work for long, in some places it did not work at all. The poverty of communications and the level of confusion were so profound on the afternoon of June 6 that some units never even formed up to join the "parade." They were not aware of the attack until after it had actually begun.

Lieutenant George Gordon, commanding a platoon in one of Berry's companies, was standing—*standing*—at the periphery of the wheat field "watching the shells as they dropped along the edge of the woods across the wheatfield." He was talking with a friend, who remarked of the shelling, "I wonder what this is about. . . . They must have something spotted over there." Several minutes passed before Captain Larsen ran up to Gordon and his friend. "Get your platoons ready immediately," he shouted. "You should have started across with the barrage." Gordon later remarked:

This was the first information we had received regarding an attack and did not know one had been planned. No objective was given as to where it was to stop and no maps had been distributed; the only thing we were sure of was the direction and we knew that.

Attacking from Lucy-le-Bocage, well south of Berry, Sibley's 3rd Battalion, 6th Marines was, in Catlin's words, "having better luck." Catlin thrilled to the sight of these men "sweeping across the open ground in four waves, as steadily and correctly as though on parade." As if to justify on some pragmatic terms the ostentatious grandeur of this procession under fire, Catlin explained: "They walked at the regulation pace, because a man is of little use in a hand-to-hand bayonet struggle after a hundred yards dash." The obvious response to this observation would have been to ask the colonel just how much use a dead man was. But who could have dared such impertinence as Catlin looked on? "My hands were clenched and all my muscles taut as I watched that cool, intrepid, masterful defiance of the German spite." He saw "no sign of wavering or breaking."

Oh, it took courage and steady nerves to do that in the face of the enemy's machine gun fire. Men fell there in the open, but the advance kept steadily on to the woods. It was then that discipline and training counted. Their minds were concentrated not on the enemy's fire but on the thing they had to do and the necessity of doing it right. They were listening for orders and obeying them. In this frame of mind the soldier can perhaps walk with even more coolness and determination than he can run. In any case it was an admirable exhibition of military precision and it gladdened their Colonel's heart.

Interviewed in October 2003, upstate New Yorker Eugene Lee—who at age 104 was then the nation's "oldest living marine"—recalled the grim journey across the wheat field Catlin watched from afar. "They split us out into formation. They had the first wave go so far. They kept on firing in the woods there. The next wave would come and jump over them and they'd go so far, and would fire till they got in the edge of the woods." The object of this leap-frog advance was to allow the first wave to cover the farther advance of the second wave, and the second to cover that of the third, and the third to cover the fourth as it finally reached the woods. Once the fourth had been delivered to the objective, the marines of the preceding waves—those who survived—would follow it in. Lee was in the third of the four human waves.

Unlike Berry's men, many of Sibley's, who had much less open field to traverse, made it to Belleau Wood. Yet their entry into the objective was somehow anticlimactic. Catlin wrote that the "Marines have a war cry that they can use to advantage when there is need of it. It is a blood-curdling yell calculated to carry terror to the heart of the waiting Hun. I am told that there were wild yells in the woods that night, when the Marines charged the machine gun nests, but there was no yelling when they went in." Catlin also noted a report that the marines "advanced on those woods crying 'Remember the *Lusitania!*' If they did so, I failed to hear it." Quite rightly, he observed that this did not "sound like the sort of thing the Marine says under the conditions." In fact, so far as he could observe, Catlin did not believe "a sound was uttered throughout the length of those four lines. The men were saving their breath for what was to follow."

Having written of this wordless entry into Belleau Wood, an entry bought at the price of many dead and wounded, the colonel of the 6th Marine Regiment feared that he had "given but a poor picture of that splendid advance." True, there "was nothing dashing about it like a cavalry charge," yet it was nevertheless "one of the finest things I have ever seen men do." Catlin fully appreciated that these marines "were men who had never before been called upon to attack a strongly held enemy position." What lay before them was a "dense woods effectively shelter-ing armed and highly trained opponents of unknown strength." Indeed, within the depths of this dark space "machine guns snarled and rattled and spat forth a leaden death. It was like some mythical monster belching smoke and fire from its lair." Yet these marines, the vast majority entirely new to combat, marched "straight against it . . . with heads up and the light of battle in their eyes."

Months after the battle, Private W. H. Smith, recovering from wounds in the Brooklyn Naval Hospital, related to Catlin what it had been like marching into Belleau Wood. He said that there "wasn't a bit of hesitation from any man. You had no heart for fear at all. Fight—fight and get the Germans was your only thought. Personal danger didn't concern you in the least and you didn't care." Smith explained that he and about sixty others had gotten ahead of the rest of the company. "We just couldn't stop despite the orders of our leaders." Reaching the edge of the woods, they "encountered some of the Hun infantry" and then "it became a matter of shooting at mere human targets." At first, it was almost easy. The marines fixed their rifle sights at three hundred yards and, "aiming through the peep kept picking off Germans. And a man went down at nearly every shot." But then the enemy "detected us and we became the objects of their heavy fire." Colonel Catlin, who had no field telephone, "felt obliged to see what was going on." He took his stand on a "little rise of ground protected by a low line of bushes about 300 yards from the woods." The position was near a road, the point at which the left flank of Thomas Holcomb's battalion made contact with the right flank of Berry's battered battalion. "The shelter trenches did not cross the road," so Catlin was fully exposed as he watched the advance through his binoculars. "Bullets," he recalled, "rained all around me, the machine gun crews near me forming a target for the Germans." The "racket of rifle and machine gun fire and bursting shrapnel and high explosives" was "like the continuous roll of some demoniacal drum, with the bass note of the heavy guns that were shelling Lucy." Through his binoculars, Catlin watched "a number of our brave lads fall" as the German machine gunners made sure to aim low, sweeping the ground, thereby "catching most of the men in the legs." Those who were thus disabled "lay right in the line of fire and many of them were killed there on the ground" whereas those "who were able to stand and keep going had the best chance." Some of these men "went through the whole fight with leg wounds received during the first ten minutes."

Vivid as his perceptions of battle were, Catlin was not destined to be an eyewitness for long. "Just about the time Sibley's men struck the woods a sniper's bullet hit me in the chest. It felt exactly as though someone had struck me heavily with a sledge. It swung me clear around and toppled me over on the ground. When I tried to get up I found that my right side was paralysed." Catlin's French interpreter, Captain Tribot-Laspierre—a "splendid fellow," Catlin called him, "who stuck to me through thick and thin"—had been "begging [Catlin] to get back to a safer place." Now he sprang out of his cover and rushed to Catlin's side. "He is a little man and I am not, but he dragged me head first back to the shelter trench some twenty or twenty-five feet away."

Like Gibbons on Berry's side of the attack, Catlin on Sibley's was more fascinated than horrified by the sensations of being wounded. "I have heard of men getting wounded who said that it felt like a red-hot iron being jammed through them before the world turned black," but nothing of the kind happened to Catlin. "I suffered but little pain and I never for a moment lost consciousness." Nor did he think of death, "though I knew I had been hit in a vital spot. I was merely annoyed at my inability to move and carry on."

The colonel took a peculiarly professional and analytical interest in the circumstances of his wounding, concluding that it had been a "chance shot and not the result of good marksmanship, for the bullet must have come some 600 yards." It passed "clean through" Catlin's right lung, "in at the front and out at the back, drilling a hole straight through me." Catlin related that ballistics experts calculated that a "bullet fired at short range—less than five hundred or six hundred yards—twists [so that] when it strikes an obstacle it wabbles." Catlin therefore reasoned that had he been shot at close range, the bullet would have "torn a piece out of my back as big as my fist." However, had the bullet been fired from a range greater than about six hundred yards, it would have been "already wabbling, and would have made a big hole in the front of my chest and perhaps would not have gone clear through." Because the holes going in and out were both small, Catlin concluded that he had been shot from a range of about six hundred yards. "[For that] I am thankful."

Catlin calmly sent word of his wounding to the command post, ordering his second in command, Lieutenant Colonel Harry Lee, to assume command of the 6th Regiment. Forty-five minutes elapsed before the regimental surgeon, Dr. Farwell, came under intense fire to Catlin's side. Farwell had brought stretcher bearers with him, but heavy shelling prevented immediate evacuation, and when gas shells began to detonate nearby, the stretcher men put a mask on the colonel. "I never knew before how uncomfortable one of those things could be. It is hard enough for a man to breathe with a lung full of blood without having one of those smothering masks clapped over his face." What gave Catlin comfort was the sound of the fire gradually receding, which told him that "Sibley's men were advancing." However, when the firing grew louder on the left, he "knew that Berry's outfit was being beaten back."

At length, the pace of the shelling eased, and four men raised Catlin's stretcher to their shoulders. "Carrying a 215-pound man on a stretcher over rough country under fire is no joke," Catlin observed, "but they got me to Lucy," then to an ambulance, and on to hospitals at Meaux and Paris. The colonel remained hospitalized until July 22, when he was sent home on leave.

In Catlin's absence, the men on Sibley's left flank, most of them, clawed their way into Belleau Wood, via its southwestern hook. On contact, the combat was a combination of close rifle fire and fierce bayonet work. Both the U.S. Army and the Marine Corps administered bayonet training, and soldiers and marines made ample use of the bayonet in the Great War—more, certainly, than they had in any previous conflict. Yet U.S. Army soldiers tended to dread the weapon, whereas marines, at least in the attack, reveled in its use. In a war fought to such a great extent by the weapons of high technology—high-explosive artillery, gas, the machine gun, the airplane, and even the tank—it was as if marines craved contact at its most warriorlike. The isolated German outposts in the southwestern end of Belleau Wood fell prey to the marines' bayonets, but the terrain, with its tangle of undergrowth, soon broke up the cohesiveness of the attacking units. Isolated and slowed, Captain Dwight Smith's company of Sibley's marines, after they had penetrated a few hundred yards into the woods, made easy marks for the German machine guns. The machine-gun fire became so intense that the attackers were deflected northward from their due-eastward push.

Another of Sibley's companies, led by Lieutenant A. H. Noble, followed Dwight Smith's men into the woods, desperately trying to maintain contact with the lead company but failing to do so amid the rugged terrain and the outpouring of machine-gun fire. As if shivered and split by the stream of fire, the left flank of Noble's company sheered off to the north—just as Smith's men had done—but the right flank, advancing along the ravine at the southern tip of Belleau Wood, continued due east. This flank consisted of two platoons, one under Lieutenant Louis Timmerman and another under a lieutenant named Hurley. The attack on the woods, which had begun in parade-order "line of sections," increasingly broke up within Belleau Wood itself. Yet, in doing so, it did not falter or flag. Instead, as companies divided into platoons and platoons into sections and sections into fire teams or even individual marines, the fragmented fight only intensified.

In Timmerman's case, his platoon soon lost contact with Hurley's, and then the sections of the platoon itself lost contact with one another. Marines set up machine-gun positions within the woods wherever they could. This was necessary, of course, but it also added to the confusion of this most chaotic combat. Timmerman and the men who were still with him passed one marine machine-gun company, so he naturally assumed that the machine-gun fire he heard to his rear was coming from them. In fact, what he heard was the sound of German machine gunners pinning down all of Smith's company along with Sibley's other two companies and the two sections of Timmerman's own platoon that had veered to the north. Unaware of this, Timmerman just kept going. In its advance, the platoon stumbled across a German outpost. The marines and the enemy were equally surprised, but it was the Germans who gave up, and Timmerman sent back the prisoners under a single man while he and the others kept moving.

That's when Timmerman got his second surprise. He was suddenly shocked to discover that he had broken through to the east side of Belleau Wood, finding himself at a point slightly to the north of Bouresches.

Just before the attack, the company commander, Lieutenant Noble, had passed on to his platoon commanders the orders he had received. They were for the platoons on the right flank to move through Belleau Wood and capture Bouresches. Like all neophyte lieutenants, Timmerman was anxious to follow orders, and he assumed everyone else was too. Finding himself and the two platoon sections with him—about twenty marines in all—on the east side of Belleau Wood, and entirely unaware that the rest of the marines in the southern end of the woods were being held down and held back by German machine guns, Timmerman experienced a moment of panic. It was not panic born of an awareness of the actual situation: that he and twenty other marines were alone in enemy territory, separated from the rest of their unit by a dense woods exploding in hostile fire. Instead, it was panic born of the fear that everyone else had made it through Belleau Wood before him and that *he* was behind in the assault on Bouresches.

Sending one wounded private—a marine named Henry—to the rear, Timmerman deployed his two sections into a line of skirmishers, sent a Corporal Larsen and Private Swenson ahead as scouts, then led his men along the ravine they had followed through the woods until they reached a wheat field. On the other side of this field, about two hundred yards away, was Bouresches. As with the wheat fields on the western face of Belleau Wood, this one (as pictured in Timmerman's diary) "was thrashing to and fro with machine gun bullets."

Timmerman watched as Larsen and Swenson reached "a sort of mound of earth parallel to our line of advance." They signaled a halt there, and Timmerman advanced his men to the mound. Suddenly, "[I] noticed that we were coming under fire from all directions," despite being "sheltered from the enemy in front."

Who was firing from the rear?

It was a profoundly disorienting moment. After no more than a minute, however, the disorientation blossomed into disbelief as Private Henry—the wounded marine Timmerman had sent to the rear—"came running back yelling something." Timmerman could not make out what Henry was trying to say, so signaled for him to come over. What he was saying was, "The woods in back of us were full of Germans." At first, the lieutenant simply did not believe him. After all, "[they] had just come through there." But the sight, sound, and sensation of "the bullets kicking up dust and landing all around our side of the barricade" soon made a believer out of him.

Clearly, Timmerman realized, he and his two sections—now reduced from twenty to "about fifteen" men—could not long stay behind a mound that offered no shelter. Timmerman yelled to his marines, ordering them back into Belleau Wood. "Luckily I hit the edge of the woods just where the Germans were."

There were seventeen German privates and two noncoms manning a pair of machine guns in a patch of low ground that led off from the ravine. The machine gunners were second-line troops, and they did not expect a swarm of marines to descend on them from the *east*. In the lead, Timmerman kicked the faces of the first two Germans he encountered, knocking both unconscious. The others, confronted with the marines' bayonets, threw down their weapons and laid themselves prostrate before the attackers. Some tore open their uniform blouses, baring their chests, as if to say in a language that required absolutely no translation, *We are unarmed!*

At this point, a sergeant from Hurley's platoon broke through Belleau Wood with a couple of marines. Timmerman put his prisoners into their custody and instructed them to take them to the rear. Still under the unshakable conviction that most of the other marines had broken through the woods and were already attacking toward Bouresches, Timmerman could not afford to be encumbered by POWs. He further assumed that capturing the machine gunners had put an end to German resistance in the south end of Belleau Wood. He therefore resumed his interrupted advance and returned to the mound. This time, machine-gun fire opened up from the town, then also from his left flank, coming from a rise just fifty yards off. To this was added fire from Timmerman's left rear as well. "I faced around and saw Swenson lying dead with a bullet hole through the forehead." Timmerman shouted, "Open fire to the right," and pointed "toward the hillock where a terrific fire was coming from." No sooner had he done this than he himself was hit on the left side of the face. "[Timmerman] fell forward thinking, 'I've got mine,'" believing that a bullet had ripped through under his eye. He lost consciousness momentarily but then "felt better." He said, "[Although] I was covered with blood I realized I had not been dangerously hit." Nevertheless, Timmerman's "men were dropping around there" and so "[Timmerman] told them to follow [him]" and, once again, they "ran back for the shelter of the woods."

Lieutenant Louis Timmerman had begun the advance on Belleau Wood commanding a platoon of fifty marines as part of a company of some two hundred. This mass of men broke apart inside the woods, leaving Timmerman with fifteen men on the other side. By the time he retreated to the eastern perimeter of Belleau Wood, shot through the face, he commanded just six marines. They hunkered down in the German machine-gun position they had captured minutes ago. Only then did it occur to him that Belleau Wood had neither been taken nor even traversed—at least not by very many of the marines who had entered it. Beyond these realizations, the lieutenant knew only that the battle, which had been ahead of him in Belleau Wood when Belleau Wood had been ahead of him, was now ahead of him in the little town of Bouresches. But the battle was also on either side of him and, not least of all, it was raging yet in the ruined tangle of trees, rocks, and ravines that now lay behind him.

CHAPTER NINE

Black Sheep and Their "Pappy"

Col. Robert Barr Smith (Ret.) and Laurence J. Yadon

He wasn't a happy man. His drinking and failed marriages reveal a portrait of someone deeply troubled in mysterious ways. But at the controls of the fighter planes he flew against the Japanese, Gregory "Pappy" Boyington was unsurpassed. He is credited with shooting down 28 enemy planes and forming a squadron that shot down 97, while sinking 28 vessels. He was shot down himself, spent 20 months in a Japanese prisoner-of-war camp, and survived. He was awarded the Medal of Honor by President Truman at the White House. This is the story of this amazing pilot and the men who flew with him.

THE MARINE FIGHTER PILOTS GREGORY "PAPPY" BOYINGTON LED INTO battle from September 1943 to January 3, 1944, widely praised him, but he was vilified by many of the men he served with some seventeen months earlier. One comrade in the Black Sheep Squadron called him the best commander of any Marine fighter squadron during the war. Yet one member of Gen. Claire Chennault's Flying Tigers said that he had a great deal of respect for most pilots in that fabled group, but not Boyington.

He ignored his children, had four troubled marriages, and often failed to pay his debts, but at the controls of a Corsair in fall 1944, he was so skilled that *Life* magazine proclaimed him "born to be a swashbuckler."

The family he joined on December 4, 1912, veered toward destruction almost from the beginning of his parents' marriage. His father, Charles Boyington, was a two-fisted drinking dentist in Coeur d'Alene, Idaho; Charles divorced Gregory's mother, Grace (Gregory) Boyington a scarce seventeen months later, claiming with some justification that Grace had been unfaithful. She married her paramour, Ellsworth Hallenbeck, who gave young Gregory his last name (without a formal adoption) and moved them all to St. Maries, a small lumber town about twenty miles away.

This was not a happy home, even at Christmas. Gregory mainly remembered Christmas as a time when his relatives spent the day drinking, brawling, and fighting. He discovered a fondness for heights early in life and often climbed to high places.

While on a school playground at age five, he saw his first airplane, a biplane flying lower and lower toward a nearby field. The pilot was pioneer aviator Clyde "Upside Down" Pangborn, who had spent World War I teaching Army Air Service cadets at Ellington Field in Houston. While his classmates went back to the schoolhouse, Gregory ran toward the plane. Pangborn's widowed mother by then lived in St. Maries, while he toured the country for the last couple of years as a partner in the Gates Flying Circus.

Either Boyington's stepfather or mother came up with the five-dollar fee, and the next morning little Gregory stood in the open cockpit throwing handbills as Pangborn flew over, fascinating the local folks. He vowed to become a Marine after the husband of his second-grade teacher paid a visit to her classroom in dress uniform, and his high school yearbook noted his letters in wrestling and membership in a leadership organization and summed him up simply: "he can't be beat."

That fall he enrolled and began studying architecture and engineering at the University of Washington, Spokane. During a Sunday drive into Seattle, he chanced upon the Boeing Aircraft Company factory and got a close look at an F-4B fighter being prepared for the Marine Corps. To him, it seemed like a living being that he and only he should take to the sky. After switching his major to aeronautical engineering, he graduated in 1934, and discovered during a brief stint at Boeing that a desk job, even in aviation, was not for him.

The next April, now married with a child due the next month, he signed up for a new program training Marine and Navy pilots on salary. There was a catch, of course: After training he would be obliged to serve three years at cadet's pay, but then would receive a commission and a $1,500 bonus, worth some $26,000 in 2016 dollars. And there was a further catch: The program was open only to single men. Since he had recently discovered that his real name was Boyington, not Hallenbeck, he enrolled as a single man named Boyington.

His first solo flight at Pensacola Naval Air Station was on July 3, 1935; while there he quarreled with Capt. Joseph Smoak, a universally disliked instructor he would see again in the Pacific three years later. But from the beginning Boyington was nearly always comfortable in the air. While learning how to execute steep dives, he even adapted an old wrestling technique for keeping his head clear by tightening his neck muscles.

But on the ground sloppy paperwork, drinking, and the news that back in Seattle his wife had found someone else began to plague him. Eventually, these problems affected his performance in the air, causing an instructor to describe him as slow to learn, but a hard worker.

A year of Marine officer's basic school at Philadelphia didn't help matters. He finished third from the bottom in a class of seventy-three, but was assigned to the 2nd Marine Aircraft Group at San Diego in January 1939. While there he honed his fighter skills, competing in exercises against several future Medal of Honor winners, and qualified for carrier duty aboard the *Yorktown*.

Boyington's drinking and problems at home persisted; he was only free in the air, or so it seemed, until a new opportunity presented itself in faraway Asia.

Former Army Air Corps captain Claire Chennault, then serving as a colonel in the Chinese Air Force and part of a delegation sent to Washington in 1940, had advocated US assistance for the Chinese fighting Japanese forces then occupying about one-third of China. Despite military opposition, President Roosevelt secretly sent one hundred fighters to China and signed an April 1941 executive order authorizing US airmen to resign and fly from Burma against the Japanese as part of an American Volunteer Group (AVG), in the pay of the Central Aircraft Manufacturing Corporation (CAMCO).

CAMCO offered large salaries and promised bonuses for every Japanese fighter brought down. CAMCO seemed custom made for Boyington, who needed more money, and was burdened by a bad marriage and longing for adventure.

Now stationed back at Pensacola Naval Air Station, Boyington was one of many who listened to a CAMCO pitch at the San Carlos Hotel on August 4, 1941, and signed up for one year, with a verbal Marine Corps assurance that he could return to service. He left in mid-September. All CAMCO recruits registered at the St Francis Hotel in San Francisco before the sea voyage west, listing their occupations in the hotel register as "missionary."

Despite such precautions, the American Volunteer Group was an open secret. By the time Boyington arrived to join nineteen other pilots waiting for a Wednesday, September 24 voyage to Burma, *Time* magazine and even Japanese radio had reported on the AVG mission. The Japanese broadcast predicted they wouldn't arrive.

The thirty-five-day voyage aboard the Dutch ship SS *Boschfontein* as "missionaries" was uneventful, although nightly blackouts served as a grim reminder of patrolling Japanese submarines that could sink them at any minute.

Real missionaries on the voyage, not knowing any better, made small talk with AVG pilots about the evangelistic challenges that awaited them.

Boyington was asked to preach the first Sunday service on September 28 but begged off.

They filled the six-day cruise to Hawaii with booze and deck tennis, compliments of CAMCO. A few hours at the sprawling Royal Hawaiian Hotel on Waikiki Beach steeled them for the long voyage to Java, in present-day Indonesia, an intermediate stop before Rangoon, Burma. Along the way, Boyington enjoyed challenging drinking mates to wrestling matches, when he wasn't insulting the missionaries. They arrived on the war front at Toungoo, Burma, fifty days after leaving San Francisco. They encountered squadrons of mosquitoes the first night.

They trained at a British airfield with the understanding that the Flying Tigers would move on to China. With one war on their hands, the Brits wanted to delay war with Japan as long as possible. While there, as a member of the 1st Squadron, Boyington developed a close relationship with Olga Greenlaw, wife of the AVG executive officer; she saw him as a man only happy in the air, working on goals larger than himself.

His first meeting with former stunt pilot Claire Chennault initially impressed Boyington, but he didn't appreciate a 5:30 a.m. wakeup to begin a crash physical training course to toughen them up after the luxury booze cruise to Rangoon. Chennault also provided captured translated Japanese flying manuals, intelligence reports, and advice on Japanese tactics based on Chennault's analysis. The AVG pilots learned that Japanese pilots generally followed flight plans but often didn't improvise to meet unanticipated challenges.

To Chennault the key to fighting the Japanese Zero was getting close enough to exploit the light armor that made the Zero more maneuverable than their own bulky P-40s. Many of the pilots, including Boyington, had trouble landing them. Boyington challenged some of Chennault's tactical doctrines almost from the day of his arrival—particularly flying the fighters in threes—but in time became a proponent of Chennault's tactics, despite their troubled personal relationship.

They became Flying Tigers when pilot Charlie Bond spotted an Australian fighter sporting a crude tiger shark drawn on its nose in a British magazine. Another AVG pilot wrote Walt Disney and arranged for a more sophisticated insignia based on the Australian idea. Meanwhile, Boyington entertained the others by pulling rickshaws, wrestling cows, and other stunts when they weren't in training. By late November at least two pilots had been killed in training accidents, but the rest of the squadron was ready to fight.

Boyington and the others learned about Pearl Harbor soon after the attack, but days passed without orders to attack the Japanese airfield just two hundred miles away.

Eleven days after the surprise Japanese attack, Boyington and the rest of the squadron bounced through buffeting winds on the 670-mile flight to Kunming, China. They were pleasantly surprised to discover that the airfield barracks had many modern conveniences, including hot showers.

Boyington and the 1st Squadron began flying routine patrols, but went into combat action on January 26 over Rangoon. They were severely outnumbered, flying two thousand feet below attacking Japanese, two of whom pounced on Boyington from behind, soon joined by a third and then more. Boyington escaped by diving low and highballing for Mingaladon, Burma, with a Japanese bullet in his arm.

Three days later he was in the air again, this time with nine other Tigers who took down sixteen of twenty opposing Japanese fighters. Boyington later claimed two of them, although no official record supports him. *Time* magazine and others proclaimed the Tigers "knights of the air" even as Boyington stewed over his personal anonymity.

His first two confirmed kills came on February 6, in a dogfight one Rangoon citizen-observer described as something akin to rowboats attacking the Spanish Armada. Despite this, Boyington was passed over for a command slot, even as his relationships with his peers and supervisors eroded. He was bored by routine patrols, paperwork, and the other routine stuff that went along with flying combat missions. Worse still, he got drunk during a personal visit by Chinese leader Chiang Kai-shek and embarrassed Chennault.

As the Japanese came nearer, Boyington and some other AVG pilots flew to Magwe, some two hundred miles north of Rangoon. By late February the entire 1st Squadron moved to Kunming, China. Early the next month Boyington was blamed, justifiably or not, for leading five planes so far off course that they ran out of fuel and crash-landed near the Indochina border. He returned and personally piloted all five planes back to Kunming at great personal danger but lost his job as vice squadron leader anyway.

Boyington broke into another pilot's liquor at Kunming on March 20, but was sober enough four days later to help attack Japanese planes on the ground at Chiang Mai, Thailand.

Boyington and nine others lifted off from a field at Namsang, Burma, before sunrise on March 24. Later he claimed to have taken out seven planes on the ground; Chennault later decided to credit all participants for the total number of planes destroyed. As a consequence, on payday Boyington was credited for 1.5 kills, but claimed to the day he died he should have been credited for at least 2.5 Japanese planes that day.

Chennault claimed that the Flying Tiger raid on Chiang Mai succeeded through teamwork and superb tactics while urging the US government to replace the long outmoded P-40s with more modern airplanes. *Time* later compared the Flying Tigers to Knute Rockne's Notre Dame football teams.

Despite such praise the Flying Tigers were less than enthusiastic when Chennault announced in early April that they soon would be escorting British bombers and supporting the Chinese infantry, rather than hunting Japanese fighters on commission.

In the meantime Boyington had received word that he was being inducted into the US Army Air Corps July 1 despite earlier verbal assurances from the Marine Corps that this would not happen. He claimed that in fact, before resigning he'd been assured that he could be reinstated if he tired of China. This all but ended his Flying Tigers career. Boyington fell down a hill while inebriated, was hospitalized for two weeks, then tried to fly a P-40 while under the influence and showed up for night watch toasted. He resigned from the AVG on April 21 and returned home, having fully expected that Chennault would throw him out anyway.

Few if any Flying Tiger pilots regretted his departure. And Chennault did nothing at all to help Boyington get back in the Marines. Instead, he encouraged the Army to draft Boyington into the Air Corps and advised the Marines to reject him.

At home he discovered that his children had been placed in his mother's care due to his wife's neglect. After working several months in the same parking garage where he paid part of his way through college, he learned on September 3, 1942, that despite Chennault's advice, the Marines were reinstating him.

After another sea voyage and several months shuffling Marine paperwork, he flew some defensive patrols over Guadalcanal, shuffled more paper until August 1943, and then got a new plane and the assignment he'd been looking for.

The F-4U Corsair had arrived in February 1943. Designed to outspeed the Japanese Zero, it also protected the pilot and fuel on board much better than the enemy plane. Boyington particularly admired the shallow angle of climb the Corsair offered. But when could he get back into action? Boyington's old friend, Brig. Gen. James "Nuts" Moore solved that problem after running out of other options. Adm. William Halsey, commander of the Pacific, needed air support for his offensive in the Solomons. Halsey's ideal solution was an aggressive fully trained Marine squadron commander with an impeccable record, but none were available.

Moore recommended that the VMF-214 Marine Fighter Squadron now on R&R in Australia following the combat death of its commander now be led by Boyington. Moore's boss, Maj. Gen. Ralph J. Mitchell, commander of the 1st Marine Aircraft Wing, was aware of Boyington's quirks but took a chance on him anyway.

The squadron was an eclectic group, but not the collection of misfits and criminals portrayed years later in the television series *Baa Baa Black Sheep*. Many had attended prestigious colleges including Princeton and Notre Dame. Others had extensive combat experience. The squadron did have its share of eccentrics: One, 1st Lt. Christopher L. Magee, flew into combat wearing a swimming suit, bowling shoes, and a bandana.

Boyington was not the oldest of the lot—that distinction belonged to thirty-four-year-old Frank Walton, the former Los Angeles police officer now in charge of squadron intelligence. And when Boyington arrived, Walton was assigned to keep him off of booze and out of trouble.

Soon after arriving in August, Boyington challenged the entire squadron except tall rangy Walton to wrestle him. When sober, Boyington pondered a serious problem. Eighteen of the twenty-four or so squadron pilots had no combat experience.

During their first meeting he compared the strengths and weaknesses of the Zero and the Corsair, emphasized the importance of staying with the squadron instead of pursuing Zeros lone-wolf style, and helped them visualize the tactics they would use in dogfights. He taught them how to confront and use fear, seek safety in numbers, and live to fight another day by resisting the often lethal temptation to do victory rolls over enemy lines. Whatever they had heard about his drunken rampages and misadventures, the young pilots around him at this first meeting showed Boyington nothing but respect. A leader, however flawed, was born that day.

Facing combat in the near future, the squadron had only a few weeks to prepare, unlike those in their wing who had trained as much as a year stateside. Boyington scavenged beat-up, worn-out Corsairs anywhere he could find them, and quickly put his men in the air on training missions, some of which ended with close calls. Robert McClurg made one landing with palm tree branches in his landing gear but became an ace with five confirmed kills.

The squadron was officially designated VMF-214 on September 7. That night or soon after, someone proposed they be called "Boyington's Bastards" over drinks. A chairborne Marine publicity officer turned that one down but approved "Black Sheep" squadron. Marine combat correspondent Penn Johnson sketched out their insignia.

They landed at Henderson Field on Guadalcanal six days after being officially organized. Plane shortages meant that individual pilots took whatever Corsair was available for the daily mission. The first Black Sheep missions were escort duty protecting B-24 Liberators in an unchallenged airfield strike on Bougainville, followed by a photo reconnaissance mission plagued by Corsair oxygen, manifold, and brake problems. But the combat action some of the Black Sheep longed for would greet them soon enough, on their third mission.

The target was Ballale, a small island near Bougainville sheltering Japanese anti-aircraft guns. Some one hundred American planes left Henderson that Thursday afternoon, September 16, to take them out.

Everyone on the flight knew that enemy fighters would do everything possible to bring as many of them down as possible.

"Tally ho!" someone yelled into the radio, just before some thirty Zeros filled the air space above the Ballale airfield, as the mostly combat-green Black Sheep pilots began the "spot, fire and evade" tactics that with some luck, might keep them alive. More than one of the newbies used the snap roll—a full-throttle dive technique Boyington had taught them—and survived to fight another day.

Boyington's first kill that day mistook him for a comrade, waggled his wings, then paid with his life. According to Boyington's action report, he scored his second victory at ten thousand feet. The Zero exploded about fifty feet away from his Corsair. Boyington climbed again, this time to eighteen thousand feet. While there he attacked a Zero that climbed, rolled on its back, and exploded. His fourth kill of the day was a trick shot; he'd been lured after one Zero, but turned and shot down the one that had been following him just the way Chennault taught him two years earlier.

He became an ace a few months later, while rescuing another American from two Zeros at about ten thousand feet, then landed at Munda, an American airbase on New Georgia Island in the Solomons, with only ten of the 237 gallons of fuel he started with.

Back at Banika where they started, he learned that all told the Black Sheep had eleven confirmed and nine probable air victories over Ballale, but Capt. Robert T. Ewing was never seen again. Daily but largely uneventful missions during the next eleven days ended on a return flight from a September 27 bomber escort mission to Kahili, near Buin on Bougainville. While returning, Boyington and six other Black Sheep pilots encountered fifty Japanese planes. He picked a Zero, went in for a confirmed kill, bagging one of four Black Sheep scores that day, but Lt. Walter Harris was lost.

And with that the small but formidable Marine public relations machine went to work, describing Boyington as "a man on his way to becoming a living legend." Soon a reporter arrived to feature Chicago-area Black Sheep, including bandana-wearing Lt. Christopher Magee, in a series of articles. He photographed several of them on September 29, the day they lost one of the best Black Sheep pilots, Lt. Robert Alexander, in a friendly fire incident near Munda. They had flown seventy-five missions in September, but more challenges were ahead.

Despite constant maintenance problems the Black Sheep and other Marine squadrons kept their Corsairs in the air throughout October, preparing the ground for large-scale attacks to come the next month.

"Major Boyington, what is your position, please?" someone asked in an accented voice over the radio on October 4, while Boyington and six other Corsair pilots were protecting dive-bombers attacking Kahili. He gave a fake position, then patrolled nearby in ambush with his squadron. Within sixty seconds Boyington scored three Zeros.

Boyington added one more to his score on October 15 in another attack on Kahili. He bagged a Zero trio in sixty seconds on October 17, when some forty Zeros rose from the airfield at Kahili the next day to attack several Corsairs the Black Sheep Squadron was using as bait. After that Boyington personally strafed the Kahili airfield, and then led the squadron back for another run in which he personally took out one of the eight Zeros destroyed.

The first six-week Black Sheep tour ended on October 19. By that time American flyers had significantly reduced the number of experienced Japanese fighter pilots still in the air.

Boyington claimed six kills in Burma combined with fourteen confirmed kills in the South Pacific. Another Marine aviator, Joe Foss, also had twenty kills, which prompted the American press to promote a competition between Boyington and Foss to Boyington's regret.

The Marines published a January 1944 booklet highlighting sixty-four points for combat pilots taught by Boyington but compiled by the Black Sheep Squadron members, rather than Boyington himself. He compared air combat to boxing matches in which the fighters maneuver strictly by reflex. Black Sheep pilots memorized the purpose of every Corsair knob and control as well as the strengths and weaknesses of the Japanese Zero. Through example Boyington taught his pilots and hundreds of others that despite its supposed invincibility, the Zero could be destroyed. He was a natural-born teacher where killing was concerned. Lt. Harold E. Segal, a pilot from another squadron, later recalled how

Boyington had saved his life by teaching Segal a specific maneuver during an evening bull session.

During a six-day R&R trip to Australia, he bumped into his old nemesis from Pensacola, Lt. Col. Joseph A. Smoak, who tried to have Boyington transferred out of his squadron. Instead, thanks to a Boyington admirer, Smoak was transferred to the same chairborne, nowhere assignment Smoak had planned for Boyington.

On November 27 the Black Sheep Squadron flew into Vella Lavella, an insect-plagued island a scarce seventy-five miles southeast of Kahili, the Japanese airfield they'd been attacking since September. The ultimate Solomon Islands target was Rabaul, some 225 miles farther.

Boyington and seven other Black Sheep led seventy-six other aircraft in a December 16 search-and-destroy sweep to Rabaul, an attack he and his boss, General Moore, had been arguing for since September. Although only eight Japanese aircraft were destroyed, four days later Boyington led forty-eight Corsairs back to Rabaul, trailing behind American bombers used as "bait" to bring up Japanese Zeros.

This time "Gramps," as some of his men now called him, dispatched one target from only fifty feet away, climbed to ten thousand feet for a second score on a Zero in mechanical difficulty, then dropped a third Zero circling the spot where the second dropped into the ocean.

His fourth kill of the day came minutes later as Boyington charged yet another formation patrolling at ten thousand feet, but was then chased into Vella Lavella by eight Zeros. The squadron began Christmas celebrations the next evening, complete with a whiskey-laced eggnog concoction.

As the daily fighter sweeps continued, Boyington downed his twenty-fifth claimed kill two days after Christmas. Newsmen now greeted him each time Boyington returned to Vella Lavella, waiting for word that he had set a new record. He hoped to get there by the time his second tour ended in early January, but was beginning to wonder whether that would happen, even though Boyington was flying two missions a day dead-tired, confiding in one letter that getting killed was the least of his worries.

He volunteered for a January 3, 1944, mission to Rabaul, and dived on a Zero from twenty-two thousand feet, to tie Rickenbacker's record. Boyington's wingman, George Ashmun, screamed, "Gramps, you got a flamer," just before Ashmun himself was surrounded and shot down by Zeros. A postwar report filed by Boyington and Black Sheep Squadron pilot Frank Walton stated that Boyington flamed two more Zeros trying to protect Ashmun, who crashed into the water near Rabaul and was never heard from again.

Boyington was now in trouble himself, sustaining shrapnel wounds even as his fuel tank exploded. Later he recalled parachuting out just before the crash as everyone else returned to base. Within hours the Black Sheep were in the air looking for him, from New Ireland to New Britain, to Bougainville, searching airfields, harbors, supply dumps, and anywhere else Boyington might be hiding. They flew their last mission as the Black Sheep Squadron on January 6.

Rumors in the days that followed placed Boyington among twenty aviators harbored by natives, on his way through Saipan to Japan, or, as his friend Frank Walton feared, executed by the Japanese. *Time* magazine reported him dead on February 21; the squadron was in effect disbanded on March 1 when the fifteen remaining Black Sheep were sent elsewhere.

Two weeks earlier on February 16, Boyington and five other prisoners were flown out of Rabaul on a Japanese bomber, only to be nearly killed during a massive American naval air attack on Truk, a base in the Caroline Islands. He'd been saved by Japanese navy interpreter Edward Honda, who had grown up in Hawaii.

The next stop was Ofuna, the notorious island prisoner of war camp near Yokohama described later by an American captive as "one big crime." Louis Zamperini, later made famous by the film *Unbroken*, was also a prisoner there at the time. During the five months Boyington was missing, the press continued to report on his possible whereabouts, including a May 1944 *Chicago Daily Tribune* article that compared him to French ace Georges Guynemer, who simply disappeared during a World War I mission. For the most part, the press and public assumed Boyington was dead; the president awarded him the Medal of Honor in March 1944.

But he was still alive. Despite intense interrogations, his living conditions improved markedly in September 1944 when he was assigned the best job in the camp, working in the kitchen, perhaps with Honda's help.

Boyington was also sober for the first time in years, unable to indulge in the off-duty drinking he'd enjoyed while not flying combat missions.

February 1945 brought a full-scale air strike against the Yokosuka naval station some twelve miles from Ofuna. The prisoners watched the action with excitement and more than a little fear. Two months later he was transferred to an equally dismal island camp at Omori as a "special" prisoner. These captives, mostly pilots, received fewer rations and none of the "privileges" enjoyed by other inmates.

As American bombings increased, the Omori prisoners began excavating caves some six miles from the camp. An inadvertent stumble on the way back brought a beating, but Japanese civilians sometimes did what they could to help the Americans, sneaking them food or dropping cigarette butts to be easily found and picked up.

Boyington, pugnacious bulldog that he was, couldn't resist baiting the guards from time to time. He once hit one with a squash without suffering any reprisal. Some Japanese guards courageously cared for the Americans. One, known to history only as Kano, snuck several special prisoners to American doctors located elsewhere in the prison for medical treatment.

Boyington later described the ever-increasing bombing of nearby Yokohama as "music." Yet it was music that caused untold thousands of rats to swim from the mainland over to the prisoner island holding the Americans, as August 6, 1945, grew closer.

That day meant nothing in particular to the guards or prisoners at Omori, until word arrived that just after eight that morning the Americans had dropped an atomic bomb on Hiroshima, killing or mortally wounding between 90,000 and 160,000 Japanese. After a second atomic bomb was dropped on Nagasaki, many Omori prisoners concluded that they would be killed.

Boyington, now held prisoner for twenty months, was one of those who dreamed about surviving. And survive he did, liberated on August 29. Four days later Boyington and the other liberated Allied prisoners watched five hundred American bombers do a slow ceremonial fly-over commemorating the victory.

He arrived back in San Francisco September 12 and met his buddies at the St. Francis Hotel for a night of revelry marking his reunion with an old friend: booze. He briefly celebrated at the St. Francis and elsewhere in San Francisco before being swept away by well-wishers.

On October 4, 1945, in Washington, Boyington and Black Sheep Squadron intelligence officer Frank Walton filed a supplemental report, officially accepted by the Marine Corps but nevertheless controversial to this day. Walton confirmed that Boyington knocked down three Zeros on January 3, 1944, rather than the sole kill reported during the war. Those two extra kills weren't mentioned in the Medal of Honor citation President Truman conferred upon Boyington at the White House the next day, but Boyington's claims of twenty-eight kills were challenged for the rest of his life.

Boyington's persistent drinking problem prompted the Marine Corps to retire him August 1, 1947, although he was not yet thirty-five. He drifted from love affair to love affair and job to job; he worked in a brewery, officiated wrestling matches, and bickered with the family he deserted over money.

"Pappy" staggered through the next thirty years without accomplishing anything. The 1958 publication of his memoir, *Baa Baa Black Sheep*, put some money in the bank, but led to the greatest controversy of his life.

Josephine Moseman, his fourth wife, was nudging him toward Alcoholics Anonymous when the first episode of the fictional television series loosely based on his memoir was broadcast nationally on September 21, 1976. During a Black Sheep reunion in Hawaii later that year, Boyington did something usually unthinkable. He apologized to everyone present.

One squadron member said that the television series only got one thing right: They flew Corsairs. Frank Walton, who corroborated Boyington's twenty-seventh and twenty-eighth kills thirty-two years earlier, complained that the NBC series had twisted significant war-making accomplishments into an inept travesty.

None of this kept Boyington from touring the country selling copies of his memoir at air shows. Sometimes he teamed with Masajiro Kawato, a Japanese pilot who claimed to be the man who shot Boyington out of the air. Other Japanese pilots acknowledged Kawato was in the battle, but said Kawato was flying cover at a higher altitude than the pilots who engaged the Black Sheep. By 1980 the barrel-chested swashbuckling bulldog who had been Pappy Boyington, plagued by medical problems self-inflicted and otherwise, was a mere shell of himself.

Worse still, a spring 1981 article by Robert Sherrod in *Fortitudine*, a newsletter of the Marine Corps Historical Program, argued Boyington's claimed twenty-eight kills should be reduced to 25.5 based on a document Sherrod discovered at Maxwell Air Force Base. Boyington responded in a published letter to *Fortitudine*, acknowledging the discrepancy in AVG records but blamed it on Chennault.

Bruce Gamble's definitive 2000 Boyington biography remarked that in the days following his August 29, 1945, liberation from Omori, he never mentioned the two extra kills the day he was shot down, but claimed them thirty-seven days later in his "supplemental" report.

The Boyington controversy has continued into the twenty-first century. Was he the underachieving swaggering braggart that some Flying Tigers made him out to be, or the skilled squadron commander who, despite his drinking excesses and exaggerations, led the Black Sheep through eighty-four days of combat downing ninety-seven planes, sinking twenty-eight vessels, and producing eight air aces?

Truth be told, he was both.

CHAPTER TEN

The Air War Over the Trenches

Eddie Rickenbacker

The battlefield horrors of World War I are described in scores of great books and stories. The battles that raged in the skies over the bitter fighting in France have been described less frequently than the infantry fighting. The autobiography of one of America's first decorated "Aces," Captain Eddie Rickenbacker, takes us into the cockpits of airmen who fought their battles where few men had ever gone.

Without formal education past age 12, Rickenbacker's early grasp of automobile mechanics served him in racing, and then in the open cockpits of early planes like the French Nieuport 23 and SPAD XIII. Rickenbacker ended WWI with a total of 26 aerial victories and the rank of major. He was called the "Ace of Ace." In 1930, one of his previous Distinguished Service Cross awards was upgraded to the Medal of Honor. Rickenbacker held many key positions in aviation and racing after the war, becoming one of the majority owners of the Indianapolis Motor Speedway. During WWII, a plane in which he was flying was forced to ditch in the Pacific. He and his surviving crew members endured three weeks on the rafts, before being rescued, in very serious shape, with the loss of 60 pounds. This amazing man went on to help create Eastern Air Lines, before retiring in 1963. He died of a stroke in 1972 while visiting Switzerland.

This excerpt from his book Flying the Fighting Circus *is one of the best accounts we have of what it was like in the early days of aviation combat.*

On September 15th the weather was ideal for flying. I left the aerodrome at 8:30 in the morning on a voluntary patrol, taking the nearest air route to the lines.

I had reached an altitude of 16,000 feet by the time I had reached the trenches. The visibility was unusually good. I could see for miles and miles in every direction. I was flying alone, with no idea as to whether other planes of our own were cruising about the sector or not. But barely had I reached a position over No Man's Land when I noticed a formation of six enemy Fokkers at about my altitude coming towards me from the direction of Conflans.

I turned and began the usual tactics of climbing into the sun. I noticed the Fokkers alter their direction and still climbing move eastward towards the Moselle. I did not see how they could help seeing me, as scarcely half a mile separated us. However, they did not attack nor did they indicate that they suspected my presence beyond continuing steadily their climb for elevation. Three complete circles they made on their side of the lines. I did the same on my side.

Just at this moment I discovered four Spad machines far below the enemy planes and some three miles inside the German lines. I decided at once they must belong to the American Second Fighting Group, at that time occupying the aerodrome at Souilly. They appeared to be engaged in bombing the roads and strafing enemy infantry from a low altitude. The

Spads of the Second Pursuit Group had but recently been equipped with bomb racks for carrying small bombs.

The leader of the Fokker Formation saw the Spads at about the same moment I did. I saw him dip his wings and stick down his nose. Immediately the six Fokkers began a headlong pique directly down at the Spads. Almost like one of the formation I followed suit.

Inside the first thousand feet I found I was rapidly overtaking the enemy machines. By the time we had reached 5,000 feet I was in a position to open fire upon the rear man. Not once had any of them looked around. Either they had forgotten me in their anxiety to get at their prey or else had considered I would not attempt to take them all on single-handed. At all events I was given ample time to get my man dead into my sights before firing.

I fired one long burst. I saw my tracer bullets go straight home into the pilot's seat. There came a sudden burst of fire from his fuel tank and the Fokker continued onwards in its mad flight—now a fiery furnace. He crashed a mile inside his own lines.

His five companions did not stay to offer battle. I still held the upper hand and even got in a few bursts at the next nearest machine before he threw himself into a vrille and escaped me. The sight of one of their members falling in flames evidently quite discouraged them. Abandoning all their designs on the unsuspecting Spads below they dived away for Germany and left me the field.

I returned to my field, secured a car and drove immediately up to the lines to our Balloon Section. I wanted to get my victories confirmed—both this one of to-day and the Fokker that I had brought down yesterday in the same sector. For no matter how many pilots may have witnessed the bringing down of an enemy plane, official confirmation of their testimony must be obtained from outside witnesses on the ground. Often these are quite impossible to get. In such a case the victory is not credited to the pilot.

Upon the tragic death of Major Lufbery, who at that time was the leading American Ace, with 18 victories, the title of American Ace of Aces fell to Lieutenant Paul Frank Baer of Fort Wayne, Ind., a member of the Lafayette Escadrille 103. Baer then had 9 victories and had never been wounded.

Baer is a particularly modest and lovable boy, and curiously enough he is one of the few fighting pilots I have met who felt a real repugnance in his task of shooting down enemy aviators.

When Lufbery fell, Baer's Commanding Officer, Major William Thaw, called him into the office and talked seriously with him regarding the opportunity before him as America's leading Ace. He advised Baer to be cautious and he would go far. Two days later Baer was shot down and slightly wounded behind the German lines!

Thereafter, Lieutenant Frank Bayliss of New Bedford, Mass., a member of the crack French Escadrille of the Cigognes, Spad 3, held the American title until he was killed in action on June 12th, 1918. Bayliss had 13 victories to his credit.

Then David Putnam, another Massachusetts boy, took the lead with 12 victories over enemy aeroplanes. Putnam, as I have said, was, like Lufbery, shot down in flames but a day or two before my last victory.

Lieutenant Tobin of San Antonio, Texas, and a member of the third Pursuit Group (of which Major William Thaw was the Commanding Officer), now had six official victories. He led the list. I for my part had five victories confirmed. But upon receiving confirmation for the two Fokkers I had vanquished yesterday and to-day, I would have my seven and would lead Tobin by one. So it was with some little interest and impatience that I set off to try to find ground witnesses of my last two battles about St. Mihiel.

Mingled with this natural desire to become the leading fighting Ace of America was a haunting superstition that did not leave my mind until the very end of the war. It was that the very possession of this title—Ace of Aces—brought with it the unavoidable doom that had overtaken all its previous holders. I wanted it and yet I feared to learn that it was mine! In later days I began to feel that his superstition was almost the heaviest burden that I carried with me into the air. Perhaps it served to redouble my caution and sharpened my fighting senses. But never was I able to forget that the life of a title-holder is short.

Eating my sandwiches in the car that day I soon ran through St. Mihiel and made my way on the main road east to Apremont and then north to Thiaucourt. I knew that there had been a balloon up near there both days and felt certain that their observers must have seen my two combats overhead.

Unfortunately the road from Apremont to Thiaucourt was closed, owing to the great number of shell-holes and trenches which criss-crossed it. After being lost for two hours in the forest which lies between St. Mihiel and Vigneulles, I was finally able to extricate myself and found I had emerged just south of Vigneulles. I was about one mile south of our trenches. And standing there with map in hand wondering where to go next to find our balloons, I got an unexpected clue.

A sudden flare of flames struck my sight off to the right. Running around the trees I caught a view of one of our balloons between me and Thiaucourt completely immersed in flames! Half-way down was a graceful little parachute, beneath which swung the observer as he settled slowly to Mother Earth!

And as I gazed I saw a second balloon two or three miles further east towards Pont-à-Mousson perform the same maneuver. Another of our observers was making the same perilous jump! A sly Heinie had slipped across our lines and had made a successful attack upon the two balloons and had made a clean getaway. I saw him climbing up away from the furious gale of anti-aircraft fire which our gunners were speeding after him. I am afraid my sympathies were almost entirely with the airman as I watched the murderous bursting of Archy all around his machine. At any rate I realized exactly how he was feeling, with his mixture of satisfaction over the success of his undertaking and of panic over the deadly mess of shrapnel about him.

In half an hour I arrived at the balloon site and found them already preparing to go aloft with a second balloon. And at my first question they smiled and told me they had seen my Fokker of this morning's combat crash in flames. They readily signed the necessary papers to this effect, thus constituting the required confirmation for my last victory. But for the victory of yesterday that I claimed they told me none of the officers were present who had been there on duty at that time. I must go to the

3rd Balloon Company just north of Pont-à-Mousson and there I would find the men I wanted to see.

After watching the new balloon get safely launched with a fresh observer in the basket, a process which consumed some ten or fifteen minutes, I retraced my steps and made my way back to my motor. The observer whom I had seen descending under his parachute had in the meantime made his return to his company headquarters. He was unhurt and quite enthusiastic over the splendid landing he had made in the trees. Incidentally I learned that but two or three such forced descents by parachute from a flaming balloon are permitted any one observer. These jumps are not always so simple and frequently very serious if not fatal injuries are received in the parachute jump. Seldom does one officer care to risk himself in a balloon basket after his third jump. And this fear for his own safety limits very naturally his service and bravery in that trying business. The American record in this perilous profession is held, I believe, by Lieutenant Phelps of New York, who made five successive jumps from a flaming balloon.

On my way to the 3rd Balloon Company I stopped to enquire the road from a group of infantry officers whom I met just north of Pont-à-Mousson. As soon as I stated my business, they unanimously exclaimed that they had all seen my flight above them yesterday and had seen my victim crash near them. After getting them to describe the exact time and place and some of the incidents of the fight I found that it was indeed my combat they had witnessed. This was a piece of real luck for me. It ended my researches on the spot. As they were very kindly signing their confirmation I was thinking to myself, "Eddie! You are the American Ace of Aces!" And so I was for the minute.

Returning home, I lost no time in putting in my reports. Reed Chambers came up to me and hit me a thump on the back.

"Well, Rick!" he said, "how does it feel?"

"Very fine for the moment, Reed," I replied seriously, "but any other fellow can have the title any time he wants it, so far as I am concerned."

I really meant what I was saying. A fortnight later when Frank Luke began his marvelous balloon strafing he passed my score in a single jump. Luke, as I have said, was on the same aerodrome with me, being a member of 27 Squadron. His rapid success even brought 27 Squadron ahead of 95 Squadron for a few days.

The following day I witnessed a typical expedition of Luke's from our own aerodrome. Just about dusk on September 16th Luke left the Major's headquarters and walked over to his machine. As he came out of the door he pointed out the two German observation balloons to the east of our field, both of which could be plainly seen with the naked eye. They were suspended in the sky about two miles back of the Boche lines and were perhaps four miles apart.

"Keep your eyes on these two balloons," said Frank as he passed us. "You will see that first one there go up in flames exactly at 7:15 and the other will do likewise at 7:19."

We had little idea he would really get either of them, but we all gathered together out in the open as the time grew near and kept our eyes glued to the distant specks in the sky. Suddenly Major Hartney exclaimed, "There goes the first one!" It was true! A tremendous flare of flame lighted up the horizon. We all glanced at our watches. It was exactly on the dot!

The intensity of our gaze towards the location of the second Hun balloon may be imagined. It had grown too dusk to distinguish the balloon itself, but we well knew the exact point in the horizon where it hung. Not a word was spoken as we alternately glanced at the second-hands of our watches and then at the eastern skyline. Almost upon the second our watching group yelled simultaneously. A small blaze first lit up the point at which we were gazing. Almost instantaneously another gigantic burst of flames announced to us that the second balloon had been destroyed! It was a most spectacular exhibition.

We all stood by on the aerodrome in front of Luke's hangar until fifteen minutes later we heard through the darkness the hum of his returning motor. His mechanics were shooting up red Very lights with their pistols to indicate to him the location of our field. With one short circle above the aerodrome he shut off his motor and made a perfect landing just in front of our group. Laughing and hugely pleased with his success, Luke jumped out and came running over to us to receive our heartiest congratulations. Within a half hour's absence from the field Frank Luke had destroyed a hundred thousand dollars' worth of enemy property! He had returned absolutely unscratched.

A most extraordinary incident had happened just before Luke had left the ground. Lieutenant Jeffers of my Squadron had been out on patrol with the others during the afternoon and did not return with them. I was becoming somewhat anxious about him when I saw a homing aeroplane coming from the lines towards our field. It was soon revealed as a Spad and was evidently intending to land at our field, but its course appeared to be very peculiar. I watched it gliding steeply down with engine cut off. Instead of making for the field, the pilot, whoever he was, seemed bent upon investigating the valley to the north of us before coming in. If this was Jeff he was taking a foolish chance, since he had already been out longer than the usual fuel supply could last him.

Straight down at the north hillside the Spad continued its way. I ran out to see what Jeff was trying to do. I had a premonition that everything was not right with him.

Just as his machine reached the skyline I saw him make a sudden effort to redress the plane. It was too late. He slid off a little on his right wing, causing his nose to turn back towards the field—and then he crashed in the fringe of bushes below the edge of the hill. I hurried over to him.

Imagine my surprise when I met him walking towards me, no bones broken, but wearing a most sheepish expression on his face. I asked him what in the world was the matter.

"Well," he replied, "I might as well admit the truth! I went to sleep coming home, and didn't wake up until I was about ten feet above the ground. I didn't have time to switch on my engine or even flatten out! I'm afraid I finished the little 'bus!"

Extraordinary as this tale seemed, it was nevertheless true. Jeffers had set his course for home at a high elevation over the lines and cutting off his engine had drifted smoothly along. The soft air and monotonous luxury of motion had lulled him to sleep. Subconsciously his hand controlled the joystick or else the splendid equilibrium of the Spad had kept it upon an even keel without control. Like the true old coach-horse it was, it kept the stable door in sight and made directly for it. Jeff's awakening might have been in another world, however, if he had not miraculously opened his eyes in the very nick of time!

The next day, September 18th, our group suffered a loss that made us feel much vindictiveness as well as sorrow. Lieutenant Heinrichs and Lieutenant John Mitchell, both of 95 Squadron, were out together on patrol when they encountered six Fokker machines. They immediately began an attack.

Mitchell fired one burst from each gun and then found them both hopelessly jammed. He signaled to Heinrichs that he was out of the battle and started for home. But at the same moment Heinrichs received a bullet through his engine which suddenly put it out of action. He was surrounded by enemy planes and some miles back of the German lines. He broke through the enemy line and began his slow descent. Although it was evident he could not possibly reach our lines, the furious Huns continued swooping upon him, firing again and again as he coasted down.

Ten different bullets struck his body in five different attacks. He was perfectly defenseless against any of them. He did not lose consciousness, although one bullet shattered his jawbone and bespattered his goggles so that he could not see through the blood. Just before he reached the ground he managed to push up his goggles with his unwounded arm. The other was hanging limp and worthless by his side.

He saw he was fairly into a piece of woodland and some distance within the German lines. He swung away and landed between the trees, turning his machine over as he crashed, but escaping further injury himself. Within an hour or two he was picked up and taken to a hospital in Metz.

After the signing of the Armistice we saw Heinrichs again at the Toul Hospital. He was a mere shell of himself. Scarcely recognizable even by his old comrades, a first glance at his shrunken form indicated that he had been horribly neglected by his captors. His story quickly confirmed this suspicion.

For the several weeks that he had lain in the Metz hospital he told us that the Germans had not reset either his jaw or his broken arm. In fact he had received no medical attention whatsoever. The food given him was bad and infrequent. It was a marvel that he had survived this frightful suffering!

In all fairness to the Hun I think it is his due to say that such an experience as Heinrichs suffered rarely came to my attention. In the large hospital in which he was confined there were but six nurses and two doctors. They had to care for several scores of wounded. Their natural inclination was to care first for their own people. But how any people calling themselves human could have permitted Heinrichs' suffering to go uncared for during all those weeks passes all understanding. Stories of this kind which occasionally came to our ears served to steel our hearts against any mercy towards the enemy pilots in our vicinity.

And thus does chivalry give way before the horrors of war—even in aviation!

Captain of the Hat-in-the-Ring Squadron
The Three-Fingered Lake is a body of water well known to the American pilots who have flown over the St. Mihiel front. It lies four or five miles directly north of Vigneulles and is quite the largest body of water to be seen in this region. The Germans have held it well within their lines ever since the beginning of the war.

At the conclusion of the American drive around St. Mihiel, which terminated victoriously twenty-two hours after it began, the lines were pushed north of Vignuelles until they actually touched the southern arm of Three-Fingered Lake. Our resistless doughboys pushing in from both directions, met each other in the outskirts of Vigneulles at two o'clock in the morning. Some fifteen thousand Boches and scores of guns were captured within the territory that had thus been pinched out.

With this lake barrier on the very edge of their lines, the Huns had adroitly selected two vantage points on their end of the water from which to hoist their observation balloons. From this position their observers had a splendid view of our lines and noted every movement in our rear. They made themselves a tremendous nuisance to the operations of our Staff Officers.

Frank Luke, the star Balloon Strafer of our group, was, as I have said, a member of the 27th Squadron. On the evening of September 18th he announced that he was going up to get those two balloons that swung above the Three-Fingered Lake. His pal, Lieutenant Wehrner, of the same squadron accompanied Luke as usual.

There was a curious friendship between Luke and Wehrner. Luke was an excitable, highstrung boy, and his impetuous courage was always getting him into trouble. He was extremely daring and perfectly blind and indifferent to the enormous risks he ran. His superior officers and his friends would plead with him to be more cautious, but he was deaf to their entreaties. He attacked like a whirlwind, with absolute coolness but with never a thought of his own safety. We all predicted that Frank Luke would be the greatest air-fighter in the world if he would only learn to save himself unwise risks. Luke came from Phoenix, Arizona.

Wehrner's nature, on the other hand, was quite different. He had just one passion, and that was his love for Luke. He followed him about the aerodrome constantly. When Luke went up, Wehrner usually managed to go along with him. On these trips Wehrner acted as an escort or guard, despite Luke's objections. On several occasions he had saved Luke's life. Luke would come back to the aerodrome and excitedly tell every one about it, but no word would Wehrner say on the subject. In fact Wehrner never spoke except in monosyllables on any subject. After a successful combat he would put in the briefest possible report and sign his name. None of us ever heard him describe how he brought the enemy machine down.

Wehrner hovered in the air above Luke while the latter went in for the balloon. If hostile aeroplanes came up, Wehrner intercepted them and warded off the attack until Luke had finished his operations. These two pilots made an admirable pair for this work and over a score of victories were chalked up for 27 Squadron through the activities of this team.

On the evening of the 18th, Luke and Wehrner set off at five o'clock. It was just getting dark. They flew together at a medium level until they reached the lake. There they separated, Luke diving straight at the balloon which lay to the west, Wehrner staying aloft to guard the sky against a surprise attack from Hun aeroplanes.

Luke's balloon rose out of the swampy land that borders the upper western edge of Three-Fingered Lake. The enemy defenses saw his approach and began a murderous fire through which Luke calmly dived as usual. Three separate times he dived and fired, dived and fired. Constantly surrounded with a hail of bullets and shrapnel, flaming onions and incendiary bullets, Luke returned to the attack the third time and finally completed his errand of destruction. The huge gas-bag burst into flames. Luke zoomed up over the balloon and looked about for his friend. He was not in view at the moment, but another sight struck Luke's searching eyes. A formation of six Fokkers was bearing down upon him from out of Germany. Perhaps Wehrner had fired the red signal light which had been the warning agreed upon, and he had failed to see it in the midst of all that Archy fire. At any rate he was in for it now.

The German Fokkers were to the west of him. The second balloon was to the east. With characteristic foolhardiness Luke determined to withdraw by way of the other balloon and take one burst at it before the Huns reached him. He accordingly continued straight on east, thus permitting the pursuing formation of Fokkers to cut him off at the south.

With his first dive Luke shot down the second balloon. It burst into towering flames, which were seen for miles around. Again he passed through a living stream of missiles fired at him from the ground, and escaped unhurt!

As he began his flight towards home he discovered that he was completely cut off by the six Fokkers. He must shoot his way through single-handed. To make it worse, three more Fokkers were rapidly coming upon him from the north. And then Luke saw his pal, Wehrner.

Wehrner had all this time been patrolling the line to the north of Luke's balloons. He had seen the six Fokkers, but had supposed that Luke would keep ahead of them and abandon his attempt at the second enemy balloon. He therefore fired his signal light, which was observed by our balloon observers but not by Luke, and immediately set off to patrol a parallel course between the enemy planes and Luke's road home. When he saw Luke dart off to the second balloon, Wehrner realized at once that Luke had not seen his signal and was unaware of the second flight of Fokkers coming directly upon him. He quickly sheered off and went forward to meet them.

What Luke saw was the aeroplane of his devoted pal receiving a direct fire from all three of the approaching Fokker pilots. The next instant it fell over in the air and slowly began to fall. Even as it hesitated in its flight, a burst of flames issued from the Spad's tank. Wehrner was shot down in flames while trying to save his comrade! It was a deliberate sacrifice of himself for his friend!

Completely consumed with fury, Luke, instead of seeking safety in flight, turned back and hurled himself upon the three Fokkers. He was at a distinct disadvantage, for they had the superiority both in altitude and position, not to mention numbers. But regardless as ever of what the chances were, Luke climbed upwards at them, firing as he advanced.

Picking out the pilot on the left, Luke kept doggedly on his track firing at him until he suddenly saw him burst into flame. The other two machines were in the meantime on Luke's tail and their tracer bullets were flashing unnoticed by his head. But as soon as he saw the end of his first enemy he made a quick renversement on number two and, firing as he came about, he shot down the second enemy machine with the first burst. The third piqued for Germany and Luke had to let him go.

All this fighting had consumed less time than it takes to tell it. The two Fokkers had fallen in flames within ten seconds of each other. With rage still in his heart Luke looked about him to discover where the six enemy machines had gone. They had apparently been satisfied to leave him with their three comrades, for they were now disappearing back towards the east. And just ahead of them Luke discerned fleecy white clouds of Archy smoke breaking north of Verdun. This indicated that our batteries were firing at enemy aeroplanes in that sector.

As he approached Verdun Luke found that five French Spads were hurrying up to attack an L.V.G. machine of the Huns, the same target at which our Archy had been firing. The six Fokkers had seen them coming and had gone to intercept them. Like a rocket Luke set his own Spad down at the L.V.G. It was a two-seater machine and was evidently taking photographs at a low altitude.

Our Archy ceased firing as Luke drew near. He hurled himself directly down at the German observer, firing both guns as he dove. The enemy machine fell into a vrille and crashed just a few hundred yards from our old Verdun aerodrome. In less than twenty minutes Lieutenant Luke had shot down two balloons, two fighting Fokkers and one enemy photographing machine—a feat that is almost unequaled in the history of this war!

Luke's first question when he arrived at our field was, "Has Wehrner come back?"

He knew the answer before he asked the question, but he was hoping against hope that he might find himself mistaken. But Wehrner had indeed been killed. The joy of Luke over his marvelous victories vanished instantly. He was told that with these five victories he had a total of eleven, thus passing me and making Luke the American Ace of Aces. But this fact did not interest him. He said he would like to go up to the front in a car and see if anything had been heard from Wehrner.

The following morning Major Hartney, Commanding Officer of our Group, took Luke and myself up to Verdun to make inquiries. Shortly after lunch the officer in charge of confirmations came to us and told Lieutenant Luke that not only had his five victories of yesterday been officially confirmed, but that three old victories had likewise been that morning confirmed, making Luke's total fourteen instead of eleven. And these fourteen victories had been gained by Frank Luke in *eight days!* The history of war aviation, I believe, has not a similar record. Not even the famous Guynemer, Fonck, Ball, Bishop or the noted German Ace of Aces, Baron von Richthofen, ever won fourteen victories in a single fortnight at the front. Any air-craft, whether balloon or aeroplane, counts as one victory, and only one, with all the armies.

In my estimation there has never during the four years of war been an aviator at the front who possessed the confidence, ability and courage that Frank Luke had shown during that remarkable two weeks.

In order to do this boy honor and show him that every officer in the Group appreciated his wonderful work, he was given a complimentary dinner that night by the Squadrons. Many interesting speeches were made. When it came Luke's turn to respond he got up laughing, said he was having a bully time—and sat down! Major Hartney came over to him and presented him with a seven days' leave in Paris—which at that time was about the highest gift at the disposal of commanding officers at the front.

Among all the delightful entertainers who came over to the front from the United States to help cheer up the fighting men, none except our own Elsie Janis, who is an honorary member of our Squadron, were quite so highly appreciated by our fellows as the Margaret Mayo Y.M.C.A. troup, which gave us an entertainment just a night or two after this. The players included such well known talent as Elizabeth Brice, Lois Meredith, Bill Morrisey, Tommy Gray and Mr. Walker—all of New York. After a hurried preparation, we cleaned up one of the hangars, prepared a stage and made a dressing room by hanging a curtain over a truck and trailer. After a merry dinner in 94's mess hall everybody crowded into the "theater," and the way the boys laughed and shouted there, during the performance, must have sounded hysterical to the actors; but to my mind this hysteria was only an outlet for the pent-up emotion and an indication of the tension and strain under which we had so long been living. At any rate it was the best show I have ever seen at the front, barring always the one evening Miss Janis appeared on our aerodrome for an entertainment.

The night of September 24th, Major Marr returned from Paris and announced that he had received orders to return to America. Shortly afterward Major Hartney handed me an order promoting me to the Command of the 94 Squadron!

My pride and pleasure at receiving this great honor I cannot put into words. I had been with 94 since its first day at the front. I was a member of this, the very first organization to go over the lines. I had seen my old friends disappear and be replaced by other pilots whom I had learned to admire and respect. And many of these had in turn disappeared!

Now but three members of the original organization were left— Reed Chambers, Thorn Taylor and myself. And I had been given the honor of leading this distinguished Squadron! It had had Lufbery, Jimmy Hall and Dave Peterson as members. And it led all the rest in number of victories over the Huns.

But did it? I walked over to the Operations Office and took a look at the records. I had a suspicion that Frank Luke's wonderful run of the past few days had put 27 Squadron ahead of us.

My suspicions were quite correct. The sober fact was that this presumptuous young 27 had suddenly taken a spurt, thanks to their brilliant

Luke, and now led the Hat-in-the-Ring Squadron by six victories! I hurried over to 94 quarters and called together all my pilots.

The half hour we had together that evening firmly fixed a resolve in the aspirations of 94's members. No other American Squadron at the front would ever again be permitted to approach so near our margin of supremacy. From that hour every man in 94 Squadron, I believe, felt that the honor of his Squadron was at stake in this matter of bringing down Huns. At all events, within a week my pilots had overtaken 27's lead and never again did any American Squadron even threaten to overtop our lead.

After a talk that night with the pilots, I went over and called the mechanics to a caucus. We had half an hour's talk together and I outlined to them just what our pilots proposed to do with their help. And they understood that it was only by their whole-souled help that their Squadron's success would be possible. How nobly these boys responded to our appeal was well proved in the weeks that followed. Rarely indeed was a dud motor found in 94 Squadron henceforward. Never did a squadron of pilots receive more faithful attendance from their helpers in the hangar than was given us by these enthusiastic air mechanics of the Hat-in-the-Ring Squadron. I honestly believe that they felt the disgrace of being second more keenly than did we pilots.

Finally, I had a long and serious conference with myself that night. After I had gone to bed I lay awake for several hours, thinking over the situation. I was compelled to believe that I had been chosen Squadron Commander because, first, I had been more successful than the other pilots in bringing down enemy aeroplanes; and second, because I had the power to make a good leader over other pilots. That last proposition caused me infinite thought. Just how and wherein could I do the best by my followers?

I suppose every squadron leader has this same problem to decide, and I cannot help but believe that on his decision as to how he shall lead his pilots depends in a great measure the extent of his success—and his popularity.

To my mind there was but one procedure. I should never ask any pilot under me to go on a mission that I myself would not undertake. I would lead them by example as well as precept. I would accompany the new pilots and watch their errors and help them to feel more confidence by sharing their dangers. Above all, I would work harder than ever I did as mere pilot. There was no question about that. My days of loafing were over!

To avoid the red-tape business at the aerodrome—the making out of reports, ordering materials and seeing that they came in on time, looking after details of the mess, the hangars and the comfort of the enlisted men—all this work must be put under competent men, if I expected to stay in the air and lead patrols. Accordingly I gave this important matter my attention early next morning. And the success of my appointments was such that from that day to this I have never spent more than thirty minutes a day upon the ground business connected with 94's operations.

Full of this early enthusiasm I went up on a lone patrol the very first morning of my new responsibility, to see how much I had changed for the better or the worse.

Within half an hour I returned to the aerodrome with two more victories to my credit—the first double-header I had so far won!

AN EVENTFUL "D" DAY

September 25th, 1918, was my first day as Captain of the 94 Squadron. Early that forenoon I started for the lines alone, flew over Verdun and Fort Douaumont, then turned east towards Etain. Almost immediately I picked up a pair of L.V.G. two-seater machines below me. They were coming out of Germany and were certainly bent upon a expedition over our lines. Five Fokker machines were above them and somewhat behind, acting as protection for the photographers until the lines were reached.

Climbing for the sun for all I was worth, I soon had the satisfaction of realizing that I had escaped their notice and was now well in their rear. I shut down my motor, put down my head and made a bee line for the nearest Fokker.

I was not observed by the enemy until it was too late for him to escape. I had him exactly in my sights when I pulled both triggers for a long burst. He made a sudden attempt to pull away, but my bullets were already ripping through his fusilage and he must have been killed instantly. His machine fell wildly away and crashed just south of Etain.

It had been my intention to zoom violently upwards and protect myself against the expected attack from the four remaining Fokkers as soon as I had finished the first man. But when I saw the effect of my attack upon the four dumbfounded Boches I instantly changed my tactics and plunged straight on through their formation to attack the photographing L.V.G.'s ahead. For the Heinies were so surprised by finding a Spad in their midst and seeing one of their number suddenly drop that the remaining three viraged to right and left. Their one idea was to escape and save their own skins. Though they did not actually pique for home, they cleared a space large enough for me to slip through and continue my dive upon the two-seaters before they could recover their formation.

The two-seaters had seen my attack and had already put down their heads to escape. I plunged along after them, getting the rear machine in my sights as I drew nearer to him. A glance back over my shoulder showed me that the four Fokkers had not yet reformed their line and were even now circling about with the purpose of again solidifying their formation. I had a few seconds yet before they could begin their attack.

The two L.V.G. machines began to draw apart. Both observers in the rear seats were firing at me, although the range was still too long for accurate shooting. I dove more steeply, passed out of the gunner's view under the nearest machine and zoomed quickly up at him from below. But the victory was not to be an easy one. The pilot suddenly kicked his tail around, giving the gunner another good aim at me. I had to postpone shooting until I had more time for my own aiming. And in the meantime the second photographing machine had stolen up behind me and I saw tracer bullets go whizzing and streaking past my face. I zoomed up diagonally out of range, made a renversement and came directly back at my first target.

Several times we repeated these maneuvers, the four Fokkers still wrangling among themselves about their formation. And all the time we were getting farther and farther back into Germany. I decided upon one bold attack and if this failed I would get back to my own lines before it was too late.

Watching my two adversaries closely, I suddenly found an opening between them. They were flying parallel to each other and not fifty yards apart. Dropping down in a sideslip until I had one machine between me and the other I straightened out smartly, leveled my Spad and began firing. The nearest Boche passed directly through my line of fire and just as I ceased firing I had the infinite satisfaction of seeing him gush forth flames. Turning over and over as he fell the L.V.G. started a blazing path to earth just as the Fokker escort came tearing up to the rescue. I put on the gas and piqued for my own lines.

Pleased as I was over this double-header, the effect it might have upon my pilots was far more gratifying to me.

Arriving at the aerodrome at 9:30 I immediately jumped into a motorcar, called to Lieutenant Chambers to come with me and we set off at once to get official confirmation for this double victory. We took the main road to Verdun, passed through the town and gained the hills beyond the Meuse, towards Etain. Taking the road up to Fort de Tavannes we passed over that bloody battlefield of 1916 where so many thousand German troops fell before French fire in the memorable Battle for Verdun. At the very crest of the hill we were halted by a French poilu, who told us the rest of the road was in full view of the Germans and that we must go no farther.

We asked him as to whether he had seen my combat overhead this morning. He replied in the affirmative and added that the officers in the adjacent fort too had witnessed the whole fight through their field glasses. We thanked him and leaving our car under his care took our way on foot to the Fort.

Two or three hundred yards of shell-holes sprinkled the ground between us and the Fort. We made our way through them, gained admittance to the interior of the Fort and in our best Pidgin French stated our errand to M. le Commandant. He immediately wrote out full particulars of the combat I had had with the L.V.G., signed it and congratulated me upon my victory with a warm shake of the hand. Having no further business at this place, we made our adieus and hastened back to our car.

Plunging through the shallowest shell-holes we had traversed about half the distance to our car, which stood boldly out on the top of the road, when a shrill whining noise made us pause and listen. The next instant a heavy explosion announced that a shell had landed about fifty yards short of us. Simultaneously with the shower of gravel and dirt which headed our way we dropped unceremoniously on our faces in the bottom of the deepest shell-hole in our vicinity.

The Huns had spotted our car and were actually trying to get its range!

Two or three times we crawled out of our hole, only to duck back at the signal of the next coming shell. After six or eight shots the Boche gunners evidently considered their target too small, for they ceased firing long enough for us to make a bolt across the intervening holes and throw ourselves into the waiting automobile. I most fervently wished that I had turned the car around before leaving it, and I shall never forget the frightful length of time it took me to get our car backed around and headed in the right direction. We lost no time in getting down that hill.

Next day was to be an important one for us and for the whole American Army. Officially it was designated as "D" day and the "Zero hour," by the same code, was set for four o'clock in the morning. At that moment the artillery barrage would begin and forty thousand doughboys who were posted along the front line trenches from the Meuse to the Argonne Forest would go over the top. It was the 26th day of September, 1918.

Precisely at four o'clock I was awakened by my orderly who informed me that the weather was good. Hastily getting out of doors, I looked over the dark sky, wondering as I did so how many of our boys it would claim before this day's work was done! For we had an important part to play in this day's operations. Headquarters had sent us orders to attack all the enemy observation balloons along that entire front this morning and to continue the attacks until the infantry's operations were completed. Accordingly every fighting squadron had been assigned certain of these balloons for attack and it was our duty to see that they were destroyed. The safety of thousands of our attacking soldiers depended upon our success in eliminating these all-watching eyes of the enemy. Incidentally, it was the first balloon strafing party that 94 Squadron had been given since I had been made its leader and I desired to make a good showing on this first expedition.

Just here it may be well to point out the difficulties of balloon strafing, which make this undertaking so unattractive to the new pilot.

German "Archy" is terrifying at first acquaintance. Pilots affect a scorn for it, and indeed at high altitudes the probabilities of a hit are small. But when attacking a balloon which hangs only 1,500 feet above the guns (and this altitude is of course known precisely to the anti-aircraft gunner) Archy becomes far more dangerous.

So when a pilot begins his first balloon attacking expeditions, he knows that he runs a gauntlet of fire that may be very deadly. His natural impulse is to make a nervous plunge into the zone of danger, fire his bullets, and get away. Few victories are won with this method of attack.

The experienced balloon strafers, particularly such daring airmen as Coolidge and Luke, do not consider the risks or terrors about them. They proceed in the attack as calmly as though they were sailing through a stormless sky. Regardless of flaming missiles from the ground, they pass through the defensive barrage of fire, and often return again and again, to attack the target, until it finally bursts into flame from their incendiary bullets.

The office charts informed me that day would break this morning at six o'clock. Consequently we must be ready to leave the ground in our machines at 5:20, permitting us thirty minutes in which to reach our objectives, and ten minutes in which to locate our individual balloons. For it is essential to strike at these well defended targets just at the edge of dawn. Then the balloons are just starting aloft, and our attacking aeroplanes are but scantily visible from below. Moreover enemy aeroplanes are not apt to be about so early in the morning, unless the enemy has some inkling of what is going on.

I routed out five of my best pilots, Lieutenants Cook, Chambers, Taylor, Coolidge and Palmer; and as we gathered together for an early breakfast, we went over again all the details of our pre-arranged plans. We had two balloons assigned to our Squadron, and three of us were delegated to each balloon. Both lay along the Meuse between Brabant and Dun. Every one of us had noted down the exact location of his target on the evening before. It would be difficult perhaps to find them before daylight if they were still in their nests, but we were to hang about the vicinity until we did find them, if it took all day. With every man fully posted on his course and objective, we put on our coats and walked over to the hangars.

I was the last to leave the field, getting off the ground at exactly 5:20. It was still dark and we had to have the searchlights turned onto the field for a moment to see the ground while we took off. As soon as we lifted into the darkness the lights were extinguished. And then I saw the most marvelous sight that my eyes have ever seen.

A terrific barrage of artillery fire was going on ahead of me. Through the darkness the whole western horizon was illumined with one mass of sudden flashes. The big guns were belching out their shells with such rapidity that there appeared to be millions of them shooting at the same time. Looking back I saw the same scene in my rear. From Luneville on the east to Rheims on the west there was not one spot of darkness along the whole front. The French were attacking along both our flanks at the same time with us in order to help demoralize the weakening Boche. The picture made me think of a giant switchboard which emitted thousands of electric flashes as invisible hands manipulated the plugs.

So fascinated did I become over this extraordinary fireworks display that I was startled upon peering over the side of my machine to discover the city of Verdun below my aeroplane's wings. Fastening my course above the dim outline of the Meuse River I followed its windings down stream, occasionally cutting across little peninsulas which I recognized along the way. Every inch of this route was as familiar to me as was the path around the corner of my old home. I knew exactly the point in the Meuse Valley where I would leave the river and turn left to strike the spot where my balloon lay last night. I did not know what course the other pilots had taken. Perhaps they had already—

Just as these thoughts were going through my mind I saw directly ahead of me the long snaky flashes of enemy tracer bullets from the ground piercing the sky. There was the location of my balloon and either Cook or Chambers was already attacking it. The enemy had discovered them and were putting up the usual hail of flaming projectiles around the balloon site. But even as the flaming bullets continued streaming upwards I saw a gigantic flame burst out in their midst! One of the boys had destroyed his gas-bag!

Even before the glare of the first had died I saw our second enemy balloon go up in flames. My pilots had succeeded beyond my fondest expectations. Undoubtedly the enemy would soon be swinging new balloons up in their places, but we must wait awhile for that. I resolved to divert my course and fly further to the north where I knew of the nest of another German observation balloon near Damvillers.

Dawn was just breaking as I headed more to the east and tried to pick out the location of Damvillers. I was piercing the gloom with my eyes when again—straight in front of my revolving propeller I saw another gush of flame which announced the doom of another enemy balloon—the very one I had determined to attack. While I was still jubilating over the extraordinary good luck that had attended us in this morning's expedition, I glanced off to my right and was almost startled out of my senses to discover that a German Fokker was flying alongside me not a hundred yards away! Not expecting any of the enemy aeroplanes to be abroad at this early hour, I was naturally upset for the moment. The next instant I saw that he had headed for me and was coming straight at my machine. We both began firing at the same time. It was still so dark that our four streams of flaming bullets cut brilliant lines of fire through the air. For a moment it looked as though our two machines were tied together with four ropes of fire. All my ammunition was of the incendiary variety for use against gas-bags. The Hun's ammunition was part tracer, part incendiary and part regular chunks of lead.

As we drew nearer and nearer I began to wonder whether this was to be a collision or whether he would get out of my way. He settled the question by tipping down his head to dive under me. I instantly made a renversement which put me close behind him and in a most favorable position for careful aim. Training my sights into the center of his fusilage I pulled both triggers. With one long burst the fight was over. The Fokker fell over onto one wing and dropped aimlessly to earth. It was too dark to see the crash, and moreover I had all thoughts of my victory dissipated by a sudden ugly jerk to my motor which immediately developed into a violent vibration. As I turned back towards Verdun, which was the nearest point to our liens, I had recurring visions of crashing down into Germany to find myself a prisoner. This would be a nice ending to our glorious balloon expedition!

Throttling down to reduce the pounding I was able just to maintain headway. If my motor failed completely I was most certainly doomed, for I was less than a thousand feet above ground and could glide but a few hundred yards without power. Providence was again with me, for I cleared the lines and made our Verdun aerodrome where one flight of the 27th Squadron was housed. I landed without damage and hastily climbed out of my machine to investigate the cause of my trouble.

Imagine my surprise when I discovered that one blade of my propeller had been shot in two by my late adversary! He had evidently put several holes through it when he made his head-on attack. And utterly unconscious of the damage I had received, I had reversed my direction and shot him down before the weakened blade gave way! The heavy jolting of my engine was now clear to me—only half of the propeller caught the air.

Lieutenant Jerry Vasconceles of Denver, Colorado, was in charge of the Verdun field on which I had landed. He soon came out and joined me as I was staring at my broken propeller. And then I learned that he had just landed himself from a balloon expedition. A few questions followed and then we shook hands spontaneously. He had shot down the Damvillers balloon himself—the same one for which I had been headed. And as he was returning he had seen me shoot down my Fokker! This was extremely lucky for both of us, for we were able each to verify the other's victory for him, although of course corroboration from ground witnesses was necessary to make these victories official.

His mechanics placed a new propeller on my Spad, and none the worse for its recent rough usage the little 'bus took me rapidly home. I landed at 8:30 on my own field. And there I heard great news. Our Group had that morning shot down ten German balloons! My victory over the Fokker made it eleven victories to be credited us for this hour's work. And we had not lost a single pilot!

As the jubilant and famished pilots crowded into the mess hall one could not hear a word through all the excited chatter. Each one had some strange and fearful adventure to relate about his morning's experiences. But the tale which aroused howls of laughter was the droll story told by Lieutenant White of the 147th Squadron.

White had searched long and earnestly for the balloon that he desired to attack. He thought himself hopelessly lost in the darkness, when off to one side he distinguished the dark outline of what he thought was his balloon. Immediately redressing his machine he tipped downwards and began plugging furious streams of flaming bullets into his target. He made a miscalculation in his distance and before he could swerve away from the dark mass ahead of him his machine had plunged straight through it!

And then he discovered that he had been piquing upon a round puff of black smoke that had just been made by a German Archy!

Frank Luke Strafes His Last Balloon

Neither side could afford to leave its lines undefended by observation balloons for a longer period than was necessary for replacements. Our onslaught of the early morning had destroyed so many of the Huns' Drachen, however, that it was quite impossible for them to get new balloons up at once, along their entire sector.

That same afternoon I flew along their lines to see what progress they were making in replacements of their observation posts. The only balloon I could discover in our sector was one which lifted its head just behind the town of Sivry-sur-Meuse. I made a note of its position and decided to try to bring it down early next morning.

Accordingly I was up again at the same hour the following day and again found the sky promised clear weather. Leaving the field at 5:30, I again took a course over Verdun in order to pick up the Meuse River there and follow it as a guide.

On this occasion I caught a grand view of No Man's Land as seen from the air by night. It was not yet daylight when I reached the lines and there I caught a longitudinal view of the span of ground that separated the two opposing armies. For upon both sides of this span of ground a horizontal line of flashes could be seen issuing from the mouth of rival guns. The German batteries were drawn up along their front scarcely a mile back of their line. And on our side a vastly more crowded line of flashes indicated the overwhelming superiority in numbers of guns that the American artillerymen were using to belabor the already vanquished

Huns. So far as my eye could reach, this dark space lay outlined between the two lines of living fire. It was a most spectacular sight. I followed down its course for a few miles, then turned again to the north and tried to find the Meuse River.

After ten minutes' flight into Germany, I realized I had crossed the river before I began to turn north and that I must be some distance inside the enemy's lines. I dropped down still lower as I saw the outlines of a town in front of me and circling above it I discovered that I had penetrated some 25 miles inside Hunland and was now over the village of Stenay. I had overshot Sivry by about twenty miles.

I lost no time in heading about towards France. Opening up the throttle, I first struck west and followed this course until I had the Meuse River again under my nose. Then turning up the river, I flew just above the road which follows along its banks. It was now getting light enough to distinguish objects on the ground below.

This Muese River highway is a lovely drive to take in the daytime, for it passes through a fertile and picturesque country. The little city of Dun-sur-Meuse stands out on a small cliff which juts into a bend of the river, making a most charming picture of what a medieval town should look like. I passed directly down Main Street over Dun-sur-Meuse and again picked up the broad highway that clung to the bank of the river. Occasional vehicles were now abroad below me. Day had broken and the Huns were up and ready for work.

It occurred to me that I might as well fly a bit lower and entertain the passing Huns with a little bullet-dodging as we met each other. My morning's work was spoiled anyway. It was becoming too late to take on a balloon now. Perhaps I might meet a general in his automobile and it would be fun to see him jump for the ditch and throw himself down on his face at the bottom. If I was fortunate enough to get him that would surely be helping along the war!

Ahead of me I saw a truck moving slowly in the same direction I was going. "Here goes for the first one!" I said to myself. I tipped down the nose of my machine and reached for my triggers.

As my nose went down something appeared over my top wing which took away my breath for an instant. There directly in my path was a huge enemy observation balloon! It was swaying in the breeze and the cable which held it to earth ran straight down until it reached the moving truck ahead of me. Then it became clear as daylight to me. The Huns were towing a new balloon up the road to its position for observation! They had just received a replacement from the supply station of Dun-sur-Meuse, and after filling it with gas were now getting it forward as rapidly as possible. It was just the target I had been searching for!

Forgetting the truck and crew, I flattened out instantly and began firing at the swaying monster in the air. So close to it had I come before I saw it that I had only time to fire a burst of fifty shots when I was forced to make a vertical virage, to avoid crashing through it. I was then but four or five hundred feet above ground.

Just as I began the virage I heard the rat-tat-tat-tat of a machine-gun fire from the truck on the road beneath me. And mingled with this drum fire I heard the sound of an explosion in the fusilage just behind my ear! One of their explosive bullets had come very close to my head and had exploded against a longeron or wire in the tail of the aeroplane! There was nothing I could do about that however, except to fly along as steadily as possible until I reached a place of safety and could make an investigation of the damage received. I cleared the side of the gas-bag and then as I passed I turned and looked behind me.

The enemy balloon was just at the point of exploding and the observer had already leaped from his basket and was still dropping through air with his parachute not yet opened. It was a very short distance to Mother Earth, and sometimes a parachute needs two or three hundred feet fall in which to fully open and check the swiftness of the falling body. I wondered whether this poor chap had any chance for his life in that short distance and just what bones he was likely to break when he landed. And then came a great burst of fire, as the whole interior of the big balloon became suddenly ignited. I couldn't resist one shout of exultation at the magnificent display of fireworks I had thus set off, hoping in the meantime that its dull glare would reach the eyes of some of our own balloon observers across the lines who would thus be in a position to give me the confirmation of my eleventh victory.

Again I decided to pay a call at Jerry Vasconcelle's field at Verdun and there get out and ascertain the extent of the damage in the tail of my Spad. Jerry welcomed me with some amusement and wanted to know whether this dropping in on him was to be a daily occurrence. Yesterday it had been a broken prop and to-day a broken tail. Before answering him I got out, and together we made a minute examination of my machine.

A neat row of bullet holes ran back down the tail of my machine. They were as nicely spaced as if they had been put in by careful measurement. The first hole was about four inches back of the pad on which my head rests when I am in the seat. The others were directly back of it at regular intervals. One, the explosive bullet, had struck the longeron that runs the length of the fusilage, and this had made the sharp explosion that I had heard at the time. The gunners on the truck had done an excellent bit of shooting!

None of the holes were in a vital part of the machine. I took off the field after a short inspection and soon covered the fifteen or sixteen miles that lay between the Verdun field and our own.

Upon landing I found very bad news awaiting me.

On the previous afternoon Lieutenant Sherry and Lieutenant Nutt, both of 94 Squadron, had gone out on patrol and had failed to come in. Long after dark their mechanics remained on the field pooping up Very lights, in the hope that they might still be searching about, trying to find their way. At last we abandoned all hope ourselves and waited for the morning's news from outside sources.

Now it had arrived and to my great joy it was in the form of a telephone call from old "Madam" Sherry himself. But his next message informed us that Nutt had been killed in combat! And Sherry himself had been through an experience that might easily have turned one's hair gray. Just before lunch time Sherry came in by automobile and told us the story of his experiences.

He and Nutt had attacked an overwhelming formation of eight Fokker machines. They had stolen up on the Heinies and counted upon getting one or two victims before the others were aware of their presence. But the attack failed and suddenly both American pilots were having the fight of their lives. The Hun pilots were not only skilful and experienced, but they worked together with such nicety that Sherry and Nutt were unable either to hold their own or to escape.

Soon each was fighting a separate battle against four enemy machines. Sherry saw Nutt go crashing down and later learned that he had been shot through the heart and killed in air. A moment later Sherry's machine received several bullets in the motor which put it immediately out of commission. Dropping swiftly to earth, Sherry saw that the Hun pilots were not taking any chances but were determined to kill him as he fell.

He was two miles and more in the air when he began his forced descent. All the way down the enemy pilots pursued him, firing through his machine continuously as it glided smoothly towards earth. Only by miracles a dozen times repeated did he escape death from their bullets. He saw the lines below him and made desperate efforts to glide his machine to our side of the fence despite the furious attempts of the Boches to prevent this escape. At last he crashed in one of the million shell-holes that covered No Man's Land of last week. His machine turned over and broke into a score of fragments, Sherry being thrown some yards away where he landed unhurt at the bottom of another shell-hole.

While he was still pinching himself to make sure he was actually unhurt he discovered his implacable enemies piquing upon him with their Fokkers and firing long bursts of bullets into his shell-hole with their machine-guns!

Sherry clung as closely to the sides of his hole as he could and watched the dirt fly up all around him as the Fokkers made dive after dive at him. It must have been like watching a file of executioners leveling their guns at one and firing dozens of rounds without hitting one. Except that in Sherry's case, it was machine-guns that were doing the firing!

Finally the Fokkers made off for Germany. Crawling out of his hole, Sherry discovered that a formation of Spads had come to his rescue and had chased the Germans homewards. And then he began to wonder on which side of the trenches he had fallen. For he had been too busy dodging Fokkers to know where his crippled machine was taking him.

One can imagine Sherry's joy when he heard a doughboy in perfectly good United States yell from a neighboring shell-hole:

"Hey guy! Where the h—'s your gas-mask?"

Madam didn't care for the moment whether he had a gas-mask or not, so glad was he to learn that he had fallen among friends and was still in the land of the living.

He quickly tumbled into the next shell-hole, where he found his new friend. The latter informed him that he was still in No Man's Land, that the German infantry were but a hundred yards away and that gas shells had been coming across that space all the afternoon. He even gave Madam his own gas-mask and his pistol, saying he guessed he was more used to gas than an aviator would be! He advised Sherry to lay low where he was until nightfall, when he would see him back into our lines. And thus Lieutenant Sherry spent the next few hours reviewing the strange episodes that flavor the career of an aviator.

Sherry finished his story with a grim recital of what had occurred when they went out next morning to recover Nutt's body. It too had fallen in No Man's Land, but the Americans had advanced a few hundred yards during the night and now covered the spot where Nutt's body lay. Sherry accompanied a squad of doughboys out to the spot where Nutt's smashed machine had lain during the night. They found poor Nutt, as I have said, with several bullets through the heart.

They extricated the body from the wreckage and were beginning to dig a grave when a shot from a hidden Hun sniper struck one of the burial party in the foot. The others jumped to their guns and disappeared through the trees. They soon returned with a look of savage satisfaction on their faces, although Sherry had not heard a shot fired. While they continued their work he strolled off in the direction from which they had returned.

Behind a trench dugout he found the German sniper who had had the yellowness to fire upon a burial party. The man's head was crushed flat with the butts of the doughboys' guns!

* ~ *

"Frank Luke, the marvelous balloon strafer of the 27th, did not return last night!"

So reads the last entry in my flight diary of September 29, 1918. Re-reading that line brings back to me the common anxiety of the whole

Group over the extraordinary and prolonged absence of their most popular member. For Luke's very mischievousness and irresponsibility made every one of us feel that he must be cared for and nursed back into a more disciplined way of fighting—and flying—and living. His escapades were the talk of the camp and the despair of his superior officers. Fully a month after his disappearance his commanding officer, Alfred Grant, Captain of the 27th Squadron, told me that if Luke ever did come back he would court-martial him first and then recommend him for the Legion of Honor!

In a word, Luke mingled with his disdain for bullets a very similar distaste for the orders of his superior officers. When imperative orders were given him to come immediately home after a patrol Luke would unconcernedly land at some French aerodrome miles away, spend the night there and arrive home after dark the next night. But as he almost invariably landed with one or two more enemy balloons to his credit, which he had destroyed on the way home, he was usually let off with a reprimand and a caution not to repeat the offense.

As blandly indifferent to reprimands as to orders, Luke failed to return again the following night. This studied disobedience to orders could not be ignored, and thus Captain Grant had stated that if Luke ever did return he must be disciplined for his insubordination. The night of September 27th Luke spent the night with the French Cigognes on the Toul aerodrome.

The last we had heard from Luke was that at six o'clock on the night of September 28th he left the French field where he had spent the night, and flying low over one of the American Balloon Headquarters he circled over their heads until he had attracted the attention of the officers, then dropped them a brief note which he had written in his aeroplane. As may well be imagined, Luke was a prime favorite with our Balloon Staff. All the officers of that organization worshiped the boy for his daring and his wonderful successes against the balloon department of their foes. They appreciated the value of balloon observation to the enemy and knew the difficulties and dangers in attacking these well-defended posts.

Running out and picking up the streamer and sheet of paper which fell near their office they unfolded the latter and read:

"Look out for enemy balloon at D-2 and D-4 positions.—Luke."

Already Luke's machine was disappearing in the direction of the first balloon which lay just beyond the Meuse. It was too dark to make out its dim outline at this distance, but as they all gathered about the front of their "office" they glued their eyes to the spot where they knew it hung. For Luke had notified them several times previously as to his intended victims and every time they had been rewarded for their watching.

Two minutes later a great red glow lit up the northwestern horizon and before the last of it died away the second German balloon had likewise burst into flames! Their intrepid hero had again fulfilled his promise! They hastened into their headquarters and called up our operations officer and announced Frank Luke's last two victories. Then we waited for Luke to make his dramatic appearance.

But Luke never came! That night and the next day we rather maligned him for his continued absence, supposing naturally enough that he had returned to his French friends for the night. But when no news of him came to us, when repeated inquiries elicited no information as to his movements after he had brought down his last balloon, every man in the Group became aware that we had lost the greatest airman in our army. From that day to this not one word of reliable information has reached us concerning Luke's disappearance. Not a single clue to his death and burial was ever obtained from the Germans! Like Guynemer, the miraculous airman of France, Frank Luke was swallowed by the skies and no mortal traces of him remain!

CHAPTER ELEVEN

December 7, 1941—
Eyewitness to Infamy

Official U.S. Navy Report Plus Eyewitness Account
Edited by Paul Joseph Travers

The expression "Where were you when . . . ?" has always been popular in American life. Today, you might be asked about 9/11, JFK's assassination, and others.

In the 1940s and into the 1950s, however, that question always revolved around a single subject. Where were you when Pearl Harbor was attacked?

Sunday, December 7, 1941, a day which President Franklin D. Roosevelt said will "live in infamy" when he addressed the nation that evening, is still an American icon. Film, books galore, anniversary remembrances—they all mark the day when the surprise attack woke up "a sleeping giant," as Japanese admiral Yamamoto described America's reaction.

There are so many varied descriptions of the action that took place on December 7, that the overall picture of what actually happened becomes blurred and fragmented. This official report from the U.S. Navy fills the need for an accurate and detailed summary of the attack on Pearl Harbor.

Somewhere in all the "facts" presented in the Navy report are the myriad acts of valor that took place that day, remembered in America's highest medals for bravery. Among those awarded the Navy's highest medal, the Navy Cross, Radioman Harry Mead recalls the action of December 7 as witnessed during the attack. He was stationed on Ford Island, when death and disaster were happening minute by minute in every direction, and when courage was as important as weapons.

THE BATTLE OF PEARL HARBOR: THE OFFICIAL ACCOUNT OF THE U.S. NAVY

On Oahu, 7 December 1941 began as another typical Sunday. It was the day of the week when military activities centered around relaxation and recreation. For military personnel, it was the time when the paradox of living in the Pacific became most evident. In this tropical paradise in the middle of the Pacific Ocean, they were preparing for a war that raged thousands of miles over the eastern and western horizons. In this island setting, it would have seemed more appropriate if the personnel were training to become tourists ready to embark on an extended vacation instead of a military campaign.

On military maps, the tiny island chain of Pearl Harbor appeared as an isolated, impenetrable fortress. The expanse of ocean surrounding the islands would certainly make it impossible for an enemy fleet to advance to them without being detected hundreds of miles at sea. Most Americans believed that their country's entrance into the global conflict would be by a formal declaration resulting from continued military aggression on the continents. Although Admiral Husband E. Kimmel, Commander in Chief, U.S. Fleet (CINCUS) and Commander in Chief, Pacific (CinCPac), warned of the possibility of a surprise air-raid attack, few people thought the Japanese had the capability to "pull it off." Most people believed that the Japanese would not attack any American forces without a formal declaration of war. The fact that Japan had attacked China in 1895 and Russia in 1904 without a formal declaration of war was dismissed as neither pertinent nor practicable. After all, this was the mid-twentieth century, and Japan was now a world power operating under the unwritten code of modern warfare. Surprisingly, no prominent U.S. military leaders excused the surprise attack on the grounds that Japan had violated its solemn agreement in the Hague Convention.

A factual narrative of the attack compiled from official navy files, military archives, congressional records, and other government sources provides insight into the immensity of death and destruction resulting from the air raid. The narrative is a list of cold, hard facts; it is a bookkeeper's ledger listing credits and debits, with a bottom line showing the losses sustained to personnel and equipment. As with any major battle, conflict, or disaster, in the Pearl Harbor attack the statistical data become the reference point to measure the total spectrum of human experiences, which gives the event its emotion, intensity, and meaning.

The U.S. Pacific Fleet

Contrary to initial reports coming from Pearl Harbor after the attack, the major part of the U.S. Pacific Fleet was not present there on 7 December 1941. A ship count showed that only about half of the fleet was anchored in the harbor. All three of the fleet aircraft carriers were elsewhere, but eight of the nine fleet battle ships were present at the time of the attack. Several ships were absent due to overhauls on the West Coast, while others were assigned to task forces on special missions.

A special task force under the command of Vice Admiral William F. Halsey on the USS *Enterprise* was about two hundred miles west of Hawaii en route to Pearl Harbor, after having delivered Marine Corps fighter planes to strengthen the defensive capability of Wake Island. The task force consisted of one aircraft carrier, three heavy cruisers, and nine destroyers. A second task force under the command of Rear Admiral J. H. Newton on the USS *Lexington* was about four hundred miles southeast of Midway, en route to deliver Marine Corps scout bombers. This task force was composed of one aircraft carrier, three heavy cruisers, and five destroyers. A third task force under the command of Vice Admiral Wilson Brown on the USS *Indianapolis* was deployed off Johnston Island to test a new type of landing craft. The task force consisted of one heavy cruiser, five destroyers, and a number of minesweepers.

In addition to these three task forces, two heavy cruisers were on convoy duty in Samoa and the Solomon Islands to protect commercial shipping to Australia, and one heavy cruiser and four destroyer mine-sweepers were conducting tactical exercises about twenty-five miles off the coast of Oahu. Two submarines were in the Midway Island area, and two others were near Wake Island. Other noncombat support ships, such as oil tankers, transports, and cargo vessels, were in transit between Hawaii and the West Coast. All ships at sea were on wartime alert and fully armed. The absence of this portion of the U.S. Pacific Fleet left the following ships in Pearl Harbor on 7 December:

eight battleships

two heavy cruisers

four ten-thousand-ton cruisers

two seven-thousand-ton cruisers

thirty destroyers

four submarines

one gunboat

nine minelayers

fourteen minesweepers

twenty-seven auxiliary vessels, such as repair ships, tenders, store ships, tugboats, and yard craft

All vessels at Pearl Harbor, except for those undergoing over haul at the Navy Yard, were in readiness condition three, as prescribed by fleet orders. This required one-quarter of the anti-aircraft batteries and their control stations to be in a ready status, with gun crews and ammunition at hand. All major combat ships were in condition "X," with two machine guns and two five-inch anti-aircraft guns in a ready status, with gun crews and ammunition at hand. In addition, all vessels were required to be on twelve-hour notice for getting underway for sea duty. The degree of closure for watertight doors and hatches was determined by the alphabet code for battle-ready status. Condition "X" was the minimum-readiness condition, whereas condition "Z" was the maximum-readiness condition, with full watertight integrity. Most of the ships in the harbor had been in port for at least a few days and were almost filled to capacity with fuel oil.

Reconnaissance

Although the high command at Pearl Harbor knew the need for aerial reconnaissance, the shortage of planes and personnel prevented commanders from establishing an effective reconnaissance system. It was estimated that a 360 degree patrol of the islands at a distance of eight hundred miles would require 84 planes on sixteen-hour flights. To perform such a patrol on a round-the-clock basis would require about 180 planes with accompanying crews. In December 1941, the planes and personnel were not available. Most of the aerial reconnaissance was conducted during combined training exercises and operations conducted by the army and navy. Other reconnaissance efforts were made by aircraft and destroyers deployed on anti-submarine searches, as well as by aircraft-carrier reconnaissance planes that escorted task forces leaving and entering Pearl Harbor. On the morning of 7 December, a small number of reconnaissance planes was in the air, and an equal number were on stand-by-ready status. Three patrol planes were scanning the fleet's operating areas, while three others remained grounded on thirty-minute notice. A submarine task force and four planes from Ford Island which were in the air took part in a joint exercise. Three Marine Corps/scout bombers at Ewa Field were on standby with two-hour notice, and 15 bombers and 15 utility planes were on standby with four-hour notice. Task forces at sea were conducting air and sea searches, as mandated by fleet orders.

High command decided that, with such a limited range for recon-naissance, the existing aerial reconnaissance was sufficient for the fleet and Oahu in a peacetime status. The belief prevailed that Japan's initial act of war would not be a surprise attack on Pearl Harbor. However, the Japanese high command was able to turn American deficiencies, miscon-ceptions, and speculative theories to its advantage, with devasting results.

Another form of aerial reconnaissance, which received considerable publicity and attention after the attack, was radar. Radar installations on the islands were considered in the experimental stage at the time of the attack. Although the navy was installing radar units as fast as they could be obtained, by the end of 1941 only a handful of ships were equipped with these long-range reconnaissance devices. At the same time, the army was in the process of installing three large field radar units, as well as six mobile units on trucks. The effectiveness of radar to detect moving objects depended on the height of both the installation and the target. Large ships in open water could be detected by shipboard radar units at a distance of twenty miles. Aircraft equipped with radar had a range of up to two hundred miles, depending on elevation.

The First Shot of the Battle

Although a number of U.S. ships claim to have fired the first shot of the Pearl Harbor attack, the distinction of having fired the first shot of the Battle of Hawaii and World War II belongs to the destroyer USS *Ward*.

At 3:45 a.m. on 7 December 1941, the minesweeper *Condor*, while making a routine sweep for magnetic mines off the channel entrance to Pearl Harbor, spotted a mysterious object riding in the water. A closer look through binoculars revealed the object to be a midget submarine. The submarine was trailing a large steel barge being towed by the minesweeper *Antares*, which was waiting for the anti-submarine net across the channel entrance to be opened. The *Condor*, equipped only for mine-sweeping, with no armament, notified the *Ward* by yardarm blinker: "Sighted submarine on westerly course speed five knots." The *Ward*, which was also on patrol duty in the area, proceeded to head on a course to cut off the submarine before she was able to make her way into the harbor. At 4:58, the submarine net gate opened to allow the *Condor* to enter the channel entrance. The net gate remained open until 6:30, when the *Antares* approached it. At this time, the unidentified submarine was spotted by the USS *Ward* and a PBY 14-P-1, which was conducting aerial reconnaissance. At 6:45, after sounding general quarters, the *Ward* opened fire on the submarine, which was operating in restricted waters. The first shot, fired by the number-one gun at a range of one hundred yards, missed its mark. The second shot, fired from the number-three gun, hit the coming tower, causing the submarine to submerge. Depth charges were then dropped over the site where the submarine was last seen. The submarine failed to surface and was believed to have been sunk. At 6:53, the *Ward* radioed the Fourteenth Naval District: "We have attacked, fired upon, and dropped depth charges upon a submarine operating in defensive sea area."

At 7:15, the USS *Ward*'s message, which had been delayed in decoding, was delivered in the duty officer of the Fourteenth Naval District. Minutes later, the same message was delivered to the duty officer, CinCPac. At 7:25, the destroyer Monaghan was ordered to get underway and investigate the submarine sighting reported by the USS *Ward*. At 7:41, CinCPac headquarters received the PBY 14-P-1 report about submarine activity off the channel entrance. Like the message delivered to the Fourteenth Naval District, this one was also delayed in decoding. The message had been logged with headquarters at 7:00. At 7:51, the Monaghan received her orders from the Fourteenth Naval District, which had been prepared at 7:25. At 7:55, the first wave of Japanese bombers made its appearance over Pearl Harbor. Another opportunity to alert the fleet was lost.

The Attack

The attack, which lasted an hour and fifty minutes, was carried out in four phases: 1) 7:45–8:25: concentrated attack by an estimated total of sixty-five torpedo planes, dive bombers, and horizontal bombers; 2) 8:25–8:40: lull in the attack and sporadic bombing and strafing runs by an estimated fifteen dive bombers; 3) 8:40–9:15: concentrated attack by an estimated total of thirty horizontal bombers and eighteen dive bombers; 4) 9:15–9:45: bombing and strafing runs by an estimated twenty-seven dive bombers; after this last attack, all planes in the area around Hawaii returned to their carriers.

Phase 1

As the preparatory signal for morning colors was being hoisted, Japanese bombers made a sudden appearance over Pearl Harbor, flying low and fast over Merry Point Landing toward Ford Island. Within seconds, nine dive bombers hit the Naval Air Station on Ford Island. Although damage to the station was not total, thirty-three of seventy navy planes parked on runways and near hangars were destroyed or severely damaged. No further attacks were directed at Ford Island, except for a direct hit on a hangar by a bomb that had been intended for the USS *California*, but fell short of its target. At almost the same time that bombs fell on Ford Island, air bases at Eva, Hickam, Wheeler, Bellows, and Kaneohe were subject to dive-bomber attacks and strafing runs. Within the first minutes of the attack, seven formidable air bases were neutralized. During and after the attack, only a token air force was able to resist the Japanese bombers or follow them out to sea on their return trip to their carriers. Although the initial attack came as a total surprise, defensive actions and maneuvers were immediate. Battleship machine guns opened fire immediately, and within five minutes nearly all anti-aircraft batteries were in action. Cruiser anti-aircraft batteries were in action within four minutes and were fired within seven minutes.

Although Pearl Harbor was hit first by dive bombers, torpedo planes inflicted the major damage during the attack's first phase. The planes launched their payloads from as low as fifty feet. The harbor's shallow water presented no obstacle because the torpedoes had been specially fitted with wooden fins to compensate for water depth. The torpedo planes made four separate attacks during this first phase. Their flight path brought them in over the southeast corner of the tank farm near Merry Point Landing and down on the decks of the ships at Battleship Row. During this phase, all outboard ships on Battleship Row received torpedo hits. The battleships USS *Arizona*, *Oklahoma*, *Nevada*, and *West Virginia* were hit first and either sunk or severely damaged.

The *Arizona* was immediately knocked out of the action. After she took several torpedoes and bombs, a higher-level bomber fired a bomb that hit near her number-two turret, which blew up her forward magazines. The ship went down so fast she did not have time to roll over on her side. Within a minute of that explosion, over one thousand men lost their lives. In the second torpedo plane attack, the *Oklahoma* took three hits and tilted to a list of 20 to 25 degrees. As the ship began to slowly roll over, men started to scramble over her starboard side. The ship continued to roll over until her masts hit bottom and stopped her roll at about 150 degrees. Many of the survivors from the *Oklahoma* made it safely to the decks of the *Maryland*, which was inboard of her. The *Maryland* escaped with relatively little damage, in comparison with the rest of the battleships. She took one bomb on the forecastle and an armor-piercing one on a hold. Her position on the inside saved her from torpedo bombers.

During the third attack in phase one, the *West Virginia* took heavy bomb and torpedo hits. The ship took so many torpedo hits that a couple passed through holes made by the first hits. One hit knocked off her rudder, which was later picked up from the harbor bottom. When a large fire broke out amidship, word was given to abandon ship. Also in the third attack, one plane flew in from the west to hit the cruiser *Helena* and the minelayer *Oglala*, both of which were at the Ten-Ten Dock. One torpedo passed beneath the outboard *Oglala* and detonated against the side of the *Helena* , buckling the side plates of the *Oglala*. Submersible pumps from the *Helena* were useless because her engineering plant had been damaged from the torpedo hit. Another bomb dropped between the two ships at around 8:00 resulted in a *Oglala*'s loss of power. With the aid of a tug and a motor launch, the *Oglala* was moved away from the *Helena* and secured behind her at the Ten Ten Dock. By 10:00, the *Oglala* had taken on so much water that she rolled over.

The fourth attack came from a wave of enemy bombers which came in over Pearl City and the Middle Lock and hit the ships moored on the opposite side of Ford Island, directly across from Battleship Row. This side of the island was the berthing place for aircraft carriers when they were in port. On this Sunday, the seaplane tender *Tangier*, the target ship

Utah, and the light cruisers *Raleigh* and *Detroit* were in their spaces. The *Detroit* and *Tangier* escaped torpedo damage, but the *Raleigh* suffered one hit and the *Utah* suffered two hits. When the *Raleigh* began to roll over, her crew put out extra lines to the quays and held her upright until the attack was over. To keep the ship upright in the water, the crew threw overboard aircraft, lockers, and any other items fastened to the ship. The *Utah*, which from the air resembled an aircraft carrier because of her concrete decks for target practice, drew the attention of Japanese pilots. After two torpedo hits, the ship began to list rapidly to port; she capsized at 8:13.

By 8:25, most of the torpedo damage to the fleet had been inflicted. All the outboard battleships along Battleship Row had received at least one direct hit from the bombing runs. The *Arizona* was a raging inferno threatening her sister ships; the stern of the *California* was on the harbor floor; the *West Virginia* was gradually sinking to the bottom; and the *Oklahoma* was in the process of rolling over. Only the *Nevada*, which had received one torpedo hit, was able to begin preparations to get underway.

Phase Two

The second phase has been termed a lull because it marked a distinctive break in between major attacks by the Japanese. During this phase, attacking aircraft made a series of sporadic bombing runs over the harbor. An estimated fifteen dive bombers participated in five attacks on ships in the Navy Yard, the *Maryland*, *Oklahoma*, and Nevada, and cruisers and destroyers anchored in various parts of the harbor. At 8:32, the *Oklahoma* capsized. Although the yard craft and other small vessels assisted the damaged ships, the larger ships in the harbor moved very little. The major action during this phase took place in the channel between Ford Island and Pearl City, where a midget submarine was sunk. The destroyer *Monaghan* was moving out of the East Loch when she passed between the *Tangier* and the seaplane tender *Curtiss* as the Japanese were firing on a midget sub that had surfaced in the harbor. The Monaghan put on flank speed, rammed the sub, and dropped two depth charges. Then the Monaghan headed out to sea, followed by the destroyer *Henley*.

Phase Three

The third phase began with the appearance of eight groups of high-altitude bombers that crossed and recrossed the harbor. Their altitude of about ten thousand feet prevented them from causing any major damage. Bombs converted from fifteen- and sixteen-inch artillery shells were dropped along Battleship Row and the Navy Yard. The *California* was hit by a fifteen-inch shell equipped with tail vanes, which penetrated to the second deck and exploded, causing a major fire. The main deck of the Curtiss was hit with a bomb, which killed twenty men and injured fifty-eight others. While bombers converged on their primary targets, numerous ships began to make their way out of the harbor. The tanker *Neosho*, which had just delivered part of her load of aviation fuel to Ford Island, pulled out between the *California* on one side and the *Maryland* and the *Oklahoma* on the other and made her way to Merry Point Landing. At the same time, the repairship Vestal, which had been bombed, and then set on fire from the *Arizona*'s burning oil fires, started to get underway, but was beached near Aiea Point when she started to sink. A few destroyers from the East Loch and a couple of cruisers from the Navy Yard also began to make their way out of the harbor. The *Nevada*, which was anchored at the northern end of Battleship Row, behind the *Arizona*, cleared her berth at 8:40 and steamed toward the harbor entrance while under attack from a determined group of dive bombers. With her bridge and superstructure in flames, she continued to make her way down the harbor channel. When Admiral William R. Furlong, aboard the *Oglaga*, feared that her sinking would block the harbor entrance, he ordered that she be deliberately grounded at Waipio Point, with the assistance of two tug boats. On the Navy Yard side of the channel, the destroyer Shaw, which was berthed in Floating Dry Dock Number Two, received a bomb hit possibly intended for the *Nevada*. The resulting fire eventually destroyed her forward magazines and produced one of the most spectacular explosions seen during the attack. In Floating Dry Dock Number One at the Navy Yard, the U.S. Pacific Fleet flagship, the USS *Pennsylvania*, as well as the destroyers *Cassin* and *Downes*, sat high and dry on keel blocks. Soon after the USS *Shaw* blew up, a bomb hit between the *Cassin* and the *Downes*, rupturing their oil tanks and causing a raging fire, which forced the crews to abandon them. At this time, the *Pennsylvania* was hit amidships by a heavy bomb, and her captain ordered the dry dock flooded in order to extinguish the fires around the *Cassin* and *Downes*. As the water level in the dry dock rose, the burning oil on the surface engulfed the ships. The heat became so intense that it set off the magazines in both destroyers, causing an explosion, which tumbled over the *Cassin* and onto the *Downes*.

Phase Four

During the fourth and final phase of the attack, an estimated twenty-seven dive bombers conducted nine strafing attacks throughout the harbor. The attacks were aimed at the nearby airfields with their remaining aircraft, and rescue workers who were assisting the disabled fleet were caught in the open. By 9:45, the last attack planes left the harbor area and returned to their carriers. The burning wreckage in the harbor and on the airfields reflected the losses in personnel and equipment. When finally tabulated on paper, the losses were worse than originally estimated immediately following the attack. In Pearl Harbor, eighteen war ships had been sunk or severely damaged. The navy lost ninety-two aircraft, including five from the carrier *Enterprise*, and had thirty-one damaged. The army lost ninety-six aircraft. The army and navy dead numbered 2,251, and almost half had been on the sunken *Arizona*. The navy listed 2,036 killed in action or fatally wounded and 759 wounded in action; the army listed 215 killed in action or fatally wounded, 360 wounded in action, and 22 missing in action. These were the figures given before the Joint Congressional Investigating Committee on 15 November 1945.

Eyewitness Account from Ford Island
By Harry Mead

Conveniently located in the center of Pearl Harbor, Ford Island was the geographical hub for the air and sea traffic of the U.S. Pacific Fleet. The island, which was large enough to accommodate an airfield, primarily served to receive aircraft carrier planes and to operate and maintain them while they were in port. The air base was also headquarters for PBY navy patrol planes and Utility Squadron One. The latter was responsible for miscellaneous duties, such as delivering mail, towing targets, and aerial photography.

Ford Island proved an ideal location for both planes and ships. Being in almost direct alignment with the channel entrance to Pearl Harbor, it offered easily accessible berthing space to larger ships, which had limited mobility and maneuverability. Just offshore of Ford Island, quays, or tiny concrete islands, provided much-needed deep-water anchorage. The docking arrangements called for battleships to the north east of Ford Island, and carriers to its northwest side. Even with the carrier force away from Pearl Harbor on the weekend of 7 December, space was at a premium. On Ford Island's northwest side, the cruisers *Detroit* and *Raleigh*, the former battleship turned target ship *Utah*, and the seaplane tender *Tangier* took up temporary residence. On the island's north east side stood the pride of the U.S. Pacific Fleet: Battleship Row. Lined up in a tight formation side by side were the *Nevada*, *Arizona*, *Tennessee*, *West Virginia*, *Maryland*, *Oklahoma* and the *California*. Also in or near this group of battleships were the *Vestal*, *Neosho* and *Avocet*.

Like other airfields on Oahu, Ford Island was one of the first targets for the original wave of Japanese dive bombers. Within minutes of the first round of bombs, the capacity of the air base at Ford Island to mount an aerial counterattack was destroyed. Those planes not destroyed by bombs and secondary explosions were chopped to pieces by continued strafing from enemy planes that swept over the island and dropped their payloads. Ford Island was even subject to attack by torpedo bombers. Numerous torpedoes that passed under their floating targets ended stuck in the muddy banks along the island's perimeter.

During and after the first wave of attack planes, men on the island prepared for what they thought would be a continued attack to finish off the rest of the fleet. Salvaging anything useful from the debris of the planes and hangars, they quickly worked to set up makeshift machine-gun emplacements and anti-aircraft fortifications. The lull between attacks was a chance to catch their breath and appraise the fate of the fleet. The view from Ford Island was anything but encouraging. Around the island was a panorama of sinking and burning ships against a background of fire and smoke. Because the backbone of the U.S. Pacific Fleet had been crushed and shattered, many on the island concluded that the rest of the fleet suffered a similar fate. Many had thought that Ford Island would be the last stronghold against a Japanese invasion force.

Immediately after the second attack, forces throughout the island regrouped for another air attack and a possible invasion by an amphibious assault force. Priorities were to assess the damage to the fleet and the ground forces and to locate and chart the movement of the Japanese attack fleet. The few remaining operational aircraft were pressed into service for aerial patrol and reconnaissance. On Ford Island, the only available planes were a few unarmed amphibians. Due to the large number of casualties suffered at the larger airfields, crews to fly the planes were as scarce as the planes themselves. Therefore, personnel were grouped together to get the planes airborne. For Radioman Second Class Harry Mead, being assigned to fly on a search mission offered the chance to see the devastation of Pearl Harbor from the ground and the air.

Seven December 1941 was a "duty day" for me. I was scheduled to relieve the supervisor of the watch in our utility wing base radio station that morning. I had showered and shaved the evening before. After I rolled out of the sack, I proceeded to the combination washroom and head to complete the usual morning ablutions. After dressing, I went down to the mess hall on the first deck of our barracks building and ate breakfast. (I really have no positive recall of this, but it was my usual routine before going to the hangar.) Finishing breakfast, I strolled leisurely down to our corrugated-sheet-steel hangar and mustered with the Duty Section.

I was twenty years old and finishing up a minority enlistment. I had joined the navy on 25 January 1939, six months after graduating from high school. My main reason for joining was to circumvent what I thought was harsh parental rule; and to go to radio school so I could learn to copy Morse code well enough to pass the Federal Communications Commission amateur radio license exam. Upon graduating from "boot camp" at Newport, Rhode Island, Naval Training Center, I was retained on board to help train two successive companies of recruits. In June 1939, after receiving an interview for suitability, I was transferred to the Naval Training Command, Norfolk, Virginia, as an applicant for Anticipher School (Radio). Graduation from this school in October 1939 found me scanning the "new assignments" (transfer) list. Before I knew it, I was bound for an old World War I, flush-deck, four-piper tin can in red-lead row in the Philly Navy Yard. Subsequently, the ship to which I was assigned was traded to the British and became the HMS *Churchill* (previously, USS *Herndon*). Through a fluke of fate, I was transferred to the West Coast to another destroyer (USS *Cushing*) in September 1940. By this time I had advanced in rating to radioman third class. Shortly after reporting aboard the *Cushing*, we departed for Pearl Harbor. My life aboard destroyers was miserable—the one feature of navy life I failed to consider before joining was seasickness. And I had a chronic case of it. In July 1941, I was transferred to Utility Squadron One (USS *Rigel*), based at Ford Island. I had to agree to extend my enlistment for two years to get this new assignment. It was worth it. No more seasickness, and I've never been bothered with airsickness.

The duty section mustered at 7:30 a.m. on the hangar deck. After mustering, my watch-stander and I walked over to the "radio shack" to relieve the watch. I had been promoted to radioman second class while aboard the Cushing and thus qualified for supervisor of the watch in the Ut Wing Base Radio Station. We relieved the watch at precisely 7:45 and were "briefed" on the previous nights messages, etc. As I recall, it had been a "dead evening" for the off-going watch.

Our base radio station was located in the southwest corner of the hangar that was closest to the new, concrete-reinforced operations building. We had an old National HRO receiver, on which we monitored the international distress frequency of five hundred kilohertz, and some other equipment used to communicate with our own aircraft, plus a teletype hooked up with CinCPac head quarters and an old wire telegraph system that was also linked to CinCPac and, I believe, to our sister squadron, VJ-2, across the field.

Prior to 7 December, CinCPac had issued an order that made it mandatory to tune in on nine hundred kilohertz in the event of an air raid in order to receive modulated continuous wave broadcasts in Morse code from CinCPac headquarters. It was customary for us to undergo periodic mock air attacks by some of the army aviation units stationed on Oahu in those days.

At 7:55 a.m. on 7 December, I heard a plane starting a power dive and immediately thought, "Oh shit! Another mock air raid. Well, I'll go outside and have a look." I opened the door leading out to the tarmac, where our planes sat in two rows, and gazed skyward towards the northwest. A plane resembling a P40 was in a dive and headed straight for the PBY hangars at the south end of Ford Island. I saw something drop off the plane and thought, "Hell! He's dropped a piece of cowling off his plane. Some mech is gonna catch hell for that." All of a sudden there was a tremendous explosion and water spewed upward like a geyser. It slowly dawned on me that the pilot had dropped a live bomb. "Boy! Now somebody's really gonna get it," I thought. The second plane corrected his dive and dropped his bomb in the middle of a row of parked PBYs. The hangar was at a sufficient distance from me and the blast so deflected that I felt no concussion. Fortunately for the personnel in that area, a new drainage ditch was being dug around the perimeter of the airfield. The hangar doors were only open about five feet, but it seemed as though forty or fifty men came running through them in less than a minute and dove into the ditch. A chief petty officer standing near me uttered an oath and said, "Those planes have the Japanese insignia. Them — bastards are bombing us!"

With that, I dashed back into the radio room and immediately set up nine hundred kilohertz on one of the available receivers. I remember portions of a message being sent concerning reports "that Japanese paratroopers are landing on Barber's Point." Later it was learned that it was one Jap pilot who had bailed out of his damaged plane.

By this time dense clouds of black smoke from burning oil in the harbor were drifting up into the sky. The noise of the bombs and torpedoes was terrible. To say that I was scared would be an understatement. I was terrified. Soon, the duty messenger came in and said, "The officer of the day says for everyone to take cover in the Operations Building."

I turned to my watch-stander, "Come on, let's get the hell outta here."

We ran over to the Operations Building with a group of other men and crouched in a stairwell, fearing the worst. I had no sooner found a spot than the messenger came by and said, "The officer of the day wants you in the radio room right away. He didn't mean for you to leave."

I got up, made my way past all the guys in the stairwell, and made a mad dash for the hangar. About halfway there, I looked up and saw a Jap plane making a pass on Battleship Row. His machine guns were winking at me, and I could see little chips of cement flying up in the air and they appeared to be heading straight for me as I ran. Just as I figured I had run out of luck, I came abreast of a four-by-four weapons carrier (truck) parked nose-in toward the hangar. Crouching down by the front bumper, I waited for the plane to pass overhead. Once it was gone, I continued to the radio room.

Inside, the officer of the day was waiting and told me, "Send a message to Maui [our other squadron, VJ-3, was located there] and tell them we're under attack. Tell 'em to take evasive action by rolling some gasoline drums out on the runway."

"Aye, Aye, Sir," I replied and set to the task. All the time I was transmitting the message (in Morse code), I could hear the rat-a-tat-tat of the bullets strafing the hangar. Apparently most of them could not penetrate the walls and roof, because of the corrugated exterior, and flew off into space.

By this time our leading chief of the radio gang had returned from shore leave and had gathered most of the radiomen in the radio room.

"I want three volunteers. You, you, and you!" he said, pointing to me and two others.

"But Chief—I've got the duty. I'm supervisor of the watch," I replied.

"I'll relieve you! Get out there and man your plane."

So that's how I got airborne that day. Our planes were rather old, Sikorsky JRS-1s. A twin-engine, parasol-wing amphibian—it was a non-combatant type of aircraft used for photographing fleet battle practice, towing targets, and carrying mail personnel. Someone gave us three Springfield rifles for defensive weapons, and we proceeded to get airborne. Our takeoff coincided with the lull between the first and second waves of attacking Jap planes.

Our pilot set a course to the south of Oahu, as ordered, and we flew a typical pre-sector search pattern looking for the Japanese fleet. Our sector was three hundred miles out, fifty miles across, and three hundred miles back to base. We didn't see a darn thing, but halfway through the mission I intercepted a message from "Benny" Benefield, in one of the other planes: "Under attack by Japanese Zero X Posn Lat (?) Long (?)." I figured, "There goes my ole liberty buddy." As luck would have it, Benny's plane emerged unscathed. Apparently the Jap was out of ammo or his guns were jammed. Upon our return to base, as we flew over Pearl Harbor in the landing pattern, the view of the harbor was horrendous. Billowing clouds of dense black smoke climbed high into the sky. Fire fighters and damage-control parties swarmed over the burning ships trying to establish order out of utter chaos. It was the most heartbreaking sight I've ever seen: our navy a shambles! The decks of the *Arizona* were awash, and Old Glory hung limp and bedraggled just barely above the water at her stern.

We landed (I don't recall the time) in the late afternoon. Almost immediately, we were put to work belting ammunition. During my absence on the search mission, machine-gun tripods had been fashioned from angle iron, sandbag emplacements had sprung up around the perimeter of the landing field, and there was a rather hushed sense of urgency and dogged determination in the air. Everyone expected another attack. We all believed that the rumor of troop ships was valid and we were bent on preparing for the worst. Invasion!

Just after dusk I was standing near one of the machine-gun emplacements. Heel-and-toe watches were in force around the perimeter of the airfield. Everyone just seemed to be waiting for the inevitable: another attack. Suddenly, in the distance came the drone of planes. We all strained to determine from which direction the sound was coming. In a very short time we made out a single plane, in the normal landing pattern, coming in for a landing. Without warning, a gunner opened up with a machine gun; tracer bullets arced toward the plane. Before you could bat an eyelash, every gun in the harbor was firing. Tracers were going every which way. Our officer of the day was having a fit running up and down the area yelling, "Cease-fire! Cease-fire! They're friendlies. Ceasefire!" All to no avail. No one could hear him for the noise of the guns. I understand one of the planes crashed near the Pearl City Tavern—a favorite hangout of some of our crew. It was learned later that they had shot down three F-4Fs from the USS *Enterprise*.

I was still wearing the enlisted white working uniform that I had donned that morning. It would be three days before I was to receive permission to leave the area and go to the barracks for a shower, shave, and fresh clothing.

Our water mains to Ford Island had been ruptured during the bombings and torpedo attacks on the battleships. Somehow they brought potable water over from the mainland in a small tank trailer for drinking purposes.

From here on my memory is not nearly so vivid. I only remember vignettes: the *Nevada* being run aground in the edge of channel to prevent her sinking and blocking the channel; an anti-aircraft battery of the USS *Curtis* getting a direct hit on a Jap torpedo plane; the USS *Solace* being towed away from over a Japanese midget two-man sub hovering neath her hull; a barge crane dropping steel netting over the sub and then raising her with the grappling hooks by the tail like a big fish; sleeping anywhere as time permitted. These things all have a tendency to run together in my mind, with no cognizance as to time of day or whether it was 7, 8, or 9 December. The passage of time dims the past. The other day I happened across the post card we were issued to send to our families right after the attack-it was preprinted with a place for check marks and room for two or three lines of text. I wrote: "Am okay, unhurt, will write when I can." I'm glad I was there, but I hope I never go through another similar incident.

On 21 March 1942, at mail call, I received a letter from my dad with a news clipping from our hometown paper (the *Bucyrus Telegraph Forum*). He kind of admonished me for not telling him about the news item in the clipping. It seems I had been awarded the Navy Cross for my actions during the attack on Pearl Harbor.

"Boy! What a joke," I thought. Apparently the public information officer of the Navy Department released the information before it became known officially in CinCPac headquarters in Pearl Harbor. I treated the entire incident as a hilarious joke, never realizing it would come true several weeks later.

On 7 April 1942, I was up on the wing of my assigned aircraft, in the hangar, restringing an antenna. We were going through a routine

120-hour check. One of the yeoman came out of the personnel office and yelled up at me.

"Hey, Mead, you gotta clean suit of whites in your locker?" "Yeah," I replied. "Why, do they want me to go into town and buy some parts?"

"No," he answered, "they want you over on the *Nevada* at 2:00 p.m. Admiral Nimitz is gonna pin the Navy Cross on you!" He then proceeded to tell me that our commissioned officer would like to ride over to the Navy Yard in my car with me. Our commissioned officer at that time was Commander Paul B. Tuzo, a tall, sparse gentleman, whom I knew by name only.

We rode the officer's motor launch from the Naval Air Station landing to the hospital landing. My car was parked in the hospital parking lot. On our drive over to the Navy Yard, the commissioned officer began relating how I should stand at attention, and after the presentation shake hands with the admiral, back step one pace, salute then about-face, and return to ranks.

The award recipients gathered on the quarter-deck of the USS *Nevada* and assembled in two ranks of twelve individuals. Directly, Admiral Nimitz and his retinue arrived and the ceremony commenced. The sun shone brightly, and a slight breeze furled and unfurled the signal flags hanging from the yardarms in a lazy, lackadaisical manner. When it came my turn, I approached the admiral, saluted smartly, and stood at rigid attention. He pinned the Navy Cross on the left breast of my jumper and grasped my hand. As we shook hands, I stared straight ahead, my eyes riveted to a distant cloud formation. I heard the admiral say, "Look at me, boy!" I shifted my gaze to those cool, pale-blue, penetrating eyes, and the twinkle there seemed to say, "Well done, lad, well done!" I thought later that the commissioned officer had coached me well, except for telling me where to look.

CHAPTER TWELVE

Legacy of Valor

Iwo Jima and John Basilone
James H. Hallas

Not far from my home in New Jersey, the tiny town of Raritan sits astride the river for which it is named. A new bridge over that river was opened in 2015, and it is called the John Basilone Veterans Memorial Bridge in honor of the hero who grew up in Raritan and is now a legend in books and in the highly regarded TV series "The Pacific."

Called "Manila John" after he enlisted in the Army and served in the Philippines, Basilone was bored by civilian life after his enlistment ended in 1938. In 1940, he joined the Marines because he thought they could help him get back to his beloved Manila. Instead, he was with the 1st Marine Division when it landed at Guadalcanal early in WWII. He was awarded the Medal of Honor for his bravery in the savage fighting there.

Blessed with movie star good looks and a winning personality, Basilone agreed to serve the war effort with a stateside tour promoting war bonds. He met a Marine lady sergeant, Lena Riggi, fell in love, and was married. He could have spent the entire rest of the war training Marines at stateside locations, but that was not to be. His persistent efforts to get back into combat resulted in his being assigned to the machine gun platoon of the 5th Marine Division. When they hit the beach at Iwo Jima in February 1945, Basilone's unit came under murderous fire from machine gun and mortar nests around Mount Suribachi. He was killed leading his own squad against entrenched positions near the airfield on the first day of the fighting. He was posthumously awarded the Navy Cross.

John Basilone did not have to be at Iwo Jima. He had already been awarded the nation's highest medal for bravery. At Guadalcanal he had taken on wave after wave of Japanese troops about to overrun his small unit's position. He was fighting with a machine gun, sometimes actually cradling the gun in his arms, with severe burns. He and a couple of other men from his platoon were the only survivors. Surely, a grateful nation could not ask for brave service beyond that.

John Basilone saw things differently. He was a fighting man who wanted to be in the action. That desire took him to Iwo Jima, and he fell there, along with 6,800 Marines killed, 26,000 wounded, in the bloodiest battle in Marine Corps history.

Basilone's widow, Lena, had to be sedated when she got the word that he was killed in action. She never remarried, and after passing in 1999 she was buried with her wedding ring still on her finger.

Today, when I stand beside the John Basilone bridge outside Raritan, over the peaceful and lovely Raritan River, surrounded by beautiful woodlands that are part of the Duke Estate, I find myself struck with a vision of a day back when Basilone was touring on his war bond effort. Nearby, the old bridge is still there, a tiny rusting thing where two of today's cars could not pass each other. John Basilone no doubt swam in the pools under this bridge, and fished in the tranquil waters. On the day I have in mind, Basilone's war bond tour was a tribute to his service. Some 20,000 people were there to honor his service and help with the war bond effort. 20,000. His heart must have swelled with great pride over the turnout.

It is difficult indeed to stand there by the old rusting bridge, the bridge John Basilone and his friends and neighbors actually used, without thinking of the wish of every Marine, Semper Fi.

February 17: The Invasion Force

Saturday, February 17, 1945, dawned clear off Iwo Jima. The seas rolled with a slight swell, while the low ceiling and intermittent squalls of the previous day had lifted, promising good visibility for aerial target spotters.

As the sun emerged on the eastern horizon, sailors aboard the great naval armada gathered offshore saw Mount Suribachi beginning to take shape, looming 550 feet over the southern tip of the pork chop–shaped land mass. The entire island was only 4.5 miles long and 2–5 miles wide at its broadest, a miserable place reeking of rotten eggs from the sulfur fumes wafting from cracks in the heated rock. To Suribachi's right stretched the two miles of beach where the 4th and 5th Marine Divisions were scheduled to land forty-eight hours later, hedged in on the right by rising cliffs that held the threat of enfilade. Black volcanic sand rose in a series of terraces behind the beaches to Iwo's airfields and an ominous interior, where 22,000 Japanese waited in pillboxes, blockhouses, tunnels, and holes, or sweltered in underground caverns carved from the soft rock.

It was for this forsaken hunk of rock and ash—dubbed "Sulfur Island" by its defenders, by virtue of its noxious emanations—that 495 ships crewed by thousands of sailors and carrying 70,000 U.S. Marines had crossed seemingly endless miles of ocean. The horizon was crowded with ships: hulking battleships dedicated to shore bombardment, agile destroyers, cruisers and aircraft carriers, and a multitude of smaller craft, each with a task to perform in that most intricate of military dances—an amphibious landing on a defended shore.

Planners had divided the 3,500 yards of shoreline extending from Suribachi to the Eastern Boat Basin on the right into 500-yard segments coded by color, from left to right: Green, Red 1 and 2, Yellow 1 and 2, and Blue 1 and 2. The 5th Marine Division would land over the three beaches on the left; the 4th Marine Division would land on the three beaches to the right. If all went according to plan, there would be 8,000 men on the beach within the first hour, 30,000 by nightfall. The 4th Division was a veteran outfit, having participated in combat at Roi-Namur, Saipan, and Tinian. The 5th Division had never fought together as a unit, but contained a large number of combat veterans, many of them culled from the disbanded Paramarine and Marine Raider outfits. The Marines were told it would take an estimated three to five days of fighting to secure the island. Some of them may even have believed it.

February 19: To the Beach at Iwo Jima

The assault troops were up and starting breakfast at about 0300, reveille in the crowded troop compartments consisting of "no bugle call," recalled Pvt. Allen R. Matthews, "but the turning on of lights and the cry, 'Hit the deck! Hit the deck!'" Breakfast consisted of the traditional steak and eggs. There were the usual jokes about being fattened up for the slaughter, but the laughter was a bit forced. The food was eaten standing up. Many men found themselves with little appetite.

The transports were in position by 0630. The bombardment began ten minutes later. At 0645 Adm. Kelly Turner ordered, "Land the Landing Force," and Marines began the process of boarding their amtracs. Many descended to the lower decks of LSTs to board the amphibious tractors, waiting in clouds of exhaust for the bow doors to open and disgorge them into the sea. Others, less fortunate, had to climb over the side and down cargo nets to the bobbing tractors. "The water was rough, and we were tossed and slammed against the side of the ship while climbing down the nets to the landing craft," recalled twenty-three-year-old Cpl. Edward D. Burow, a veteran of Guadalcanal. "Many men were injured trying to jump down into the landing craft. I remember most of the Marines were violently sick from the motion of the landing craft bouncing in the rough sea, and the black, noxious fumes from the engines that just made matters worse. I remember thinking that this was a hell of a way for some of us to spend the last moments of our lives, throwing up and violently ill."

The first three waves were boated and circling at the Line of Departure, two miles offshore, by 0815. At 0830 the Central Control Vessel dipped her pennant and the first wave of armored amtracs headed for Iwo's smoking shore, followed by a second wave of LVTs carrying 1,360 assault troops. Eight more waves began to form up behind them, scheduled to land at five-minute intervals. On the inside ramp of one landing craft, the last thing the occupants would see before it crashed down on the beach, someone had painted, "Too Late to Worry."

THE JOHN BASILONE STORY

The landing was only hours old when word began to circulate among disbelieving Marines clinging to isolated shell holes and ruined enemy pillboxes amid the rain of enemy fire: "John Basilone is dead." If anyone still needed a reminder of the peril, this was it—for if Gunnery Sgt. John Basilone could be killed, then no one was immune to sudden death.

When "Manila John" Basilone joined the 5th Marine Division in January 1944, he was already a national hero, entitled to wear the starred ribbon of the Medal of Honor, his face familiar to millions of Americans from newspaper and magazine photos. He could have sat out the war basking in public adulation. Instead, he ended up wading to his death through the volcanic ash of Iwo Jima. And he was there by choice.

Born November 4, 1916, in Buffalo, New York, Johnny Basilone grew up with ten brothers and sisters in a two-bedroom duplex on the wrong side of the tracks in Raritan, New Jersey. His father, Salvatore, was a tailor who had emigrated from Italy in 1902 in search of a better life. "Dad worked seventy hours a week as a tailor in his own business in Somerville to put food on the table," recalled John's younger sister, Mary. "Once he made our family doctor a fancy overcoat in return for John and me to have our tonsils out. Counting my grandmother, he had thirteen mouths to feed."

Friends later recalled Johnny as a good-natured cut-up, a jug-eared mop-top who wasn't above stealing apples or saving himself a dime by sneaking into the downtown movie theater. "People often ask me what kind of person Johnny was when he was growing up," said Mary Basilone. "I tell them he was a happy-go-lucky kid who wanted to sing opera. He had a twinkle in his eye that the nuns at our school loved. He knew all the operas and he'd sing them to my mother while she was cooking."

Not much of a student, and with the Basilone family facing hard times, John quit school at age fifteen after finishing the eighth grade at St. Bernard's parochial. The nuns might have enjoyed the twinkle in his eye, but the departure of the high-spirited youth with the wide grin probably came as something of a relief. Johnny Basilone had tended to resist the discipline of the classroom and his lowest marks were always in "conduct." His eighth-grade yearbook listed his hobby as "chewing gum," his life's ambition to be "an opera singer," and his current status as "the most talkative boy" in his class.

Freed from academia, Basilone found work as a caddy at the Raritan Valley Country Club for forty cents a day. When winter arrived, he got a job working on a laundry truck—then lost it when the boss caught him napping on a pile of clothes. One night in 1934, sitting around the family dinner table, he announced, "I'm joining the army." The decision changed his life. During a three-year hitch that took him to the Philippines, he fell in love with Manila and the girls and the good times in the bars along Dewey Boulevard. Along the way, he did some middleweight boxing and became an expert in the workings of the .30-caliber water-cooled Browning heavy machine gun.

When his enlistment was up in 1938, Basilone returned to Raritan, where he worked for a year as a laborer at the Calco Chemical plant. He then moved in with his sister in Reisterstown, Maryland, and got a job installing propane gas tanks. Bored silly, in July 1940 he quit his job and enlisted in the Marine Corps, with the idea that he would get back to his beloved Manila more quickly with the Marines. Tough guy that he was, he couldn't bring himself to tell his mother he had reenlisted—his father had to break the news for him, his sister recalled.

A return to Manila was not to be, but Basilone's incessant tales about his previous tour of duty in the Philippines quickly earned him the nickname "Manila John" among his Marine buddies. "You would have thought he was the mayor of Manila," remarked one Marine of Basilone's nostalgic stories. By 1942 when the 1st Marine Division landed on Guadalcanal, Basilone was serving as a sergeant in the heavy weapons company of the 7th Marines. He was very good at his job. "He was absolutely a genius with machine guns," recalled fellow Marine Richard Greer.

Left on Samoa during the initial Marine landing on Guadalcanal, Basilone's regiment did not come ashore until September 18. The situation on Guadalcanal was still very much in doubt, and the 4,262 men in the 7th Marines were almost immediately engaged in heavy fighting. Despite the American reinforcement, Japanese pressure on the Marine line continued, and Henderson Field, the crucial island airstrip, remained vulnerable. The night of October 24, Basilone's machine gunners were placed in defensive positions on Edson's Ridge, screening the inland side of Henderson Field. Manila John was in charge of fourteen men and four .30-caliber machine guns in support of Company C in the center of the American line. Earlier that same day, a Japanese officer had been spotted examining the Marine positions through binoculars. Everybody knew it was only a matter of time before the ridge came under attack.

A drenching rain pelted down as darkness closed over Marine positions on October 24. Basilone's Marines were wet, but their guns and ammunition were dry, well sheltered by the ponchos of men who knew a working weapon was more important than a comfortable Marine. Basilone sat barefooted in his muddy foxhole, having kicked off his boondockers because his feet had been wet for weeks and they "itched like hell," he said later. At 2130 a Marine outpost phoned in from the sopping jungle beyond the perimeter. "Colonel," whispered an apprehensive Marine to Battalion Commander Lewis B. "Chesty" Puller. "There are about 3,000 Japs between me and you."

Enemy probes began at about 2200. Then, about an hour after midnight, the 9th Company of the 3rd Battalion of the Japanese 29th Regiment charged out of the soaking jungle directly toward "Manila John" Basilone's machine guns. "When the first wave came at us, the ground just rattled!" recalled Basilone. "We kept firing and drove them back, but our ammunition was getting low so I left the guns and started running to the next outfit to get some more."

Despite the toll exacted by Marine guns, the enemy attacks continued. A slight incline in front of Basilone's position forced the Japanese to expose themselves as they attempted to knock out the machine guns. With that small advantage, the Marines piled up the enemy dead. But as the hours wore on, the enemy's numbers began to tell. One of the Marine machine-gun sections suddenly went silent. A runner ducked into Basilone's gun pit. "They got the guns on the right," he informed Basilone.

Basilone realized the enemy attack would pour through the hole left by the now silent machine-gun position if something wasn't done quickly. "I took off up the trail to see what had happened," recalled Basilone. "I found [Pvt. Cecil H.] Evans there. He had a rifle by him and was screaming at the Japs to come!" Aside from the defiant Evans, there wasn't much to stop the Japanese. Both machine guns were inoperable and it was only a matter of time before the Japanese rolled through. Hustling back to his own position, Basilone grabbed a water-cooled machine gun—90 pounds of gun and tripod—and shouted to two Marines, "Follow me!" As they scrambled back to the overrun position, they bumped into a group of about eight Japanese. The Marines mowed them down in a wild melee, and kept going.

Setting up in the abandoned pit, the new crew opened up with their gun, while Basilone went to work on the two inoperable weapons. One gun had been ruined; the other was jammed. He worked by feel in the darkness. "Bullets were smacking into the sandbags," he recalled. The rain had stopped, and in the lulls as he worked, he could hear the *thwack thwack* as the Japanese cut the barbed wire out front.

He finally managed to clear the gun, fed in a new belt of ammo, and opened up to his front. The other crew fed ammo to the guns while Basilone fired. "The Japs were still coming at us and I rolled over from one gun to the other, firing them as fast as they could be loaded," he recalled.

"The ammunition belts were in bad shape from being dragged on the ground. I had to scrape mud out of the receiver. They kept coming and we kept firing. We all thought our end had come. Some Japs would sneak through the lines and behind us. It got pretty bad because I'd have to stop firing every once in a while and shoot one behind me with my pistol." As the bodies heaped up, Basilone's men crept out front to roll the corpses down the slope and clear their fields of fire.

Ammunition again began to run low. "I'm going back for ammo," Basilone told his crew. With Japanese filtering through everywhere, Basilone, still shoeless, headed back to an ammunition point 150 yards to the rear, where he grabbed six belts of ammo, draped the 14-pound belts over his shoulders, and struggled back to the muddy gun pit on the ridge. "That lousy last 100 yards," he said later. "I thought it would never end!"

Eight separate Japanese attacks were made against the American line before the fighting tapered off at about 0700 on October 25. In the morning, the legendary Col. Chesty Puller came across Basilone lying in a foxhole with thirty-eight dead Japanese strewn around, almost at arm's length. They didn't come much tougher than Puller, but even he was impressed. "Nice work," he remarked. An estimated 1,200 Japanese were killed in the assault on the 7th Marines that night. "At dawn our guns were burned out," observed Basilone. "Altogether we got rid of 26,000 rounds. After that, I discovered I was hungry, so I went to the CP to see about getting chow. All we could get was crackers and jam."

PFC Nash Phillips, who lost a hand fighting alongside Basilone during the night, was surprised when the sergeant materialized beside him at the aid tent early that morning. "He was barefooted and his eyes were red as fire," remembered Nash. "His face was dirty black from gunfire and lack of sleep. His shirtsleeves were rolled up to his shoulders. He had a .45 tucked into the waistband of his trousers. He'd just dropped by to see how I was making out—me and the others in the section. I'll never forget him."

Wet, muddy, and exhausted, the kid from the wrong side of the tracks found he was the hero of the hour. His courage and tenacity had kept his machine guns operating, "contributing in large measure to the virtual annihilation of a Japanese regiment," noted his subsequent citation. In recognition of his actions, Basilone received the Medal of Honor from Gen. A. A. Vandegrift on June 23, 1943, in Australia. His machine-gun company expressed their admiration by collecting $200 to buy the former laundry truck worker a watch. "I am very happy, for the other day I received the Congressional Medal of Honor, the highest award you can get in the armed forces," the sergeant wrote to his parents.

Returning to the United States in September, Johnny Basilone was greeted as a national hero. Raritan held "Basilone Day" on September 19 and presented him with a $500 bond. He spent several months touring the country on a war bond drive. Curly-haired, personable, and quick with a boyish grin, he was a photographer's dream.

He hated it.

"I felt pretty embarrassed every time I spoke," he admitted later. A lieutenant assigned to escort the hero during the tour recalled asking him if he owned a set of dress blues. "What d'ya think I am, lieutenant," Basilone retorted, "a Navy Yard Marine?"

Though not comfortable with his celebrity, the fawning movie stars, and the pop of the flashbulbs, Basilone's tour raised $1.4 million in war bond pledges. "After about six months of tours and speeches, I found myself doing guard duty at Washington, D.C. Navy Yard," Basilone said later. Once again, he was bored. "Washington was a pleasant place," he admitted. "But I wasn't very happy. I wanted to get back to the machine guns. I felt out of things."

The Marine Corps offered to make him an officer and let him spend the rest of the war in Washington, but Basilone had endured enough. He was just a "plain Marine," he said. He wanted to get back into the war. "I ain't no officer, and I ain't no museum piece," he remarked. "I belong back with my outfit." He reiterated that his great ambition was to be present at Manila's recapture. "I kept thinking of how awful it would be if some Marines made a landing on Dewey Boulevard and Manila John Basilone wasn't among them," he observed slyly.

The Marine Corps turned down his repeated requests to rejoin a line outfit. But Basilone persisted, and finally, in late 1944, the Corps relented. Gunnery Sgt. John Basilone joined a machine-gun platoon of the 27th Marines, 5th Marine Division. "We tried to keep him from going," recalled his brother Carlo. "I said, 'Johnny, it's a miracle you got out of Guadalcanal.' I had a hunch Johnny wasn't coming back. He knew it too. But he still went. He wasn't afraid."

Fellow Marines who expected a brawny giant capable of firing heavy machine guns off hand were surprised to find that the heroic sergeant was only five feet eight and a half inches tall, weighing in at 158 pounds, an unpretentious sort who spoke with the "dems" and "doses" of his Jersey grade-school education. He also sported two tattoos: one on the upper right arm incongruously (considering his New Jersey background) depicted the head and shoulders of a full-blown Wild West girl in blue and red; the left depicted a sword plunged into a human heart, all entwined with stars and flowers and a ribbon reading, "Death before Dishonor." He didn't make much of his Medal of Honor, but his fame had benefits—especially on liberty. "When you went out with him, everyone paid for your drinks," recalled Sgt. Clinton Watters. "We walked out of places and left them on the table. You just couldn't drink them all."

Cpl. William D. Lansford recalled the first time he saw Basilone in one of Camp Pendleton's slop chutes, describing him as "a jug-eared young gunny who wore his cap sideways, drank beer with the gusto of a millionaire guzzling champagne and laughed so infectiously that you couldn't help liking him on sight." Asked about his future plans, Basilone indicated to *Leatherneck Magazine* that he intended to return to civilian life after the war. "I've got a girl back east and, thanks to the people of my hometown, Raritan, N.J., I have enough money invested in war bonds to get a start in civilian life as soon as the shooting is over," he remarked. "It'll either be a restaurant or a farm. I haven't decided which."

The "girl back east," whoever she was, was in for a surprise. Basilone's eye was caught by a female Marine, Sgt. Lena Riggi, who worked as a cook at Camp Pendleton. Three years older than Basilone, the daughter of Italian immigrants who operated a small farm in Portland, Oregon, Riggi did not seem impressed with her admirer, but Basilone persisted. "He was very attentive," recalled one of Riggi's friends. They were married July 10, 1944, at St. Mary's Church in Oceanside. They honeymooned at the Riggi family onion farm in Portland. Basilone happily talked about a future that included buying a ten-bedroom house and putting "a kid in each room." Thirty-two days later, the 5th Marine Division received its orders. The division was shipping out. Their destination was Hawaii, and then, five months later, Iwo Jima. From Pearl Harbor, Basilone sent his mother a photo of himself in uniform with the note, "Tell Pop his son is still tough."

Just how tough was witnessed by PFC Chuck Tatum on the beach at Iwo Jima, the morning of D-Day, February 19. Tatum, who had never been in combat before, was huddled in the sand debating what to do next as enemy fire rained down all around, when he noticed "a lone Marine walking back and forth on the shore among hundreds of prone figures, kicking asses, shouting his profane displeasure and demanding, 'Move out! Get your butts off the beach!'" It was Manila John Basilone.

Basilone and the executive officer of the 27th Marines made their way toward Tatum, booting the huddled men and shouting, "Move out! Move out! Get the fuck off the beach you dumb sons-of-bitches." Basilone directed Tatum and his machine gun toward a reinforced-concrete block-house to their front. A field piece concealed in the fortification was firing down the beach to their right. Basilone coordinated the assault on the structure. As Tatum covered them with fire from his machine gun, other Marines got close enough to toss demolitions into the blockhouse; then a flamethrower operator stuck his nozzle through an aperture and cut loose.

Eighteen-year-old Tatum suddenly realized that Basilone was standing over him, releasing the machine gun from the tripod. "Get the belt and follow me," he screamed in Tatum's ear. The youngster followed Basilone at a run to the top of the blockhouse, just as a knot of burning Japanese scrambled out the rear entrance. Holding the machine gun by its "Basilone Bail" (a specially adapted handle the gunny had devised for the barrel of the weapon to make it easier to use), Manila John mowed them down. "It was a mercy killing," observed Tatum.

Ninety-three minutes after coming ashore, Basilone's small group found itself on the runway of Airfield No. 1, about 500 yards in from the landing beach and less than halfway across the narrow neck of the island. Coming under heavy fire on the open runway, the Marines started to fall back. Basilone told them to dig in and hold their ground. "I'll go back for more men," he said. He disappeared in the direction of the beach.

Not half an hour later, Tatum lifted his head to see a small knot of Marines heading toward the runway with Basilone in the lead. They were seventy-five yards from his shell hole when a Japanese mortar shell plummeted down, knocking them to the ground like so many rag dolls. The shell exploded at Basilone's feet, sending metal tearing into his groin, neck, and left arm. His brother's fears had been realized: Johnny Basilone's luck had finally run out. If not killed instantly, he died within minutes.

At about noon, the executive officer of the 2nd Battalion, 26th Marines saw Basilone's close friend, CWO John Daniels. "Gunnery Sergeant Basilone is laying dead at the end of the first airstrip," he told him. Daniels went out to the runway and found Basilone there with three other C Company Marines cut down by mortar fire. The dead gunny was just "a thin, pallid kid," recalled Cpl. Bill Lansford, who wasn't entirely convinced at first that it was really Basilone lying there. "His helmet was half off and he lay face up, arched over his combat pack, with his jacket torn back and his mouth open. He looked incredibly thin, like an undernourished kid with his hands near his stomach as though it hurt," observed Lansford.

Over the next few hours, word filtered along the line. Basilone was dead. They couldn't believe it, recalled Tatum. But it was true. A graves registration detail pulled Basilone's poncho from his backpack and wrapped him in it, and the hero of Guadalcanal eventually joined the growing line of dead Marines awaiting burial in Iwo's black volcanic sand. Lena Basilone got the bad news on March 7, her thirty-second birthday; she had to be sedated. She lived until 1999, never remarrying. "It's sad what happened," Basilone's brother Carlo said years later. "I told Johnny to stay home, after all he went through, but that wasn't enough. I always had a feeling he wasn't going to come home."

For his actions in the first hour and a half of the Iwo Jima assault, Gunnery Sgt. John Basilone was awarded a posthumous Navy Cross. He was the only enlisted Marine in World War II to receive the nation's two highest awards for valor, and to this day his memory as a fighting Marine is revered and held up as an example in the Corps. Following the war, his remains were removed from the 5th Marine Division cemetery on Iwo Jima and reinterred at Arlington National Cemetery, where he rests today in section 12-384 under a simple marble marker engraved with a rendering of the Medal of Honor.

Marines would again walk the streets of Manila. But John Basilone would not be among them.

Editor's Note: The Invasion of Iwo Jima proved to be the most costly Marine battle in history. There were 26,000 casualties, 6,800 killed. Of the Island's 21,000 Japanese defenders, only 210 were taken prisoner. Japanese defenses not only included artillery, mortar and machine-gun positions on the heights of Mt. Suribachi, overlooking the beaches, but a network of tunnels totaling 17 miles under the Island. In addition the black, volcanic sand covering the beaches made movement agonizingly slow for the gear-laden Marines. Where there was death and suffering, there was also great courage. More Medals of Honor were issued for Iwo Jima than any single battle in history.

CHAPTER THIRTEEN

The Rough Riders

San Juan Hill

Theodore Roosevelt

In a life filled with adventure, political success, and personal heartbreak, Theodore Roosevelt capped his years, 1858–1919, with written accounts of virtually everything he experienced. Our 26th president produced a prodigious forty-two books and countless magazine articles on everything ranging from ranch life to explorations in the Amazon jungle. His book The Rough Riders *details his military experiences with that famous unit in Cuba, including the action that made the Roosevelt name synonymous with the words "San Juan Hill." On January 16, 2001—four days before he would leave office—President Bill Clinton held a ceremony in the Roosevelt Room of the White House. Attended by many Roosevelt family members,*

the president presented the Medal of Honor to Tweed Roosevelt, Teddy's great-grandson. The citation reads:

Lieutenant Colonel Theodore Roosevelt distinguished himself by acts of bravery on 1 July 1898, near Santiago de Cuba, Republic of Cuba, while leading a daring charge up San Juan Hill. Lieutenant Colonel Roosevelt, in total disregard for his personal safety, and accompanied by only four or five men, led a desperate and gallant charge up San Juan Hill, encouraging his troops to continue the assault through withering enemy fire over open countryside. Facing the enemy's heavy fire, he displayed extraordinary bravery throughout the charge, and was the first to reach the enemy trenches, where he quickly killed one of the enemy with his pistol, allowing his men to continue the assault. His leadership and valor turned the tide in the Battle for San Juan Hill. Lieutenant Colonel Roosevelt's extraordinary heroism and devotion to duty are in keeping with the highest traditions of military service and reflect great credit upon himself, his unit, and the United States Army.

Here, in Roosevelt's own words, excerpted from The Rough Riders *is the story of what happened on San Juan Hill.*

Just before leaving Tampa we had been brigaded with the First (white) and Tenth (colored) Regular Cavalry under Brigadier-General S. B. M. Young. We were the Second Brigade, the First Brigade consisting of the Third and Sixth (white), and the Ninth (colored) Regular Cavalry under Brigadier-General Sumner. The two brigades of the cavalry division were under Major-General Joseph Wheeler, the gallant old Confederate cavalry commander.

General Young was—and is—as fine a type of the American fighting soldier as a man can hope to see. He had been in command, as Colonel, of the Yellowstone National Park, and I had seen a good deal of him in connection therewith, as I was President of the Boone and Crockett Club, an organization devoted to hunting big game, to its preservation, and to forest preservation. During the preceding winter, while he was in Washington, he had lunched with me at the Metropolitan Club, Wood being one of the other guests. Of course, we talked of the war, which all of us present believed to be impending, and Wood and I told him we were going to make every effort to get in, somehow; and he answered that we must be sure to get into his brigade, if he had one, and he would guarantee to show us fighting. None of us forgot the conversation. As soon as our regiment was raised General Young applied for it to be put in his brigade. We were put in; and he made his word good; for he fought and won the first fight on Cuban soil.

Yet, even though under him, we should not have been in this fight at all if we had not taken advantage of the chance to disembark among the first troops, and if it had not been for Wood's energy in pushing our regiment to the front.

On landing we spent some active hours in marching our men a quarter of a mile or so inland, as boat-load by boat-load they disembarked. Meanwhile one of the men, Knoblauch, a New Yorker, who was a great athlete and a champion swimmer, by diving in the surf off the dock, recovered most of the rifles which had been lost when the boat-load of colored cavalry capsized. The country would have offered very great difficulties to an attacking force had there been resistance. It was little but a mass of rugged and precipitous hills, covered for the most part by dense jungle. Five hundred resolute men could have prevented the disembarkation at very little cost to themselves. There had been about that number of Spaniards at Daiquiri that morning, but they had fled even before the ships began shelling. In their place we found hundreds of Cuban insurgents, a crew of as utter tatterdemalions as human eyes ever looked on, armed with every kind of rifle in all stages of dilapidation. It was evident, at a glance, that they would be no use in serious fighting, but it was hoped that they might be of service in scouting. From a variety of causes, however, they turned out to be nearly useless, even for this purpose, so far as the Santiago campaign was concerned.

We were camped on a dusty, brush-covered flat, with jungle on one side, and on the other a shallow, fetid pool fringed with palm-trees. Huge land-crabs scuttled noisily through the underbrush, exciting much interest among the men. Camping was a simple matter, as each man carried all he had, and the officers had nothing. I took a light mackintosh and a tooth-brush. Fortunately, that night it did not rain; and from the palm-leaves we built shelters from the sun.

General Lawton, a tall, fine-looking man, had taken the advance. A thorough soldier, he at once established outposts and pushed reconnoitering parties ahead on the trails. He had as little baggage as the rest of us. Our own Brigade-Commander, General Young, had exactly the same impedimenta that I had, namely, a mackintosh and a tooth-brush.

Next morning we were hard at work trying to get the stuff unloaded from the ship, and succeeded in getting most of it ashore, but were utterly unable to get transportation for anything but a very small quantity. The great shortcoming throughout the campaign was the utterly inadequate transportation. If we had been allowed to take our mule-train, we could have kept the whole cavalry division supplied.

In the afternoon word came to us to march. General Wheeler, a regular game-cock, was as anxious as Lawton to get first blood, and he was bent upon putting the cavalry division to the front as quickly as possible. Lawton's advance guard was in touch with the Spaniards, and there had been a skirmish between the latter and some Cubans, who were repulsed. General Wheeler made a reconnaissance in person, found out where the enemy was, and directed General Young to take our brigade and move forward so as to strike him next morning. He had the power to do this, as when General Shafter was afloat he had command ashore.

I had succeeded in finding Texas, my surviving horse, much the worse for his fortnight on the transport and his experience in getting off, but still able to carry me.

It was mid-afternoon and the tropic sun was beating fiercely down when Colonel Wood started our regiment—the First and Tenth Cavalry and some of the infantry regiments having already marched. Colonel Wood himself rode in advance, while I led my squadron, and Major Brodie followed with his. It was a hard march, the hilly jungle trail being so narrow that often we had to go in single file. We marched fast, for Wood was bound to get us ahead of the other regiments, so as to be sure of our place in the body that struck the enemy next morning. If it had not been for his energy in pushing forward, we should certainly have missed the fight. As it was, we did not halt until we were at the extreme front.

The men were not in very good shape for marching, and moreover they were really horsemen, the majority being cowboys who had never done much walking. The heat was intense and their burdens very heavy. Yet there was very little straggling. Whenever we halted they instantly took off their packs and threw themselves on their backs. Then at the word to start they would spring into place again. The captains and lieutenants tramped along, encouraging the men by example and word. A good part of the time I was by Captain Llewellen, and was greatly pleased to see the way in which he kept his men up to their work. He never pitied or coddled his troopers, but he always looked after them. He helped them whenever he could, and took rather more than his full share of hardship and danger, so that his men naturally followed him with entire devotion. Jack Greenway was under him as lieutenant, and to him the entire march was nothing but an enjoyable outing, the chance of fight on the morrow simply adding the needed spice of excitement.

It was long after nightfall when we tramped through the darkness into the squalid coast hamlet of Siboney. As usual when we made a night camp, we simply drew the men up in column of troops, and then let each man lie down where he was. Black thunder-clouds were gathering. Before they broke the fires were made and the men cooked their coffee and pork, some frying the hardtack with the pork. The officers, of course, fared just as the men did. Hardly had we finished eating when the rain came, a regular tropic downpour. We sat about, sheltering ourselves as best we could, for the hour or two it lasted; then the fires were relighted and we closed around them, the men taking off their wet things to dry them, so far as possible, by the blaze.

Wood had gone off to see General Young, as General Wheeler had instructed General Young to hit the Spaniards, who were about four miles away, as soon after daybreak as possible. Meanwhile, I strolled over to Captain Capron's troop. He and I, with his two lieutenants, Day and Thomas, stood around the fire, together with two or three non-commissioned officers and privates; among the latter were Sergeant Hamilton Fish and Trooper Elliot Cowdin, both of New York. Cowdin, together with two other troopers, Harry Thorpe and Munro Ferguson, had been on my Oyster Bay Polo Team some years before. Hamilton Fish had already shown himself one of the best non-commissioned officers we had. A huge fellow, of enormous strength and endurance and dauntless courage, he took naturally to a soldier's life. He never complained and never shirked any duty of any kind, while his power over his men was great. So good a sergeant had he made that Captain Capron, keen to get the best men under him, took him when he left Tampa—for Fish's troop remained behind. As we stood around the flickering blaze that night I caught myself admiring the splendid bodily vigor of Capron and Fish—the captain and the sergeant. Their frames seemed of steel, to withstand all fatigue; they were flushed with health; in their eyes shone high resolve and fiery desire. Two finer types of the fighting man, two better representatives of the American soldier, there were not in the whole army. Capron was going over his plans for the fight when we should meet the Spaniards on the morrow, Fish occasionally asking a question. They were both filled with eager longing to show their mettle, and both were rightly confident that if they lived they would win honorable renown and would rise high in their chosen profession. Within twelve hours they both were dead.

I had lain down when toward midnight Wood returned. He had gone over the whole plan with General Young. We were to start by sunrise toward Santiago, General Young taking four troops of the Tenth and four troops of the First up the road which led through the valley; while Colonel Wood was to lead our eight troops along a hill-trail to the left, which joined the valley road about four miles on, at a point where the road went over a spur of the mountain chain and from thence went downhill toward Santiago. The Spaniards had their lines at the junction of the road and the trail.

Before describing our part in the fight, it is necessary to say a word about General Young's share, for, of course, the whole fight was under his direction, and the fight on the right wing under his immediate supervision. General Young had obtained from General Castillo, the commander of the Cuban forces, a full description of the country in front. General Castillo promised Young the aid of eight hundred Cubans, if he made a reconnaissance in force to find out exactly what the Spanish strength was. This promised Cuban aid did not, however, materialize, the Cubans, who had been beaten back by the Spaniards the day before, not appearing on the firing-line until the fight was over.

General Young had in his immediate command a squadron of the First Regular Cavalry, two hundred and forty-four strong, under the command of Major Bell, and a squadron of the Tenth Regular Cavalry, two hundred and twenty strong, under the command of Major Norvell. He also had two Hotchkiss mountain guns, under Captain Watson of the Tenth. He started at a quarter before six in the morning, accompanied by Captain A. L. Mills, as aide. It was at half-past seven that Captain Mills, with a patrol of two men in advance, discovered the Spaniards as they lay across where the two roads came together, some of them in pits, others simply lying in the heavy jungle, while on their extreme right they occupied a big ranch. Where General Young struck them they held a high ridge a little to the left of his front, this ridge being separated by a deep ravine from the hill-trail still farther to the left, down which the Rough Riders were advancing. That is, their forces occupied a range of high hills in the form of an obtuse angle, the salient being toward the space between the American forces, while there were advance parties along both roads. There were stone breastworks flanked by block-houses on that part of the ridge where the two trails came together. The place was called Las Guasimas, from trees of that name in the neighborhood.

General Young, who was riding a mule, carefully examined the Spanish position in person. He ordered the canteens of the troops to be filled, placed the Hotchkiss battery in concealment about nine hundred yards from the Spanish lines, and then deployed the white regulars, with the colored regulars in support, having sent a Cuban guide to try to find Colonel Wood and warn him. He did not attack immediately, because he knew that Colonel Wood, having a more difficult route, would require a longer time to reach the position. During the delay General Wheeler arrived; he had been up since long before dawn, to see that everything went well. Young informed him of the dispositions and plan of attack he made. General Wheeler approved of them, and with excellent judgment left General Young a free hand to fight his battle.

So, about eight o'clock Young began the fight with his Hotchkiss guns, he himself being up on the firing-line. No sooner had the Hotchkiss one-pounders opened than the Spaniards opened fire in return, most of the time firing by volleys executed in perfect time, almost as on parade. They had a couple of light guns, which our people thought were quick firers. The denseness of the jungle and the fact that they used absolutely smokeless powder, made it exceedingly difficult to place exactly where they were, and almost immediately Young, who always liked to get as close as possible to his enemy, began to push his troops forward. They were deployed on both sides of the road in such thick jungle that it was only here and there that they could possibly see ahead, and some confusion, of course, ensued, the support gradually getting mixed with the advance. Captain Beck took A Troop of the Tenth in on the left, next Captain Galbraith's troop of the First; two other troops of the Tenth were on the extreme right. Through the jungle ran wire fences here and there, and as the troops got to the ridge they encountered precipitous heights. They were led most gallantly, as American regular officers always lead their men; and the men followed their leaders with the splendid courage always shown by the American regular soldier. There was not a single straggler among them, and in not one instance was an attempt made by any trooper to fall out in order to assist the wounded or carry back the dead, while so cool were they and so perfect their fire discipline, that in the entire engagement the expenditure of ammunition was not over ten rounds per man. Major Bell, who commanded the squadron, had his leg broken by a shot as he was leading his men. Captain Wainwright succeeded to the command of the squadron. Captain Knox was shot in the abdomen. He continued for some time giving orders to his troops, and refused to allow a man in the firing-line to assist him to the rear. His First Lieutenant, Byram, was himself shot, but continued to lead his men until the wound and the heat overcame him and he fell in a faint. The advance was pushed forward under General Young's eye with the utmost energy, until the enemy's voices could be heard in the entrenchments. The Spaniards kept up a very heavy firing, but the regulars would not be denied, and as they climbed the ridges the Spaniards broke and fled.

Meanwhile, at six o'clock, the Rough Riders began their advance. We first had to climb a very steep hill. Many of the men, foot-sore and weary from their march of the preceding day, found the pace up this hill too hard, and either dropped their bundles or fell out of line, with the result that we went into action with less than five hundred men—as, in addition to the stragglers, a detachment had been left to guard the baggage on shore. At the time I was rather inclined to grumble to myself about Wood setting so fast a pace, but when the fight began I realized that it had been absolutely necessary, as otherwise we should have arrived late and the regulars would have had very hard work indeed.

Tiffany, by great exertions, had corralled a couple of mules and was using them to transport the Colt automatic guns in the rear of the regiment. The dynamite gun was not with us, as mules for it could not be obtained in time.

Captain Capron's troop was in the lead, it being chosen for the most responsible and dangerous position because of Capron's capacity. Four men, headed by Sergeant Hamilton Fish, went first; a support of twenty men followed some distance behind; and then came Capron and the rest of his troop, followed by Wood, with whom General Young had sent Lieutenants Smedburg and Rivers as aides. I rode close behind, at the head of the other three troops of my squadron, and then came Brodie at the head of his squadron. The trail was so narrow that for the most part the men marched in single file, and it was bordered by dense, tangled jungle, through which a man could with difficulty force his way; so that to put out flankers was impossible, for they could not possibly have kept up with the march of the column. Every man had his canteen full. There was a Cuban guide at the head of the column, but he ran away as soon as the fighting began. There were also with us, at the head of the column, two men who did not run away, who, though non-combatants—newspaper correspondents—showed as much gallantry as any soldier in the field. They were Edward Marshall and Richard Harding Davis.

After reaching the top of the hill the walk was very pleasant. Now and then we came to glades or rounded hill-shoulders, whence we could look off for some distance. The tropical forest was very beautiful, and it was a delight to see the strange trees, the splendid royal palms and a tree which looked like a flat-topped acacia, and which was covered with a mass of brilliant scarlet flowers. We heard many bird-notes, too, the cooing of doves

and the call of a great brush cuckoo. Afterward we found that the Spanish
guerrillas imitated these bird-calls, but the sounds we heard that morning,
as we advanced through the tropic forest, were from birds, not guerrillas,
until we came right up to the Spanish lines. It was very beautiful and very
peaceful, and it seemed more as if we were off on some hunting excursion
than as if we were about to go into a sharp and bloody little fight.

Of course, we accommodated our movements to those of the men in
front. After marching for somewhat over an hour, we suddenly came to a
halt, and immediately afterward Colonel Wood sent word down the line
that the advance guard had come upon a Spanish outpost. Then the order
was passed to fill the magazines, which was done.

The men were totally unconcerned, and I do not think they realized
that any fighting was at hand; at any rate, I could hear the group nearest
me discussing in low murmurs, not the Spaniards, but the conduct of a
certain cow-puncher in quitting work on a ranch and starting a saloon
in some New Mexican town. In another minute, however, Wood sent
me orders to deploy three troops to the right of the trail, and to advance
when we became engaged; while, at the same time, the other troops,
under Major Brodie, were deployed to the left of the trail where the
ground was more open than elsewhere—one troop being held in reserve
in the centre, besides the reserves on each wing. Later all the reserves
were put into the firing-line.

To the right the jungle was quite thick, and we had barely begun to
deploy when a crash in front announced that the fight was on. It was
evidently very hot, and L Troop had its hands full; so I hurried my men
up abreast of them. So thick was the jungle that it was very difficult to
keep together, especially when there was no time for delay, and while I
got up Llewellen's troops and Kane's platoon of K Troop, the rest of K
Troop under Captain Jenkins, which, with Bucky O'Neill's troop, made
up the right wing, were behind, and it was some time before they got into
the fight at all.

Meanwhile, I had gone forward with Llewellen, Greenway, Kane,
and their troopers until we came out on a kind of shoulder, jutting over a
ravine, which separated us from a great ridge on our right. It was on this
ridge that the Spaniards had some of their entrenchments, and it was just

beyond this ridge that the Valley Road led, up which the regulars were at that very time pushing their attack; but, of course, at the moment we knew nothing of this. The effect of the smokeless powder was remarkable. The air seemed full of the rustling sound of the Mauser bullets, for the Spaniards knew the trails by which we were advancing, and opened heavily on our position. Moreover, as we advanced we were, of course, exposed, and they could see us and fire. But they themselves were entirely invisible. The jungle covered everything, and not the faintest trace of smoke was to be seen in any direction to indicate from whence the bullets came. It was some time before the men fired; Llewellen, Kane, and I anxiously studying the ground to see where our opponents were, and utterly unable to find out.

We could hear the faint reports of the Hotchkiss guns and the reply of two Spanish guns, and the Mauser bullets were singing through the trees over our heads, making a noise like the humming of telephone wires; but exactly where they came from we could not tell. The Spaniards were firing high and for the most part by volleys, and their shooting was not very good, which perhaps was not to be wondered at, as they were a long way off. Gradually, however, they began to get the range and occasionally one of our men would crumple up. In no case did the man make any outcry when hit, seeming to take it as a matter of course; at the outside, making only such a remark as: "Well, I got it that time." With hardly an exception, there was no sign of flinching. I say with hardly an exception, for though I personally did not see an instance, and though all the men at the front behaved excellently, yet there were a very few men who lagged behind and drifted back to the trail over which we had come. The character of the fight put a premium upon such conduct, and afforded a very severe test for raw troops; because the jungle was so dense that as we advanced in open order, every man was, from time to time, left almost alone and away from the eyes of his officers. There was unlimited opportunity for dropping out without attracting notice, while it was peculiarly hard to be exposed to the fire of an unseen foe, and to see men dropping under it, and yet to be, for some time, unable to return it, and also to be entirely ignorant of what was going on in any other part of the field.

It was Richard Harding Davis who gave us our first opportunity to shoot back with effect. He was behaving precisely like my officers, being on the extreme front of the line, and taking every opportunity to study with his glasses the ground where we thought the Spaniards were. I had tried some volley firing at points where I rather doubtfully believed the Spaniards to be, but had stopped firing and was myself studying the jungle-covered mountain ahead with my glasses, when Davis suddenly said: "There they are, Colonel; look over there; I can see their hats near that glade," pointing across the valley to our right. In a minute I, too, made out the hats, and then pointed them out to three or four of our best shots, giving them my estimate of the range. For a minute or two no result followed, and I kept raising the range, at the same time getting more men on the firing-line. Then, evidently, the shots told, for the Spaniards suddenly sprang out of the cover through which we had seen their hats, and ran to another spot; and we could now make out a large number of them.

I accordingly got all of my men up in line and began quick firing. In a very few minutes our bullets began to do damage, for the Spaniards retreated to the left into the jungle, and we lost sight of them. At the same moment a big body of men who, it afterward turned out, were Spaniards, came in sight along the glade, following the retreat of those whom we had just driven from the trenches. We supposed that there was a large force of Cubans with General Young, not being aware that these Cubans had failed to make their appearance, and as it was impossible to tell the Cubans from the Spaniards, and as we could not decide whether these were Cubans following the Spaniards we had put to flight, or merely another troop of Spaniards retreating after the first (which was really the case), we dared not fire, and in a minute they had passed the glade and were out of sight.

At every halt we took advantage of the cover, sinking down behind any mound, bush, or tree trunk in the neighborhood. The trees, of course, furnished no protection from the Mauser bullets. Once I was standing behind a large palm with my head out to one side, very fortunately; for a bullet passed through the palm, filling my left eye and ear with the dust and splinters.

No man was allowed to drop out to help the wounded. It was hard to leave them there in the jungle, where they might not be found again until the vultures and the land-crabs came, but war is a grim game and there was no choice. One of the men shot was Harry Heffner of G Troop, who was mortally wounded through the hips. He fell without uttering a sound, and two of his companions dragged him behind a tree. Here he propped himself up and asked to be given his canteen and his rifle, which I handed to him. He then again began shooting, and continued loading and firing until the line moved forward and we left him alone, dying in the gloomy shade. When we found him again, after the fight, he was dead.

At one time, as I was out of touch with that part of my wing commanded by Jenkins and O'Neill, I sent Greenway, with Sergeant Russell, a New Yorker, and trooper Rowland, a New Mexican cow-puncher, down in the valley to find out where they were. To do this the three had to expose themselves to a very severe fire, but they were not men to whom this mattered. Russell was killed; the other two returned and reported to me the position of Jenkins and O'Neill. They then resumed their places on the firing-line. After a while I noticed blood coming out of Rowland's side and discovered that he had been shot, although he did not seem to be taking any notice of it. He said the wound was only slight, but as I saw he had broken a rib, I told him to go to the rear to the hospital. After some grumbling he went, but fifteen minutes later he was back on the firing-line again and said he could not find the hospital—which I doubted. However, I then let him stay until the end of the fight.

After we had driven the Spaniards off from their position to our right, the firing seemed to die away so far as we were concerned, for the bullets no longer struck around us in such a storm as before, though along the rest of the line the battle was as brisk as ever. Soon we saw troops appearing across the ravine, not very far from where we had seen the Spaniards whom we had thought might be Cubans. Again we dared not fire, and carefully studied the new-comers with our glasses; and this time we were right, for we recognized our own cavalry-men. We were by no means sure that they recognized us, however, and were anxious that they should, but it was very difficult to find a clear spot in the jungle from which to signal; so Sergeant Lee of Troop K climbed a tree and from its summit waved the troop guidon. They waved their guidon back, and as our right wing was now in touch with the regulars, I left Jenkins and O'Neill to keep the connection, and led Llewellen's troop back to the path to join the rest of the regiment, which was evidently still in the thick of the fight. I was still very much in the dark as to where the main body of the Spanish forces were, or exactly what lines the battle was following, and was very uncertain what I ought to do; but I knew it could not be wrong to go forward, and I thought I would find Wood and then see what he wished me to do. I was in a mood to cordially welcome guidance, for it was most bewildering to fight an enemy whom one so rarely saw.

I had not seen Wood since the beginning of the skirmish, when he hurried forward. When the firing opened some of the men began to curse. "Don't swear—shoot!" growled Wood, as he strode along the path leading his horse, and everyone laughed and became cool again. The Spanish outposts were very near our advance guard, and some minutes of the hottest kind of firing followed before they were driven back and slipped off through the jungle to their main lines in the rear.

Here, at the very outset of our active service, we suffered the loss of two as gallant men as ever wore uniform. Sergeant Hamilton Fish at the extreme front, while holding the point up to its work and firing back where the Spanish advance guards lay, was shot and instantly killed; three of the men with him were likewise hit. Captain Capron, leading the advance guard in person, and displaying equal courage and coolness in the way that he handled them, was also struck, and died a few minutes afterward. The command of the troop then devolved upon the First Lieutenant, young Thomas. Like Capron, Thomas was the fifth in line from father to son who had served in the American army, though in his case it was in the volunteer and not the regular service; the four preceding generations had furnished soldiers respectively to the Revolutionary War, the War of 1812, the Mexican War, and the Civil War. In a few minutes Thomas was shot through the leg, and the command devolved upon the Second Lieutenant, Day (a nephew of "Albemarle" Cushing, he who sunk the great Confederate ram). Day, who proved himself to be one of our most efficient officers, continued to handle the men to the best possible advantage, and brought them steadily forward. L Troop was from the Indian Territory. The whites, Indians, and half-breeds in it, all fought with equal courage. Captain McClintock was hurried forward to its relief with his Troop B of Arizona men. In a few minutes he was shot through the leg and his place was taken by his First Lieutenant, Wilcox, who handled his men in the same soldierly manner that Day did.

Among the men who showed marked courage and coolness was the tall color-sergeant, Wright; the colors were shot through three times.

When I had led G Troop back to the trail I ran ahead of them, passing the dead and wounded men of L Troop, passing young Fish as he lay with glazed eyes under the rank tropic growth to one side of the trail. When I came to the front I found the men spread out in a very thin skirmish line, advancing through comparatively open ground, each man taking advantage of what cover he could, while Wood strolled about leading his horse, Brodie being close at hand. How Wood escaped being hit, I do not see, and still less how his horse escaped. I had left mine at the beginning of the action, and was only regretting that I had not left my sword with it, as it kept getting between my legs when I was tearing my way through the jungle. I never wore it again in action. Lieutenant Rivers was with Wood, also leading his horse. Smedburg had been sent off on the by no means pleasant task of establishing communications with Young.

Very soon after I reached the front, Brodie was hit, the bullet shattering one arm and whirling him around as he stood. He had kept on the extreme front all through, his presence and example keeping his men entirely steady, and he at first refused to go to the rear; but the wound was very painful, and he became so faint that he had to be sent. Thereupon, Wood directed me to take charge of the left wing in Brodie's place, and to bring it forward; so over I went.

I now had under me Captains Luna, Muller, and Houston, and I began to take them forward, well spread out, through the high grass of a rather open forest. I noticed Goodrich, of Houston's troop, tramping along behind his men, absorbed in making them keep at good intervals from one another and fire slowly with careful aim. As I came close up to the edge of the troop, he caught a glimpse of me, mistook me for one of his own skirmishers who was crowding in too closely, and called out, "Keep your interval, sir; keep your interval, and go forward."

A perfect hail of bullets was sweeping over us as we advanced. Once I got a glimpse of some Spaniards, apparently retreating, far in the front, and to our right, and we fired a couple of rounds after them. Then I became convinced, after much anxious study, that we were being fired at from some large red-tiled buildings, part of a ranch on our front. Smokeless powder, and the thick cover in our front, continued to puzzle us, and I more than once consulted anxiously the officers as to the exact whereabouts of our opponents. I took a rifle from a wounded man and began to try shots with it myself. It was very hot and the men were getting exhausted, though at this particular time we were not suffering heavily from bullets, the Spanish fire going high. As we advanced, the cover became a little thicker and I lost touch of the main body under Wood; so I halted and we fired industriously at the ranch buildings ahead of us, some five hundred yards off. Then we heard cheering on the right, and I supposed that this meant a charge on the part of Wood's men, so I sprang up and ordered the men to rush the buildings ahead of us. They came forward with a will. There was a moment's heavy firing from the Spaniards, which all went over our heads, and then it ceased entirely. When we arrived at the buildings, panting and out of breath, they contained nothing but heaps of empty cartridge-shells and two dead Spaniards, shot through the head.

The country all around us was thickly forested, so that it was very difficult to see any distance in any direction. The firing had now died out, but I was still entirely uncertain as to exactly what had happened. I did not know whether the enemy had been driven back or whether it was merely a lull in the fight, and we might be attacked again; nor did I know what had happened in any other part of the line, while as I occupied the extreme left, I was not sure whether or not my flank was in danger. At this moment one of our men who had dropped out, arrived with the information (fortunately false) that Wood was dead. Of course, this meant that the command devolved upon me, and I hastily set about taking charge of the regiment. I had been particularly struck by the coolness and courage shown by Sergeants Dame and McIlhenny, and sent them out with small pickets to keep watch in front and to the left of the left wing. I sent other men to fill the canteens with water, and threw the rest out in a long line in a disused sunken road, which gave them cover, putting two or three wounded men, who had hitherto kept up with the fighting-line, and a dozen men who were suffering from heat exhaustion—for the fighting and running under that blazing sun through the thick dry jungle was heart-breaking—into the ranch buildings. Then I started over toward the main body, but to my delight encountered Wood himself, who told me the fight was over and the Spaniards had retreated. He also informed me that other troops were just coming up. The first to appear was a squadron of the Ninth Cavalry, under Major Dimick, which had hurried up to get into the fight, and was greatly disappointed to find it over. They took post in front of our lines, so that our tired men were able to get a rest, Captain McBlain, of the Ninth, good-naturedly giving us some points as to the best way to station our outposts. Then General Chaffee, rather glum at not having been in the fight himself, rode up at the head of some of his infantry, and I marched my squadron back to where the rest of the regiment was going into camp, just where the two trails came together, and beyond—that is, on the Santiago side of—the original Spanish lines.

The Rough Riders had lost 8 men killed and 34 wounded, aside from two or three who were merely scratched and whose wounds were not reported. The First Cavalry, white, lost 7 men killed and 8 wounded; the Tenth Cavalry, colored, 1 man killed and 10 wounded; so, out of 964 men engaged on our side, 16 were killed and 52 wounded. The Spaniards were under General Rubin, with, as second in command, Colonel Alcarez. They had two guns, and eleven companies of about 100 men each: three belonging to the Porto Rico regiment, three to the San Fernandino, two to the Talavero, two being so-called mobilized companies from the mineral districts, and one a company of engineers; over 1,200 men in all, together with two guns.

General Rubin reported that he had repulsed the American attack, and Lieutenant Tejeiro states in his book that General Rubin forced the Americans to retreat, and enumerates the attacking force as consisting of three regular regiments of infantry, the Second Massachusetts and the Seventy-first New York (not one of which fired a gun or were anywhere near the battle), in addition to the sixteen dismounted troops of cavalry. In other words, as the five infantry regiments each included twelve companies, he makes the attacking force consist of just five times the actual amount. As for the "repulse," our line never went back ten yards in any place, and the advance was practically steady; while an hour and a half after the fight began we were in complete possession of the entire Spanish position, and their troops were fleeing in masses down the road, our men being too exhausted to follow them.

General Rubin also reports that he lost but seven men killed. This is certainly incorrect, for Captain O'Neill and I went over the ground very carefully and counted eleven dead Spaniards, all of whom were actually buried by our burying squads. There were probably two or three men whom we missed, but I think that our official reports are incorrect in stating that forty-two dead Spaniards were found; this being based upon reports in which I think some of the Spanish dead were counted two or three times. Indeed, I should doubt whether their loss was as heavy as ours, for they were under cover, while we advanced, often in the open, and their main lines fled long before we could get to close quarters. It was a very difficult country, and a force of good soldiers resolutely handled could have held the pass with ease against two or three times their number. As it was, with a force half of regulars and half of volunteers, we drove out a superior number of Spanish regular troops, strongly posted, without suffering a very heavy loss. Although the Spanish fire was very heavy, it does not seem to me it was very well directed; and though they fired with great spirit while we merely stood at a distance and fired at them, they did not show much resolution, and when we advanced, always went back long before there was any chance of our coming into contact with them. Our men behaved very well indeed—white regulars, colored regulars, and Rough Riders alike. The newspaper press failed to do full justice to the white regulars, in my opinion, from the simple reason that everybody knew that they would fight, whereas there had been a good deal of question as to how the Rough Riders, who were volunteer troops, and the Tenth Cavalry, who were colored, would behave; so there was a tendency to exalt our deeds at the expense of those of the First Regulars, whose courage and good conduct were taken for granted. It was a trying fight beyond what the losses show, for it is hard upon raw soldiers to be pitted against an unseen foe, and to advance steadily when their comrades are falling around them, and when they can only occasionally see a chance to retaliate. Wood's experience in fighting

Apaches stood him in good stead. An entirely raw man at the head of the regiment, conducting, as Wood was, what was practically an independent fight, would have been in a very trying position. The fight cleared the way toward Santiago, and we experienced no further resistance.

That afternoon we made camp and dined, subsisting chiefly on a load of beans which we found on one of the Spanish mules which had been shot. We also looked after the wounded. Dr. Church had himself gone out to the firing-line during the fight, and carried to the rear some of the worst wounded on his back or in his arms. Those who could walk had walked in to where the little field-hospital of the regiment was established on the trail. We found all our dead and all the badly wounded. Around one of the latter the big, hideous land-crabs had gathered in a gruesome ring, waiting for life to be extinct. One of our own men and most of the Spanish dead had been found by the vultures before we got to them; and their bodies were mangled, the eyes and wounds being torn.

The Rough Rider who had been thus treated was in Bucky O'Neill's troop; and as we looked at the body, O'Neill turned to me and asked, "Colonel, isn't it Whitman who says of the vultures that 'they pluck the eyes of princes and tear the flesh of kings'?" I answered that I could not place the quotation. Just a week afterward we were shielding his own body from the birds of prey.

One of the men who fired first, and who displayed conspicuous gallantry, was a Cherokee half-breed, who was hit seven times, and of course had to go back to the States. Before he rejoined us at Montauk Point he had gone through a little private war of his own; for on his return he found that a cowboy had gone off with his sweetheart, and in the fight that ensued he shot his rival. Another man of L Troop who also showed marked gallantry was Elliot Cowdin. The men of the plains and mountains were trained by life-long habit to look on life and death with iron philosophy. As I passed by a couple of tall, lank, Oklahoma cowpunchers, I heard one say, "Well, some of the boys got it in the neck!" to which the other answered with the grim plains proverb of the South: "Many a good horse dies."

Thomas Isbell, a half-breed Cherokee in the squad under Hamilton Fish, was among the first to shoot and be shot at. He was wounded no less than seven times. The first wound was received by him two minutes after he had fired his first shot, the bullet going through his neck. The second hit him in the left thumb. The third struck near his right hip, passing entirely through the body. The fourth bullet (which was apparently from a Remington and not from a Mauser) went into his neck and lodged against the bone, being afterward cut out. The fifth bullet again hit his left hand. The sixth scraped his head and the seventh his neck. He did not receive all of the wounds at the same time, over half an hour elapsing between the first and the last. Up to receiving the last wound he had declined to leave the firing-line, but by that time he had lost so much blood that he had to be sent to the rear. The man's wiry toughness was as notable as his courage.

We improvised litters, and carried the more sorely wounded back to Siboney that afternoon and the next morning; the others walked. One of the men who had been most severely wounded was Edward Marshall, the correspondent, and he showed as much heroism as any soldier in the whole army. He was shot through the spine, a terrible and very painful wound, which we supposed meant that he would surely die; but he made no complaint of any kind, and while he retained consciousness persisted in dictating the story of the fight. A very touching incident happened in the improvised open-air hospital after the fight, where the wounded were lying. They did not groan, and made no complaint, trying to help one another. One of them suddenly began to hum, "My Country, 'Tis of Thee," and one by one the others joined in the chorus, which swelled out through the tropic woods, where the victors lay in camp beside their dead. I did not see any sign among the fighting men, whether wounded or unwounded, of the very complicated emotions assigned to their kind by some of the realistic modern novelists who have written about battles. At the front everyone behaved quite simply and took things as they came, in a matter-of-course way; but there was doubtless, as is always the case, a good deal of panic and confusion in the rear where the wounded, the stragglers, a few of the packers, and two or three newspaper correspondents were, and in consequence the first reports sent back to the coast were of a most alarming character, describing, with minute inaccuracy, how we had run into ambush, etc. The packers with the mules which carried the rapid-fire guns were among those who ran, and they let the mules go in the jungle; in consequence the guns were never even brought to the firing-line, and only Fred Herrig's skill as a trailer enabled us to recover them. By patient work he followed up the mules' tracks in the forest until he found the animals.

Among the wounded who walked to the temporary hospital at Siboney was the trooper, Rowland, of whom I spoke before. There the doctors examined him, and decreed that his wound was so serious that he must go back to the States. This was enough for Rowland, who waited until nightfall and then escaped, slipping out of the window and making his way back to camp with his rifle and pack, though his wound must have made all movement very painful to him. After this, we felt that he was entitled to stay, and he never left us for a day, distinguishing himself again in the fight at San Juan.

Next morning we buried seven dead Rough Riders in a grave on the summit of the trail, Chaplain Brown reading the solemn burial service of the Episcopalians, while the men stood around with bared heads and joined in singing, "Rock of Ages." Vast numbers of vultures were wheeling round and round in great circles through the blue sky overhead. There could be no more honorable burial than that of these men in a common grave—Indian and cowboy, miner, packer, and college athlete—the man of unknown ancestry from the lonely Western plains, and the man who carried on his watch the crests of the Stuyvesants and the Fishes, one in the way they had met death, just as during life they had been one in their daring and their loyalty.

On the afternoon of the 25th we moved on a couple of miles, and camped in a marshy open spot close to a beautiful stream. Here we lay for several days. Captain Lee, the British attaché, spent some time with us; we had begun to regard him as almost a member of the regiment. Count von Gotzen, the German attaché, another good fellow, also visited us. General Young was struck down with the fever, and Wood took charge of the brigade. This left me in command of the regiment, of which I was very glad, for such experience as we had had is a quick teacher. By this time the men and I knew one another, and I felt able to make them do themselves justice in march or battle. They understood that I paid no heed to where they came from; no heed to their creed, politics, or social standing; that I would care for them to the utmost of my power, but that I demanded the highest performance of duty; while in return I had seen them tested, and knew I could depend absolutely on their courage, hardihood, obedience, and individual initiative.

There was nothing like enough transportation with the army, whether in the way of wagons or mule-trains; exactly as there had been no sufficient number of landing-boats with the transports. The officers' baggage had come up, but none of us had much, and the shelter-tents proved only a partial protection against the terrific downpours of rain. These occurred almost every afternoon, and turned the camp into a tarn, and the trails into torrents and quagmires. We were not given quite the proper amount of food, and what we did get, like most of the clothing issued us, was fitter for the Klondyke than for Cuba. We got enough salt pork and hardtack for the men, but not the full ration of coffee and sugar, and nothing else. I organized a couple of expeditions back to the seacoast, taking the strongest and best walkers and also some of the officers' horses and a stray mule or two, and brought back beans and canned tomatoes. These I got partly by great exertions on my part, and partly by the aid of Colonel Weston of the Commissary Department, a particularly energetic man whose services were of great value. A silly regulation forbade my purchasing canned vegetables, etc., except for the officers; and I had no little difficulty in getting round this regulation, and purchasing (with my own money, of course) what I needed for the men.

One of the men I took with me on one of these trips was Sherman Bell, the former Deputy Marshal of Cripple Creek, and Wells-Fargo Express rider. In coming home with his load, through a blinding storm, he slipped and opened the old rupture. The agony was very great and one of his comrades took his load. He himself, sometimes walking, and sometimes crawling, got back to camp, where Dr. Church fixed him up with a spike bandage, but informed him that he would have to be sent back to the States when an ambulance came along. The ambulance did not come until the next day, which was the day before we marched to San Juan. It arrived after nightfall, and as soon as Bell heard it coming, he crawled out of the hospital tent into the jungle, where he lay all night;

and the ambulance went off without him. The men shielded him just as school-boys would shield a companion, carrying his gun, belt, and bedding; while Bell kept out of sight until the column started, and then staggered along behind it. I found him the morning of the San Juan fight. He told me that he wanted to die fighting, if die he must, and I hadn't the heart to send him back. He did splendid service that day, and afterward in the trenches, and though the rupture opened twice again, and on each occasion he was within a hair's breadth of death, he escaped, and came back with us to the United States.

The army was camped along the valley, ahead of and behind us, our outposts being established on either side. From the generals to the privates all were eager to march against Santiago. At daybreak, when the tall palms began to show dimly through the rising mist, the scream of the cavalry trumpets tore the tropic dawn; and in the evening, as the bands of regiment after regiment played "The Star-Spangled Banner," all, officers and men alike, stood with heads uncovered, wherever they were, until the last strains of the anthem died away in the hot sunset air.

CHAPTER FOURTEEN

Blood in the Hills

The Story of Khe Shanh,
the Most Savage Fight of the Vietnam War

Robert Maras and Charles W. Sasser

The fact that American servicemen and -women fought bravely in Vietnam is given testimony by their blood that has leached into the soil of that country. Testimony of that blood is readily at hand, for those willing to listen, and it is written on two black granite walls that meet at an angle between the Washington Monument and the Lincoln Memorial on the peaceful banks of the Potomac River in our nation's capital.

The names of 58,209 Americans inscribed on the Vietnam Veterans Memorial are powerful reminders of the extreme sacrifices a relative few Americans were making while their fellow citizens lived on in peace and prosperity, attending classes, getting married and raising their children, pursuing careers and chasing personal interests.

Every year now some 2.5 million people come to the memorial. They touch the names, trace them sometimes on bits of paper. Some of them kneel, some pray, most cry. They leave little gifts: a picture, a note, flowers, teddy bears.

The wall was built in 1982, and the statue of the three servicemen was added in 1984. The statue of the Vietnam Women's Memorial was added in 1993.

Robert "Bobby" Maras was a 19-year-old PFC machine gunner in the Weapons Platoon of Gulf Company, 3rd Marines, in the savage fighting in the hills at Khe Sanh in the Vietnam War in 1967. He survived the war and went on to write—with the help of Charles W. Sasser—the most complete and compelling story of the entire Khe Sanh campaign, one of the most memorable in U.S. military history.

In his preface to the book, Maras describes a visit to the Vietnam Memorial Wall:

The Wall and its names have generated a unique ritual called "rubbing." Relatives, friends, and loved ones come to The Wall with a sheet of paper, which they place over the selected name and rub with wax crayon or graphite pencil to make a memento.

Sergeant Crawford, Tony, and I were etching our eighteenth name from the stone when we heard sniffling and weeping. Startled, we looked turned to discover a small crowd gathered behind us to watch.

"How did you know so many guys who died in the war?" someone asked.

Tony turned away to hide the tears in his eyes. Sergeant Crawford's face resembled stone. I lowered my head.

"They were all from our battalion at Khe Sanh," I said.

IT WAS A RESTLESS NIGHT IN THE RAVINE. GOLF AND ECHO COMPANIES had been lucky in today's brief encounter. None of our people were killed and everybody walked back out of it with only a few suffering minor wounds that Magilla and the other Docs patched up without need of a medevac to send them to the rear.

The crunch of twigs, a whisper of moving branches, the scurry of some small creature through the weeds put everybody's nerves raw and rubbing against his backbone. Stationed at the buttress of a rain forest giant with Tony, I struggled to suppress panic alarm in the motor response areas of a very tired nervous system, to control a natural instinct to breathe too fast and too shallowly. Fear, I scolded myself, was a handy warning system, nothing more.

Muscles ached, eyes stung, skin and clothing were caked with sweat and dirt. My ears rang from today's explosions and I dared not trust my hearing as I strained to distinguish monsters in the night from the harmless sounds of nature. Imagination was a terrible thing to waste—and none of us was wasting it. A number of times, unable to sleep during our 50-50, either Tony or I heard the tiger-heavy noise of men stalking us through the forest. A pattern to their movements—*Step, step, pause. . . . Step, step, pause.*

"Somebody's out there," Tony whispered, his breathing fast and sharp.

"No, no. It's your turn to sleep. I'll keep watch."

"Sleep? You gotta be shitting me, Maras."

So, together we stared into the long night, eyes wide.

Elsewhere, guys with less discipline and more imagination, unable to restrain their natural impulses for self-preservation, beguiled by threatening movement in the surrounding jungle, would toss grenades that split apart the night. Somebody else would blast off with an M-16. That brought platoon leaders up and shouting their fool heads off.

"Cease fire, damnit! Cease fire!"

How was a guy supposed to get any sleep with all this racket, providing, of course, he was inclined to sleep?

"Maras, do you ever pray?"

"Not much before," I admitted. "Now I pray every day."

Like the old World War II guys said, there were no atheists in foxholes. "God," I promised, "I'll never take life for granted again—"

If You'll get me out of this. That last part went unsaid. I just *thought* it. You don't bargain with God or fate.

Exhausted, we finally catnapped on and off in turns. Tony opened one eye to greet the dawn.

"Good morning, Vietnam!" he managed half-heartedly as he got up on his knees to piss in place against our tree.

The sun broke over the misty green peaks of the Wicked Sisters of the North and South. Last night's thick blanket of fog engulfed all but the tops of the hills whose foreheads stuck up above in soft early light that helped cover blemishes and damages inflicted by prep fire.

Back home, on a morning like this, the most important decision I might have to make was what to have for breakfast. "Mom, let's have eggs and bacon. No, make that oatmeal."

Linda and I hadn't lived together but for our honeymoon and those few weeks we spent in the motel on the beach at Pendleton where I attended Basic Infantry Training and where she baked a cherry pie.

Of course, at home, decisions weren't about life and death. My next-door neighbor wasn't apt to take a pot shot at me with his deer rifle, nor was the Neighborhood Watch Committee organizing to overrun the block and eat my brain.

For those who fight for life, I had scribbled on the C-rat carton at Khe Sanh the day BLT 2/3 arrived in these hills, *it has a special flavor the protected shall never know.* That *special flavor* was becoming more difficult to define as the Hill Fights dragged on. It was becoming . . . *bitter.*

Warplanes stacked up in air space over Khe Sanh as prepping fire against the hills resumed. Aerial bombing blasted the tops and sides of both 881S and 881N, shaking earth and sky and making trees rattle against each other like skeletons. Artillery followed as planes cleared the AO. The hills absorbed a total of 166 aircraft sorties dumping over a half-million pounds of ordnance and 1,500 artillery rounds.

At 1015 hours, Captain Sheehan received orders from Colonel Pappy to commence the operation, our objective once again the hill knob on 881N's northeastern slope. The 1st Platoon, Lieutenant Hesser's, led off again. Tony and I tagged along as a machine gun team with PFC Taylor's 1st Squad in Lieutenant Mac's 3rd Platoon. Taylor still resented Corporal Dye's failure to live long enough to take over his responsibilities.

"He would have to go and get himself killed," Taylor fussed.

Golf Company moved easily but cautiously along the narrow ridge that led toward the hill knob. To the right the ground fell away into Crawford's Draw, to the left it began to swell into 881N.

Hand signals flashed. Damn, it was a scorcher of a day, geared down as we were with weapons, ammo, packs. I was soon sweating like a pig, no offense to the Pig. Tony trailed along, puffing from exertion and the weight of 3.5 rocket rounds he carried. Over to our left, I spotted Rainey and Kilgore with his Starlite-mounted M-16 sneaking along in a half-crouch, weapons ready, eyes big and glaring beneath their helmets. You bet they were scared. We were all scared. We were also *Marines*, and we would do our job.

War in Vietnam was nothing like the world wars of I and II with their large-scale operations of thousands all hitting a beach at the same time, or taking a town or an island, or seizing a range of hills. Here, there was a feeling of isolation in relatively small units moving more or less separately. I knew that Echo was off to our flank, but I had no idea which flank nor what it was doing. Same thing with units at 881S. While BLT 2/3 was tasked with taking 881N, other outfits, probably elements of the Walking Dead and perhaps our Foxtrot 2/3, were assigned to 881S. Aside from when air and artillery worked over the hills, I experienced war as that portion of it that occurred immediately around me and my squad or platoon. In that aspect, battle for the individual Marine in Vietnam was very personal and confined.

Tony was a bulkier man than my lean 150 pounds. He soon drained his canteen. I still had half of my water left. I offered it to him during a break. I was afraid he would become dehydrated again. He licked his dry lips and shook his head.

"Damn, Tony. Take it. What, you think I got syphilis or something?"

He swigged and handed the canteen back. "Better ration what's left, Maras, or we'll be sucking the dew off toads."

Golf entered an area of thick woods and dense brush. During the last break, Lieutenant Mac's Third Herd Platoon had relieved Hesser up front of the company. Our point man, currently Lance Corporal James Boda, who was giving our faithful Indian scout a break, forged a path through the woods and soon came to the edge of a small clearing, on the other side of which rose the hill knob just below our taller objective. He halted and took a knee to scan for the enemy.

"Maras, I got a bad feeling again," Tony mentioned.

"Probably indigestion from the spaghetti you copped off me."

Boda stepped into the clearing and rushed to the far side with 2nd Squad right behind. PFC Taylor's 1st Squad emerged next with Lieutenant Mac and his RTO, Bill Vlasek, Tony, and me. We footed into the clearing like mice scampering across a barn floor, followed by 3rd Squad bringing up Tailend Charlie.

Tony's "bad feeling" was right on again. Suddenly, a violent blast of AK-47 and automatic fire erupted from the vicinity of the knob, catching many of us in the open and cutting through our ranks like through a crop of field cane. Marines dropped, riddled with lead. I yelled at Tony to follow me to cover while other guys went to ground where they were.

Bullets whip-snapped around my head. Some gook had spotted my machine gun. I hit the dirt only a few paces into the edge of the woods, but kept going, crawling on my elbows with the Pig cradled in my arms and Tony still in my wake, rounds snapping and whining above our heads and chopping off green foliage that showered down on us.

Vlasek, Lieutenant Mac's RTO, was one of the first to fall, a bullet in his temple. The lieutenant stripped the badly wounded and unconscious man of his radio and took cover among the gnarled roots of the nearest tree. PFC Tom Huckaba overheard McFarlane radioing Captain Sheehan, whose command element traversed back and forth between Golf Company and Echo.

"Skipper, I got a number of wounded up here. My radioman's down."

"Don't worry, Mac," came the calm response. "We'll get you out. We're calling up the sixty mike-mikes."

While a 60mm mortar crew moved up, Lieutenant Mac's 3rd blasted back at the knob with everything we had, even though the brush and trees made it impossible to select targets. Still, anything was better than lying on the ground sucking our thumbs and waiting to be slaughtered. I let loose the Pig and kept squeezing the trigger to burp out three-round bursts that avoided overheating the barrel. I carried a spare in my pack, but this was no time to burn out a barrel and have to try to replace it.

"Yeah! Yeah!" Tony cheered, blasting away with his M-16 in between feeding me ammo.

While 3rd Platoon kept the enemy occupied, Golf's other two platoons seized the opportunity to charge across the clearing to enter the fight. Lieutenant Hesser's 1st Platoon moved into a nearby patch of woods on a rise off to my left that had been previously plowed up by artillery. Lance Corporal Bill Roldan's Mattie Mattel jammed. Instead of dropping to seek cover, he bent over to work on the rifle's cocking lever. An NVA shot him through the chest and he collapsed.

Lieutenant Hesser darted forward and dragged Roldan out of the line of fire while shouting, "Corpsman! Corpsman up!"

From the corner of my eye, I observed Magilla Gorilla, unarmed except for a .45 pistol strapped to his waist, spring from cover and head toward Roldan with his aid bag. At close to two hundred pounds on a six-four frame, he provided a prime target. A year ago he was playing high school football in Phoenix, Arizona. Now, he dodged through a hail of enemy fire clutching his bag like it was a football and he had goal to go. We regarded our Navy corpsmen as angels of mercy who responded to the sounds of guns while everyone else ducked for cover.

Magilla skidded up to Roldan on his belly, already unsnapping the cover of his aid bag to get at his bandages. At the same time, Catherine the French photojournalist ran forward and dived into a shallow shell crater nearby from which she proceeded to capture on film a series of images that would become some of the most famous of the Vietnam War. They showed big redheaded Vernon Wike on his knees in the middle of a fierce firefight bandaging the unconscious Marine.

The following photos showed him looking up with rage and sorrow etched on his face as Roldan died from the bullet that had pierced his heart and lungs. Wike grabbed his dead friend's M-16 off the ground, cleared the jam, and, roaring at the top of his lungs, jumped up to charge the hillside.

I happened to glance his way. "No, Magilla!" I yelled. "*No! Get down! We need you!*"

Someone else noticed what was going on and bellowed a second warning, "Don't do it, Doc. J.K.'s been hit over here and needs help."

That caused Magilla to pause. Duty came first over personal vengeance. Wike ran back to render aid to Lance Corporal J.K. Johnson, who lay crumpled and semiconscious on the ground while bullets cracked all around him.

My attention returned to the ongoing battle, attracted by unnatural movement in shrubbery not one hundred meters to my front, almost down my throat. A bush appeared to open and close. I recalled the spider traps during Hotel Company's bloody contest in the draw. NVA fighters were masters at the art of camouflage. But I had this guy dead to rights, with the operative term being *dead*. I felt a certain cold anticipation as I paused to wait for the bush to open again and its tenant to show himself.

I hovered over the Pig, sights centered on the bush. Presently, the leaves parted. A pith helmeted head and shoulders appeared. In a rush of adrenaline and satisfaction, I laid on the trigger and burned through a half-belt of 7.62. The guy's chest fluttered with black starbursts. His body launched backwards, electrified, his arms and legs flailing in what appeared to be attempted flight.

Except he wasn't going anywhere, ever again.

This was my first confirmed KIA. In most firefights, everybody was shooting and no one was certain of who killed who. But this time, I was face to face with the guy. I saw scraggly hair on his chin, one of his eyes larger than the other, a small scar on his cheek—and I squeezed the trigger and watched him die.

I felt nothing for his death except a slight elation that he would kill no more Marines.

"I wasted his ass," I said calmly to Tony.

He was calm in return. "I know. I saw."

Time has no meaning in a firefight, is somehow truncated. A battle that lasts for an hour might seem two minutes—or two minutes feel like a day. This one ended in a series of artillery explosions before 60mm mortars could go into action on our behalf. Both the enemy's big guns and ours opened up simultaneously and stomped geysers of fire and destruction all over the slope. Our artillery from Khe Sanh tried to kill the enemy out only a few hundred meters in front of us and save our asses. The NVA's big guns from over by Laos attempted to kill us and save *their* asses. Our lines were so close, perhaps even mingled here and there, that it was difficult to tell whose shells were killing whom. What a fucked up mess this was turning out to be.

I felt no fear. What I felt was sheer *terror* as deadly shrapnel buzzed and cut through the brush, indiscriminately seeking targets on both sides. Out front, exploding shells walked directly toward Tony and me, step by step. And like Nancy Sinatra sang about her boots, they were gonna walk all over us.

I grabbed Tony. "Get the hell out of here. Follow me!"

The look in his eyes—early signs of shock.

"Tony? Damn it!"

"Yeah, yeah. Go!"

The two of us scooted through the grass like a pair of lizards on amphetamine, not knowing where we were going. Just *going*. Anywhere but here.

Old soldiers and Marines always said you never heard or saw the round with your number on it. They were wrong. I heard the shell coming in like an elephant trumpeting and blistering as it hurtled from the sky. It thudded to the ground where Tony and I were lying not two seconds ago. It shook the earth when it exploded. I became like a flea trying to hold onto a dog shaking itself after coming out of the water.

What felt like the blast from a furnace nearly ripped off my arm. Or so I thought. I yelped with sudden excruciating pain. Tony cried out in almost the same instant.

"*I'm hit!*"

My first thought was of the rotting dead gook I almost pissed on in the trees. Man, I hoped nobody saw me looking like that.

GET ON THE CHOPPER

If it was your time to die, it was your time. Death could come right out of the sky and kill you in an instant. Apparently, this wasn't my time. Nor Tony's. We lay together in the grass where we had fallen and assessed our wounds while bullets and shrapnel continued to saturate the air over our heads. With overwhelming relief I realized I still had my arm and other parts.

A shrapnel fragment had first struck my 781 web gear, slicing the strap, before it lodged just above my elbow. The piece of steel glowed red hot and cauterized the flesh around it, staying most of the bleeding. The wound still hurt like hell, and bled a little more when I snatched the fragment out of my arm, burning my fingers and prompting an involuntary stream of curses.

Tony groaned. "This is no time to blaspheme God," he warned.

Surprising how calm a man could be when wounded, as long as it wasn't deemed life threatening. Your poor body might be riddled from hostile intent, but fellow Marines weren't likely to coddle you and let you stew about it. Man up. Keep a stiff upper lip, you're not dying.

Tony was hit in the outer thigh. It bled like a sonofabitch, saturating his utility trousers. We quickly ascertained, however, that no vital vein or artery was involved. I ripped open a battle dressing and applied pressure to the ugly gash.

"I guess we got Purple Hearts coming," I mentioned. "Peggy'll change her mind when you come home a wounded hero."

"Piss on her."

Corpsman Lloyd Heath must have seen us take the hits. He rushed over. After patching us up, he decided our wounds were serious enough to warrant our going to the rear and a pre-designated casualty collection point. We slithered on our bellies to a thicket of trees that provided some protection near the clearing we crossed before everything started. A couple of other Marines were already there, one shot through the meaty part of his back, his torso wrapped in OD bandages, the other lying on the ground with blood oozing through lips already turning blue. Appeared he had a sucking chest wound and would have to be evacuated immediately if he was going to survive.

Tony and I exchanged looks. These guys were our buddies since Okinawa. And now—?

"Damn!" I exhaled, the expletive all but drowned out by the sounds of battle. "*Damn!*"

Corpsman Heath looked me right in the eye for emphasis. "Maras," he said, "you and Leyba get out of here while you can. It's gonna get much worse in these hills before it gets better. Your wounds are enough to get you out. Here are your tags."

He affixed casualty "Get out of Dodge!" tags to our jackets. More cries for help rose from the direction of the hill knob.

"I have to go," the corpsman said. He dumped bandages in Tony's lap where he leaned against a tree. "It's a flesh wound, Leyba. Put more pressure on it and tie a knot in the crevette. You'll be fine."

Then he was gone back toward the sound of guns. A few minutes later, while we were still contemplating what came next, Gunny Janzen crab-legged through the trees seeking volunteers to help bring out the other wounded and escort or carry them down the ridgeline to a clearing that we might use as an LZ for medevacs. Tom Huckaba and Dennis Johnson were with him.

"We'll go," I volunteered. It just came out, no pre-thought involved. Afterwards, I chastised myself for being some kind of fool to go back out there after we had barely escaped with our lives.

Tony shot me a "What the hell?" look.

Gunny hesitated. "How bad?" he asked, indicating our injuries.

"We can do it," I said. "We'll be flying out on the chopper anyhow. We need to make sure some of the other wounded guys go with us."

He nodded solemnly. "You're good Marines," he said.

My elbow throbbed something awful and threatened to lock up. Tony was limping. Nonetheless, the two of us plus Huckaba and Johnson zig-zagged toward the knob where the ambush occurred and our company corpsmen had more casualties than they could cope with by themselves. Cries and screams for help resounded throughout the brush. It was a matter of picking out a cry and rushing toward it while at the same time dodging bullets snapping past our heads.

Private James Golden was the first casualty we came upon. He had taken a round in the spine and seemed paralyzed. Tony and I took him while Huckaba and Johnson scrambled toward another summons for help.

One of the corpsmen had already patched up Golden and left him for us to carry out. His eyes full of pleading and suffering stared inward as Tony and I, keeping low, rolled the private into his poncho, gathered up the ends in an emergency litter, labored to our feet, and headed for the collection point carrying the fallen Marine between us. Through the lead and steel hailstones, dodging and ducking. Not knowing if we would make it or not.

Huckaba and Johnson brought in another casualty, whose face the poncho covered. I didn't look to see who it was, nor did I ask. I didn't want to know. Not now. Tony and I headed out again.

Get past this. Get through this alive and we're outta here.

"Maras, I thought you'd have learned by now not to volunteer for anything in the Marine Corps," Tony scolded.

He didn't mean it. If I hadn't offered our services, he would have. Somebody had to bring the WIAs to safety. Besides, Tony and I were best buddies and partners. We did everything together—slept together, bitched together, fought together, were even wounded together.

By the time we collected our casualties, Captain Sheehan was calling off the assault for the second day in a row. The enemy force apparently proved much larger and stronger than anticipated. First off, he called for our artillery to cease fire. Mixed together like everyone was on the battlefield, shelling might be doing as much damage to our own men as to the enemy.

The company broke contact with platoons covering each other in another "strategic withdrawal," leaving our dead out there where they fell. Four or five that we knew of. Maybe more. The urgency now was in getting our WIAs out. Elements of Echo Company had secured the LZ in the clearing. Medevac choppers were on their way in.

PFC Vlasek, Lieutenant Mac's radioman who took a round through the temple at the start of the ambush, was still breathing, but just barely. A hoarse, disconcerting sound. Magilla Gorilla had wrapped his head up like a mummy's, leaving only openings for his eyes, nose, and mouth. Tony and I slung our weapons across our backs and hoisted him in his poncho and started back with him from the casualty collection point to the medevac LZ. By this time the fight at the knob was pretty much over, leaving only scattered rifle shots in residue.

Storm clouds had been gathering for most of the day beyond the hills. Flashes of lightning stabbed out of the roiling skies as the column of walking wounded and those carried in makeshift litters wended our way across the clearing and down the slope and over to the ridgeline for medevac pickup. Golf Company guarded our rear in case the NVA might not have had enough and attempted to pursue.

A light rain started falling, making footing even more precarious. Wind rattled in the trees, but wind was a big improvement over the previous rattle of bullets. The sky darkened to almost night. Thunder rumbled. Lightning struck the remains of forest giants on top of the hills.

I figured the storm was God's way of saying He had seen enough of this shit.

My one good arm, Tony's bad leg, the walking wounded hobbling along reminded me of the *Yankee Doodle Dandy* skit in school where kids bandaged like soldiers of the Revolutionary War shuffled along to the beating dirge of drums.

Tony and I were breathing heavily under the weight of our load, the further awkwardness of our wounds and keeping Vlasek's IV bag aloft on a stick and the line free and open. I slipped and fell on a wet upgrade, dumping our unconscious patient out of his poncho and into the mud. His mummy bandages slipped off to reveal his face as we lifted him back onto the poncho. Tony jumped back.

"Oh, God!"

I had witnessed unimaginable horrors in the brief time since 2/3 landed at Red Beach, of violence and madness, of men mangled, brutalized, and slaughtered. Sergeant Hard during Vietnam training in Okinawa had tried to prepare us.

"You're going to see things," he said. "Horrible scenes. Dead men. Some of them your buddies. But remember one thing: You are Marines. Marines don't quit. Marines *can't* quit."

Lee Marvin the movie star, he said, was a Marine during World War II. "I knew I was going to be killed," Marvin said. "I just wanted to die in the very best outfit. There are ordinary corpses—and then there are Marine corpses. I figured on the first-class kind and hitched up."

Frozen in horror, Tony and I stared at what remained of Vlasek's face, stared while thunder banged across the sky, lightning strobed, and a few guns still cracked from the bad place we left behind. Hardly enough remained of the young Marine's face to recognize him. Just a red, gory mass of tissue and bone fragments from the temples down, a monster mask out of which breath rattled and blew bubbles of bloody fluids.

Tony, all choked up, murmured, "Maras. . . . Thank God we're getting out of here."

I heard a chopper coming in. "Let's get him to the LZ."

Tony prayed all the way. So did I. "Lord, please? Let him die."

No way would he survive, not with gray brain matter dribbling from his skull. I wouldn't want to live like this. A vegetable. Neither would Vlasek. A compassionate God would let him die.

We got him to the chopper as it came in fast, whipping rain showers with its rotors, hovering a foot or so off the grass while we loaded casualties aboard. Magilla Gorilla was there.

"Get on the helicopter," the crew chief ordered, looking directly at Tony and me. "You've got your tags."

I hesitated. Magilla came over. "Get on the chopper," he encouraged. "You two have done your part. Now save yourselves."

I had that fabled million-dollar wound. All I had to do was climb aboard that aircraft and Tony and I were out of here.

Still, I hesitated. Tony looked anxious. Sergeant Crawford wouldn't have left with such a puny wound. I thought of Captain Sheehan, Bill Rainey, Ramirez, Burnham and Kilgore, the Gunny, Lieutenant Mac, Magilla and Heath. All of them. Staying behind, being Marines while I bailed out on them. *Semper Fi* had to mean something.

"Maras?" Tony's voice quivered.

I drew in a deep breath. Damn! I was about to do the dumbest thing I had ever done in my entire life. I tore the casualty tag off my jacket and handed it to Magilla.

"Take it. I've got my gun. I can still shoot. I'm going back. See you later, Tony."

Tony couldn't believe it. "What? Maras, you stupid bastard."

I headed down the ridge to where Golf was digging in again for another night and another try at the hill tomorrow. Not looking back, the Pig slung forward for possible action. Above the ominous rumble of thunder, I overheard Tony saying to Magilla, "He'll never make it without me. I have to go with him."

We returned to the fight together, walking side by side, our utilities stained with our blood and the blood of others, not talking as the gathering storm lashed at our faces, gale winds shrieked in the trees, and thunder sounded like the bombardment of enemy hills.

We heard later that Vlasek died before the chopper reached the *Princeton*'s sick bay.

Sources

"The Brave Men" from *Goodbye Darkness*, by William Manchester, Little, Brown and Company Inc., 1979.

"Hell in a Very Small Place" from *We Were Soldiers Once . . . And Young*, by Lt. Gen. Harold G. Moore (Ret.) and Joseph L. Galloway, Random House Inc., 1992.

"Into the Fire" from the book *Ploesti, the Most Fateful Mission of World War II*, by Duane Schultz, Westholme Publishing, 2007.

"Sergeant York" from the book *Sergeant York and His People*, by Sam K. Cowin, Funk & Wagnalls, 1922.

"Long Rifle" from the book *Long Rifle, A Sniper's Story in Iraq and Afghanistan*, by Joe LeBleu, Lyons Press, 2009.

"Capturing a Locomotive" from the book *Capturing a Locomotive*, by William Pettinger, 1881.

"The Boys from Shangri-La," from *The Greatest Air Aces Stories Ever Told*, Lyons Press, 2017.

"Miracle at Belleau Wood" from the book *Miracle at Belleau Wood*, by Alex Axelrod, Lyons Press, 2010.

"Black Sheep and Their 'Pappy'" from *The Greatest Air Aces Stories Ever Told*, Lyons Press, 2017.

"Air War Over the Trenches" from the book *Fighting the Flying Circus*, by Eddie Rickenbacker, Frederick A. Stokes, 1919.

"Eyewitness to Infamy" from the book *Eyewitness to Infamy, An Oral History of Pearl Harbor,* December 7, 1941, edited by Paul Joseph Travers, Lyons Press, 1991 and 2016; the account "Ford Island" by Harry Mead is from the same book.

"Legacy of Valor" from *Uncommon Valor on Iwo Jima*, by James H. Hallas, Stackpole Books/Globe Pequot, 2016.

"San Juan Hill" from the book *The Rough Riders*, by Theodore Roosevelt, 1899.

"Blood in the Hills" from the book *Blood in the Hills, the Story of Khe Sanh*, by Robert Maras and Charles W. Sasser, Lyons Press, 2017.